©Master Key
to the GRE

Volume 2

Number Properties
& Algebra

Made by
Sherpa Prep

Master Key to the GRE: Number Properties & Algebra.

ISBN: 978-0-9966225-0-9

© 2017 Sherpa Prep.

Register Your Book!

To access the online videos that come with this book, please go to:

www.SherpaPrep.com/Activate

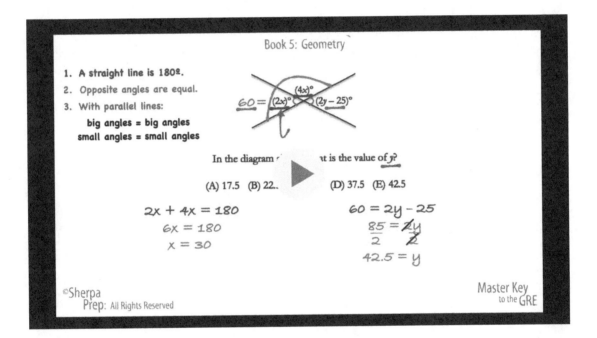

When registering:

Be sure to provide the **same** last name and shipping address that you used to purchase this book or to enroll in your GRE course with Sherpa Prep!

Register @ www.SherpaPrep.com/Activate

Master Key by
Sherpa Prep

Dear Student,

Thank you for purchasing Sherpa Prep's guide to <u>Number Properties & Algebra</u>. We know that preparing for the GRE can be a grueling and intimidating process. The fact that you've chosen us to assist you is deeply appreciated.

This series of books is the culmination of nearly three decades of experience teaching the GRE on a daily basis. We think you'll find that experience and expertise reflected in the pages that follow.

As with any undertaking of this size, there are a number of people who deserve special recognition. First among them is Nasheed Amin, who critiqued <u>Master Key to the GRE</u> in its entirety and whose insightful recommendations significantly enhanced all five volumes. We would also like to recognize the contributions of Bronwyn Bruton, Shawn Magnuson, Seth Alcorn, and Jessica Rider Amin. Without their assistance, this project would not have been possible. Finally, we would like to extend our gratitude to the students and instructors of Sherpa Prep, whose feedback, questions, and experiences lie at the heart of these materials.

Good luck with your preparation! If we can be of further assistance, please reach out to us at **jay@sherpaprep.com** or **nafeez@sherpaprep.com**. We'd love to hear from you.

On behalf of everyone at Sherpa Prep,

Jay

Nafeez

Jay Friedman
Founder
Sherpa Prep

Nafeez Amin
President
Sherpa Prep

Table of Contents

Volume 2

Number Properties & Algebra

Chapter 1

Introduction to the GRE

Introduction

To be discussed:

Master Key to the GRE

Get a sense of how to use our books, how to study properly for the GRE, and how to access our online video content.

1 Choosing the Right Guide	**4** Proper Study Habits
2 Why Master Key is Special	**5** The App
3 How to Use Our Guides	**6** Register Your Book!

The Structure & Scoring System

Read about the structure and scoring system of the GRE. Learn how to sign up for the exam and report your scores.

7 The Structure of the GRE	**9** Registering for the GRE
8 The Scoring System	**10** Reporting & Canceling Scores

Navigating the Exam

Get an in-depth sense of how the GRE's scoring system works and what you can do to maximize your performance on test day.

11 How the Exam Works	**13** Strategy & Time Management
12 The Scoring Algorithm	**14** Practice Tests

Intro to Quantitative Reasoning

Before you get started, educate yourself about the sort of math you'll find on the GRE and the four ways in which the exam formats its math questions.

15 Content Overview	**18** Numeric Entry Questions
16 Problem Solving Questions	**19** Quantitative Comparisons
17 "Select One or More" Questions	**20** Before You Get Started

Master Key to the GRE

(1) Choosing the Right Guide – If you're like most people preparing to take the GRE, you probably have little sense of what differentiates one GRE guide from another.

• You may think that all GRE guides are more or less the same, or that the guides you see in bookstores are the most comprehensive on the market.

> ➤ The basic story is that most guides fall into one of two categories: "strategy-based" or "content-based".

• **The guides that you find in bookstores are almost always strategy-based.** In general, strategy-based guides provide:

1. A brief discussion of each question type that you find on the GRE.
2. A small set of suggestions for approaching these question types.
3. A collection of one hundred or so practice questions with some brief solutions.

• You also tend to find instructions on how to register for the GRE and report your scores; advice for the test day experience; and a few appendices that review vocabulary and elementary math principles.

> ➤ You won't find a lot of "know-how", however, in strategy-based guides. **The focus of such books is test-taking advice, not education.**

• The latest "premier" guide of one well-known test-prep provider, for example, devotes just nineteen pages to explaining math concepts.

• This said, you will find some useful ideas for taking the exam strategically, among them: ways to use the answer choices to your advantage; advice on how to pace yourself; and recommendations on how to read.

> ➤ In our experience, learning these sorts of strategies is helpful for most test-takers. Unfortunately, **they will not help you attain a strong GRE score, on their own.**

• If you do not know how to solve the problems you find on your exam, you will not do well, regardless of how well you can eliminate irrational answers, pace yourself, or otherwise "game" the exam.

➤ In contrast, **content-based guides teach the "know-how" you need** to solve exam questions without guessing.

• Such guides generally devote several pages of discussion to most of the major topics tested by the GRE.

• At the end of each discussion, you tend to find a set of section-ending exercises that allow you to practice what you've studied. As a result, content-based guides almost always have far more practice questions than their strategy-based counterparts.

➤ In our view, **this sort of approach is critical to success on the GRE**. It may not be the only thing you need to succeed, but it is the most important.

• Think about it logically for a moment. Is there any other exam you would dare take without learning its content beforehand?

• Of course not. Yet students regularly "prep" for the GRE using books that do not review the content of the exam. It takes years to graduate from college, and some admissions committees weigh GRE scores more heavily than grade point averages. Isn't an exam that means so much worth preparing for properly?

➤ Unfortunately, there a number of drawbacks to the content-based guides currently available for the GRE.

• For starters, **these guides almost always ignore the tactics recommended by strategy-based guides**, tactics that we believe are an asset to any test taker.

• What's more, such guides rarely tell you how frequently a particular topic is tested. Knowing which topics to study is important if you only have limited time to prepare for the GRE!

➤ Most importantly, none of the guides actually teach you EVERYTHING tested by the GRE.

• While most cover the major topics found on a typical exam, **none cover the vast array of rare and advanced concepts that you need to grasp if you're hoping to score <u>above</u> the 90th percentile.**

(2) Why Master Key Is Special – <u>Master Key to the GRE</u> is the only guide to the GRE that will teach you everything you need to attain a perfect score.

• Whether you're looking for help with advanced concepts, or are starting from scratch, our materials will have what you need.

> ➤ **We start by assuming you know NOTHING.** Everything is laid out for you as if you haven't done math in years.

• Each chapter focuses on a specific topic, such as Fractions, Rates, or Triangles, and opens with a thorough discussion of its simplest, most fundamental concepts.

• Bit by bit, we gradually explore ALL the wrinkles associated with that topic, so that you can solve problems involving sophisticated nuances, not just easy problems.

> ➤ At the ends of our chapters, you'll find a treatment of **every RARE and ADVANCED concept tested by the GRE**.

• You won't find these topics discussed anywhere else. <u>Master Key to the GRE</u> is the only resource that covers them.

• We know that some of you only need help solving the most difficult questions — the questions that determine who scores ABOVE the 90th percentile. We've made sure that our guides teach <u>everything</u>, so that students in your position get all the support they need.

> ➤ To keep things simple, we discuss math in **language that's EASY to understand** and focus on **SMART strategies for every level of material**.

• In writing <u>Master Key to the GRE</u>, we were determined to make our guides helpful for everyone, not just math geeks.

• We are GRE specialists who have spent our entire professional careers making math ACCESSIBLE to students who hate it. **These books are the culmination of over three decades of daily classroom instruction.** No matter how difficult a topic may be, we walk you through each concept, step by step, to ensure that everything makes sense.

> ➤ Along the way, **we sprinkle in hundreds of SHORTCUTS and TRICKS** that you won't find in any other guide.

• We know that TIME is a major concern for many test-takers, so we've included every time-saving strategy out there to help you "beat the clock".

- We don't care how well you think you know math. These shortcuts will save you valuable minutes, no matter what your current skill level may be.

  ➤ To complement our content-oriented approach, the first volume of <u>Master Key to the GRE</u> devotes **an entire chapter to something we call "Plan B" strategies**.

- A "Plan B" strategy is a strategy that can help you deduce a correct answer when you don't know how to solve a problem.

- Such "tricks of the trade" are sometimes encountered in mainstream strategy-based guides. No other guide, however, features a collection like the one we've put together here. We've got all of the tricks, not just a few.

  ➤ We also complement our content-oriented approach by telling you **how FREQUENTLY the GRE tests every concept** — something no other guide does.

- We know that most people don't have the time to study everything and aren't looking for a perfect score — just a score that's good enough to get them into the school of their choice.

- So, we let you know which topics are <u>commonly tested</u> and which ones are not so that you can determine for yourself which topics are worth your time.

  ➤ Additionally, **we organize our discussions by level of DIFFICULTY**, as well as by topic.

- As we see it, test-takers deserve to know which topics they need to master in order to get elite scores and which topics they can afford to skip if they're only looking for above average scores.

- Our hope is that by organizing our material in this way, you'll be able to limit your efforts to material that is right for you.

  ➤ In total, <u>Master Key to the GRE</u> includes **nearly ONE THOUSAND practice questions**. That's more than any other resource out there.

- Like our teaching sections, our practice questions are sorted by difficulty, as well as by topic, so that you can focus on any level of material and on any topic that you like.

- Moreover, nearly a quarter of these questions involve the most rare or advanced topics tested by the GRE. So if you're looking for a lot of help with diabolical fare, you'll find it here.

➢ Most of the solutions to these questions come in the form of **ANIMATED VIDEOS, which you can play on any computer, tablet, or smart phone**.

• We understand that the short, written explanations found in other GRE handbooks are often insufficient for students who find math challenging.

• By providing you with video solutions, we are able to talk you through our practice problems, every step of the way, so that you can follow along easily and see where your solution went wrong.

➢ In many cases, you'll find that our animated videos discuss **multiple ways to solve a question**.

• In math, there is often more than one way to solve a problem. Not all of these approaches, however, are equally efficient.

• Our videos discuss the best of these approaches to ensure that you're exposed to a solution that's not only fast and simple, but also works well with your way of thinking.

➢ We know that <u>Master Key to the GRE</u> is the most expensive GRE guide on the market.

• It's anywhere from $60 to $100 dollars more expensive than most of the alternatives out there. That's a lot of money.

• But let us ask you this. Which would rather have: an extra $60 to $100 dollars or the GRE scores that you need?

➢ Remember, it took you years to graduate from college, and many admissions committees weigh GRE scores more heavily than your grade point average.

• Isn't an exam that means so much worth the cost of a college textbook? Of course it is.

• If you're still not certain, **we encourage you to compare our materials to anything else** that you can find. Whether you're looking for help with advanced material or something a little less extreme, we have no doubt that you'll see why <u>Master Key to the GRE</u> is worth the difference.

(3) How to Use Our Guides – As mentioned, <u>Master Key to the GRE</u> has been designed to help you solve EVERY question on the GRE.

• It explains ALL of the TOUGH concepts that no other GRE prep book attempts to cover, not just the easy ones.

> ➢ Depending on your goals, however, you may NOT need to master everything. Not every program requires a perfect score. In fact, most don't require anything close.

• If you've yet to do so, we strongly encourage you to contact the programs you're interested in to see what sort of scores they require.

• Knowing "how high" to set the bar will give you a sense of whether you need to cover everything or just the core material. (Remember, we'll tell you how frequently each topic is tested!)

> ➢ Every volume of <u>Master Key to the GRE</u> has been designed to help someone starting from SCRATCH to build, step by step, to the most challenging material.

• Thus, Chapter 1 is intended to precede Chapter 2, and the same is true for each volume: <u>Arithmetic & "Plan B" Strategies</u> (Vol. 1) is intended to precede <u>Number Properties & Algebra</u> (Vol. 2).

• The chapters, however, are largely independent of one another, as are the books, so you're welcome to skip around if you only need help with a few key topics or are short on time.

> ➢ As you study, bear in mind that you DON'T have to master one topic before studying another.

• If you have a hard time with something, put it aside for a day or two. It can take one or two "exposures" for a concept to "click" – especially if it's new or tricky.

• You also don't need to solve all 1,000 of our practice problems. If you're comfortable with a topic, feel free to skip the questions marked "fundamental" to save time.

> ➢ Finally, remember that our ADVANCED materials are intended for students in need of PERFECT scores.

• If that's not you, don't waste your time! Questions involving advanced topics are generally rare for the GRE, so if you'd be thrilled with a score around the 90th percentile, you're more likely to achieve it by focusing on questions and materials involving core concepts.

(4) Proper Study Habits – Whatever your goals may be for the GRE, it's important that you work consistently.

• Studying a little EVERY DAY is the best way to retain what you're learning and to avoid the burn out that comes with studying too intensely for too long.

  ➢ In a perfect world, we'd have you study about an hour a day during the workweek and one to two hours a day on the weekends.

• Unfortunately, we know that such a schedule is unrealistic for some people. If you can't find an hour each day, at least DO SOMETHING!

• Even 5 minutes a day can help you stave off rust and prevent the cycle of guilt and procrastination that comes from not studying.

  ➢ If you can, do your best to AVOID CRAMMING. Much of what you'll be studying is boring and technical. It will take "elbow grease" to master.

• We truly question how much of this information can be absorbed in a few short weeks or in study sessions that last three or four hours.

• In our experience, most students who do too much too rapidly either burnout or fail to absorb the material properly.

  ➢ To avoid "study fatigue", SWITCH things up. Spend part of each day studying for the math portion of the exam and part for the verbal portion.

• And do your best to incorporate at least part of your study routine into your daily life.

• If you can study 30 minutes out of every lunch break and a few minutes out of every snack break, we think you'll find that you have more time to prepare than you might believe. We also think you'll find the shorter study sessions more beneficial.

  ➢ As you study, be sure to bear in mind that QUALITY is just as important as QUANTITY.

• Many test-takers believe that the key to success is to work through thousands of practice questions and to take dozens of exams. This simply isn't true.

• While working through practice questions and taking exams are important parts of preparing for the GRE, doing so does not mean that you are LEARNING the material.

> ➤ It is equally important that you LEARN from your MISTAKES. Whenever you miss a practice question, be sure to watch the video explanation that we've provided.

• Then, redo the problem yourself. Once you feel that you've "got it", come back to the problem two days later.

• If you still get it wrong, add the problem to your "LOG of ERRORS" and redo it every few weeks. Keeping track of tricky problems and redoing them MORE THAN ONCE is a great way to learn from your mistakes and to avoid similar difficulties on your actual exam.

> ➤ As you prepare, keep the REAL exam in mind. The GRE tests your ability to recognize concepts under TIMED conditions. Your study habits should reflect this.

• If it takes you 3 minutes to solve a problem, you may as well have missed that problem. 3 minutes is too much time to spend on a problem during an actual exam. Be sure to watch the video solutions for such problems and to redo them until you can solve them quickly.

• Likewise, bear in mind that you will take the GRE on a COMPUTER, unless you opt to take the paper-based version that is administered only three times a year.

> ➤ So adopt GOOD HABITS now. Whenever you practice, avoid doing things you can't do on a computer, such as writing atop problems or underlining key words.

• And make a NOTECARD whenever you learn something. The cards don't have to be complicated – even a sample problem that illustrates the concept will do.

• As your studying progresses, it can be easy to forget concepts that you learned at the beginning of your preparation. Notecards will help you retain what you've learned and make it easy for you to review that material whenever you have a few, spare minutes.

> ➤ Finally, do your best to keep your emotions in check. It's easy to become overconfident when a practice exam goes well or to get down when one goes poorly.

• The GRE is a tough exam and improvement, for most students, takes time.

• In our experience, however, test-takers who prepare like PROFESSIONALS — who keep an even keel, who put in the time to do their assignments properly, and who commit to identifying their weaknesses and improving them – ALWAYS achieve their goals in the end.

(5) The App – <u>Master Key to the GRE</u> is available in print through Amazon or through our website at **www.sherpaprep.com/masterkey**.

• It's also available as an app for iPhones and iPads through Apple's App Store under the title <u>GRE Math by Sherpa Prep</u>.

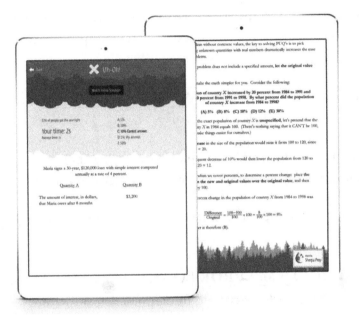

  ➢ Like the printed edition, the app comes with access to all of our LESSONS, practice QUESTIONS, and VIDEOS.

• And, like any book, it allows you to BOOKMARK pages, UNDERLINE text, and TAKE NOTES.

• Unlike a book, however, it also allows you to design practice quizzes, create study lists, make error logs, and keep statistics on just about everything.

  ➢ The **DESIGN a PRACTICE QUIZ** feature lets you make quizzes in which you select the TOPICS, the NUMBER of questions, and the DIFFICULTY.

• It also allows you to SHUFFLE the questions by topic and difficulty and to SET a TIMER for any length of time.

• For example, you can make a 30-minute quiz comprised of fifteen intermingled Ratio, Rate, and Overlapping Sets questions, in which all the questions are advanced. Or you can make a 10-minute quiz with just ten Probability questions, of which some are easy and others are intermediate. You can pretty much make any sort of quiz that you like.

➢ AFTER each quiz, you get to REVIEW your performance, question by question, and to view video solutions.

• You also get to see the difficulty level of your quiz questions, as well as the time it took you to answer each of them.

• You even get to COMPARE your performance to that of other users. You see how frequently other users were able to solve the questions on your quiz and how long it took them, on average, to do so.

➢ As you read through our lessons, the $\boxed{\textbf{MAKE a STUDY LIST}}$ feature allows you to form a personalized study list.

• With the tap of a button, you can add any topic that you read about to an automated "to do" list, which organizes the topics you've selected by chapter and subject.

• From your study list, you can then access these topics instantly to revisit them whenever you need to.

➢ Similarly, the $\boxed{\textbf{CREATE an ERROR LOG}}$ feature allows you to compile a list of practice problems you wish to redo for further practice.

• Every time you answer a question, you can add it to this log, regardless of whether you got the question right or wrong, or left it blank.

• By doing so, you can keep track of every problem that you find challenging and redo them until they no longer pose a challenge.

➢ Finally, the app $\boxed{\textbf{TRACKS your PERFORMANCE}}$ at every turn to help you identify your strengths and weaknesses.

• In addition to the data from your practice quizzes, the app provides key information on how you're performing, by TOPIC and across DIFFICUTLY LEVELS.

• So if you want to know what percentage of advanced level Algebra questions you're answering correctly, the app can tell you. Likewise, if you want to know what percentage of intermediate level Triangle questions you're answering correctly, the app can tell you that too.

➢ The app offers the first volume of <u>Master Key to the GRE</u> for $\boxed{\textbf{FREE}}$. The other four volumes retail for $9.99 apiece.

(6) Register Your Book! – Every volume of <u>Master Key to the GRE</u> comes with six months of free access to our collection of video solutions.

- If you have a print edition of <u>Master Key</u>, you'll need to Register your book(s) to access these videos.

  ➤ To do so, please go to **www.sherpaprep.com/activate** and enter your email address, last name, and shipping address.

- **Be sure to provide the SAME last name and shipping address that you used to purchase your copy of <u>Master Key to the GRE</u>.**

- If you received your books upon enrolling in a GRE prep course with Sherpa Prep, be sure to enter the same last name and shipping address that you used to enroll.

  ➤ Once you've entered this information, you will be asked to create an account password.

- Please RECORD this password! You will need it to login to our website whenever you choose to watch our videos.

- Our login page can be found at **www.sherpaprep.com/videos**. We recommend that you BOOKMARK this page for future visits.

  ➤ If your registration is Unsuccessful, please send your last name and shipping address to **sales@sherpaprep.com**.

- We will confirm your purchase manually and create a login account for you.

- In most cases, this process will take no more than a few hours. Please note, however, that requests can take up to 24 hours to fulfill if you submit your request on a U.S. federal holiday or if we are experiencing extremely heavy demand.

  ➤ Six months after your date of registration, your video access to <u>Master Key to the GRE</u> will come to an end.

- An additional six months of access can be purchased at a rate of $9.99 per book. To do so, simply login at **www.sherpaprep.com/videos** and follow the directions.

About the GRE

(7) The Structure of the GRE – Before examining the content of the GRE, let's take a moment to discuss how the exam is structured and administered.

• The GRE is a computer-based exam that is offered world-wide on a daily basis.

> ➢ The test consists of six sections and takes around 3 hours and 45 minutes to complete (not including breaks).

• These sections are as follows:

    I. An Analytical Writing section containing two essays.
    II. Two Verbal Reasoning sections.
    III. Two Quantitative Reasoning sections.
    IV. One Unidentified Research section.

• The Analytical Writing section is always first, while **the other five sections may appear in ANY order**. You get a 10-minute break between the third and fourth sections, and a 1-minute break between the other test sections.

> ➢ The Unidentified Research section **does NOT count towards your score** and is either a Verbal Reasoning section or a Quantitative Reasoning section.

• Unfortunately, the Unidentified Research section is designed to look exactly like the other sections — there is no way to spot it.

• As such, you must take all five sections seriously. Even though one of them will not count towards your score, there is no way of knowing which section that is.

> ➢ Finally, some exams have an **Identified Research section** in place of the Unidentified Research section.

• This section is marked "For Research Purposes" and does not count towards your score. If your exam has an Identified Research section, it will appear at the end of the test.

• On the following page, you'll find a breakdown of all six sections. Notice that every Quantitative Reasoning section has 20 questions and is 35 minutes long.

- Similarly, notice that every Verbal Reasoning section also has 20 questions but is only 30 minutes long.

  ➤ When viewing the table below, remember that **the order of sections 2 through 6 is RANDOM**. These sections can occur in any order.

- This means that the Unidentified Research section can be ANY section after the first and that you might get two Quantitative sections in a row (or two Verbal sections)!

Section	Task	Number of Questions	Time	Note
1	Analytical Writing	Two Essays	30 minutes per essay	
2	Verbal Reasoning	20	30 minutes	
3	Quantitative Reasoning	20	35 minutes	
10-minute break				
4	Verbal Reasoning	20	30 minutes	
5	Quantitative Reasoning	20	35 minutes	
6	Unidentified Research	20	30 or 35 minutes	Not scored

- Also remember that that Unidentified Research section may be replaced with an Identified Research section. If so, the Identified Research section will appear at the end of the test.

<u>**(8) The Scoring System**</u> – After your GRE has been completed and graded, you will receive three scores:

1. A Verbal Reasoning score.
2. A Quantitative Reasoning score.
3. An Analytical Writing score.

• **Both the Verbal Reasoning and Quantitative Reasoning scores are reported on a scale from 130 to 170, in one-point increments**.

➤ The Analytical Writing score is reported on a scale from 0 to 6, in half-point increments.

• A score of NS (no score) is given for any measure in which no questions (or essay prompts) are answered.

• In addition to these scaled scores, you will also receive percentile rankings, which compare your scores to those of other GRE test-takers.

➤ Before applying to graduate school or business school, you should have a basic sense of what constitutes a good score and what constitutes a bad score.

• Currently, **an average Verbal Reasoning score is 151, an average Quantitative Reasoning score is 152, and an average Analytical Writing score is approximately 3.5**.

• Roughly two-thirds of all test-takers receive a score within the following ranges:

1. Verbal Reasoning: 142 to 159
2. Quantitative Reasoning: 143 to 161
3. Analytical Writing: 3 to 4.5

➤ As a loose guideline, these ranges suggest that any score in the 160s is fairly exceptional and that any score in the 130s may raise a red flag with an admissions committee.

• The same goes for Analytical Writing scores higher than 4.5 or lower than 3. In fact, only 7 percent of test-takers receive a score above 4.5 and only 9 percent receive a score below 3.

• You can find a complete concordance of GRE scores and their percentile equivalents on page 23 of this document: **http://www.ets.org/s/gre/pdf/gre_guide.pdf**.

➤ As you prepare for the GRE, we strongly encourage you to research the programs to which you plan to apply.

• Get a general sense of what sorts of scores your programs are looking for. See whether they have "cutoff" scores below which they no longer consider applicants.

• Knowing what you need to achieve is important. If your program needs an elite math score, it's best to know immediately so that you can make time to prepare properly!

➤ In some cases, you'll find the information you need online. In many cases, however, you'll need to contact your program directly.

• If you are reluctant to do so, bear this in mind: many programs are more forthcoming about scores in person or over the phone than they are by email or on the internet.

• Moreover, it never hurts to make contact with a prospective program. Saying "hi" gives you a chance to ask important questions and — if you can present yourself intelligently and professionally — to make a good impression on a potential committee member.

➤ If a school tells you they are looking for applicants with an average score of 160 per section, remember that such quotes are only averages!

• Some applicants will be accepted with scores below those averages and some will be turned down with scores above them.

• An average is simply a "ballpark" figure that you want to shoot for. Coming up short doesn't guarantee rejection (particularly if the rest of your application is strong), and achieving it doesn't ensure admission.

➤ Unfortunately, not all programs are willing to divulge average or "cutoff" GRE scores to the public.

• If that's the case with a program you're interested, here are some general pointers to keep in mind:

1. Engineering, Economics, and Hard Sciences programs are likely to place far more emphasis on your Quantitative Reasoning score than your other scores.

2. The more prestigious a university it is, the more likely its programs will demand higher scores than comparable programs at other schools.

3. Public Health, Public Policy, and International Affairs programs likely require very strong scores for all three portions of the GRE.

4. Education, Sociology, and Nursing programs are less likely to require outstanding scores.

➢ Should you wish to get a sense of average GRE scores, by intended field of study, you can do so here: **http://www.ets.org/s/gre/pdf/gre_guide_table4.pdf**.

• When viewing these scores, remember that these are the scores of INTENDED applicants!

• The average score of ACCEPTED applicants is likely to be higher for many programs — in some cases, much higher.

➢ Finally, it's worth noting that many programs use GRE scores to determine which applicants will receive SCHOLARSHIPS.

• When contacting programs, be sure to ask them about the averages or "cutoffs" for scholarship recipients.

• And if you find it difficult to study for an exam that has little to do with your intended field of study, just remember: strong GRE scores = $$$!

(9) Registering for the GRE – The GRE is administered via computer in over 160 countries on a near daily basis.

- This means that you can that you take the GRE almost ANY day of the year.

  ➤ To register, you must create a personalized GRE account, which you can do online at **http://www.ets.org/gre/revised_general/register/**.

- When creating your account, the NAME you use must MATCH the name you use to register for the GRE.

- **It must also match the name on your official identification EXACTLY!** If it doesn't, you may be prohibited from taking the exam (without refund).

  ➤ We encourage you to schedule a date that gives you ample time to prepare properly. Don't choose a random date just to get it over with!

- If possible, wait until you score a few points higher than your target score at least TWO TIMES in a row on practice exams. Doing so will ensure that you're ready to take the exam.

- When scheduling the time of day, **don't schedule an 8 a.m. exam if you are not accustomed to waking up at 6:30 a.m. or earlier**. The exam is challenging enough. Don't take it when you're likely to be groggy or weary!

  ➤ If you plan to take the exam on a specific date, register at least one month in advance. Exam centers have limited capacity, so dates can fill up quickly, especially in the fall.

- On the day of the test, be sure to bring your official identification and your GRE admission ticket.

- Once you register for the exam, your admission ticket can be printed out at any time through your personalized GRE account online.

  ➤ Finally, if you need to reschedule or cancel your exam date, you must do so no later than FOUR days before your test date. (Ten days for individuals in mainland China.)

- This means that a Saturday test date must be canceled by Tuesday and that an April 18th test date must be canceled by April 14th.

- You can find more information on canceling or rescheduling a test date here: **http://www.ets.org/gre/revised_general/register/change**.

(10) Reporting & Canceling Scores – Immediately upon completing your exam, you will be given the opportunity to cancel your scores or to report them.

- If you choose to cancel your scores, they will be deleted irreversibly.

  ➢ Neither you nor the programs to which you're applying will see the numbers. Your official score report, however, will indicate a canceled test.

- In general, there's almost no reason to cancel your scores.

- **The GRE has a Score Select option that allows you to decide which scores to send if you've taken the GRE more than once**. Thus, if you take the exam a second time (or a third time), you can simply choose which set of scores to report.

  ➢ If you choose to report your scores, you will immediately see your unofficial Quantitative Reasoning and Verbal Reasoning scores.

- Roughly 10 to 15 days after your test date, you will receive an email notifying you that your official scores and your Analytical Writing score are available.

- To view them, simply go to the personalized GRE account you created to register for the exam.

  ➢ You won't need to memorize any school CODES to send your scores while at the test center.

- Such codes will be accessible by computer, should you wish to report your scores when you're there. To get the code for a particular program, you'll need:

  1. The name of the college (e.g. College of Arts & Sciences).
  2. The name of the university.
  3. The city and state of its location.

- As long as you have this information for each of your programs, you'll have everything you need to send out your score reports on the spot.

  ➢ **Your OFFICIAL and UNOFFICIAL scores are unlikely to differ**. If they do, the difference will almost surely be a single point.

- For example, your Verbal Reasoning score may rise from a 157 to a 158 or your Quantitative Reasoning score may dip from a 162 to a 161.

• The scores you receive on test day are an estimate comparing your performance with previous data. The official scores compare your performance with those of everyone who took that particular exam – hence the potential discrepancy.

> **Your official scores will be valid for FIVE years**. For example, a test taken on August 2nd, 2015 will be valid until August 1st, 2020.

• Over the course of those five years, your scaled scores will never change. The percentiles, however, may shift marginally.

• Thus, a scaled Verbal Reasoning score of 162 may equate to the 89th percentile in 2015. Come 2018, however, that 162 may equate to a 91st percentile.

> On test day, after viewing your unofficial scores, you will be given a choice at the test center.

• You can choose NOT to send your scores at that time or to send **free score reports** to as many as FOUR graduate programs or fellowship sponsors.

• If you choose to send out score reports at the test center, you will be given two further options:

1. The **Most Recent** option – send your scores from the test you've just completed.
2. The **All** option – send the scores from all the GREs you've taken in the last five years.

> After your test date, you can send additional score reports for a fee. **For each report**, you will be given the options above.

• **You will also be given the option to send your scores from just one exam OR from ANY exams you've taken over the last five years.**

• You cannot, however, choose your best Quantitative Reasoning score from one exam and your best Verbal Reasoning score from another. When sending scores, you must send all the scores you receive on a particular exam date.

> ➤ Given all of these options, **here's our advice**. First, NEVER cancel your scores. There's no point.

• Even if you believe you've had a bad performance, you may as well learn how you did. You never know — you might even be pleasantly surprised.

• If your scores are great, you're done. Send out your scores on test day to take advantage of the four free score reports.

> ➤ If you feel you can do better, retake the exam as soon as possible. Don't let your hard work go to waste.

• Anyone can have a bad day, misplay their time, or make an uncharacteristic number of careless errors.

• **You can retake the exam every 21 days** and up to 5 times within any 12-month period, so you won't have to wait long.

> ➤ Upon receiving your second set of scores, use the Score Select option on test day to determine which set of scores to send for free (or to send both sets).

• In the unpleasant event that you take the exam more than twice, consider utilizing the Score Select option the day after your last exam.

• This will allow you to send the single set of scores (or pair of scores) that puts you in the best possible light. Of course, if that last score is awesome, use the four free score reports to send out your most recent scores while you're at the test center!

Navigating the Exam

(11) How the Exam Works – Although the GRE is administered on computer, the exam has been designed to mimic the experience of a traditional, paper-based standardized test.

• This means that you can:

    ☑ Skip questions and return to them later.
    ☑ Leave questions blank.
    ☑ Change or edit an answer.

• You can even "flag" questions with a check mark as a reminder to revisit them before time expires. (As with a paper-based exam, however, you cannot return to a section once that section ends.)

    ➤ If you took the GRE before 2011, you'll notice that this format differs dramatically from the one you remember.

• **The exam is no longer adaptive on a question-by-question basis**, so the problems don't get harder if you answer a prior problem correctly.

• In fact, you can now preview every question within a section the moment that section begins. (If you like, you can even do the problems in reverse order.)

    ➤ There are, however, a few differences between the way the GRE works and that of most paper-based standardized tests.

• First, the questions in each section do NOT get progressively harder.

• Unlike, say, the SAT, where the first questions within a section are generally easy and the last questions within a section are generally hard, **the difficulty of GRE questions varies throughout a particular section**. In other words, a section might start with a hard question and end with an easy question.

    ➤ Furthermore, the GRE has a "Review Screen" that allows you to see which questions you've answered and which ones you haven't.

• The Review Screen can also be used to see which questions you've flagged for further review. (A very helpful feature!)

➢ **Finally, the GRE adapts on a section-by-section basis**. If you perform well on your first quantitative section, your second quantitative section will be harder.

• Likewise, if you do not perform well on your first quantitative section, your second quantitative section will be easier.

• The verbal sections work this way, too. The quantitative and verbal sections, however, are independent of one another. A strong performance on a verbal section will not result in more difficult quantitative sections, or vice versa.

➢ According to our experiments with the GRE's official test software, **how you perform on your first quantitative section can produce 1 of 3 results.**

• The same is true of your performance on the first verbal section:

Approximate # of Correct Questions on First Section	Difficulty Level of Second Section
0 to 6	Easy
7 to 13	Medium
14 to 20	Hard

• In some exams, it might take 15 correct answers to end up with a hard second section. In others, it might take 13. The correlation between the number of questions you get right and the difficulty level of your second section, however, generally matches the chart above.

➢ Our experiments also indicate that **the difficulty of the questions that you get right has no bearing on the difficulty level of the second section.**

• In other words, getting any 14 (or so) questions correct will give you a hard second section — it doesn't matter whether those questions are the hardest 14 or the easiest 14.

• It also doesn't matter how quickly you answer anything. There are no bonus points for solving problems quickly.

➢ It should, however, be noted that **a hard second section is not comprised entirely of hard questions,** nor an easy second section entirely of easy questions.

• The questions in ANY section span a range of difficulties. A hard second section simply has a greater number of hard questions than an easy one. Thus, if you receive easy questions in your second quantitative section, it does not mean that you've done poorly!

(12) The Scoring Algorithm – Exactly how the GRE is scored is a closely guarded secret.

• From the official practice test software, however, it's clear that Quantitative Reasoning and Verbal Reasoning scores are essentially the byproducts of two factors:

1. How many questions you answer correctly.
2. Whether your second sections are easy, medium, or hard.

• As you may recall from our discussion of the structure of the GRE, every exam has two Quantitative Reasoning sections and two Verbal Reasoning sections that count.

➢ Since each of these sections has 20 questions, every GRE has 40 Quantitative Reasoning questions and 40 Verbal Reasoning questions.

• As you may also recall, each of these measures is scored on a 41-point scale (from 130 to 170). This means, that **each question is essentially worth 1 point**.

• Thus, to get a Quantitative Reasoning score of 170, you likely need to answer all 40 questions correctly. Each question that you get wrong more or less subtracts 1 point from your score.

➢ In analyzing the practice test software, however, it's also apparent that there are deductions for failing to achieve a hard or medium second section.

• In general, these deductions range from 1 to 3 points.

• For example, if you were to get 11 questions correct on your first Quantitative Reasoning section, your score would be lowered 9 points on account of the 9 questions you got wrong or left blank since the exam treats blank and incorrect answers equally. (**There is NO PENALTY for getting problems wrong, so always GUESS when you're stuck!**)

➢ Your 11 correct answers, however, would also result in a second section of medium difficulty.

• Thus, your score would be lowered an additional 1 to 3 points for failing to make it to the hard section.

• Likewise, if you were to answer only 4 questions correctly in your first Quantitative Reasoning section, your score would be lowered 16 points for the blank or incorrect answers, 1 to 3 points for failing to make it to the hard section, and another 1 to 3 points for failing to make it to the medium section.

➢ Thus, a test taker who gets 10 questions right in each of his or her Quantitative Reasoning sections would likely receive a score from 147 to 149.

• The 20 questions left blank or answered incorrectly would deduct 20 points from the total score.

• Failing to make it to the hard section would deduct an additional 1 to 3 points. Subtracted from 170 (a perfect score), this would leave a final score of 147 to 149:

170	A perfect score
10	10 missed questions in section 1
10	10 missed questions in section 2
− 1 to 3	The penalty for not reaching the hard section
147 to 149	

➢ In all likelihood, the scoring algorithm considers a few other factors as well.

• For example, when exam-makers opt to include a greater number of difficult questions on a particular exam, they likely slide the scale for that exam 1 to 2 points in order to normalize its data with past exams that contain fewer difficult questions.

• From what we've seen, however, the dynamics described above will predict your score perfectly in most instances.

(13) Strategy & Time Management – Given the factors we've just discussed, there are several tactics that we recommend when taking the GRE.

1. SKIP around.

• It doesn't matter which questions you get right, so you may as well work on the questions that are easiest for you first.

> **Don't waste your time on a question that you don't understand or that confuses you.**

• Engaging such questions will only take time from questions that may be easier for you. If you come across something that makes you nauseous, FLAG IT and double back after you've solved the questions that you know how to solve.

2. FOCUS on your FAVORITE 15.

• As we've seen, there are potentially harsh deductions for failing to achieve a hard or medium second section.

> Since reaching the hard second section generally demands a minimum of 13 to 15 correct responses, we encourage you to focus your efforts on the 15 easiest questions.

• You shouldn't ignore the hardest 5 questions, but you should save them for last. **If you don't think you can answer 15 questions correctly, focus your efforts on the easiest 10 questions.** Landing in the lowest tier can devastate your score.

3. GUESS on questions that you don't understand.

• We've also seen that an incorrect answer is no worse than a blank answer, so you may as well guess on anything that you don't understand and flag it for further review. Remember, there's no penalty for guessing!

> As you'll see, **there's either a 1 in 5 chance or a 1 in 4 chance of guessing most GRE questions correctly.**

• Those chances increase if you can eliminate a couple of answer choices through logic. If you have time left over, you can return to the questions you've flagged after you've answered everything else.

4.   REMEMBER the ⌈"Two-and-a-Half Minute Rule"⌉.

• Over the years at Sherpa Prep, we've noticed that test-takers who take more than 2.5 minutes to solve a question do so correctly only 25% of the time.

> Given that there are usually five answers to choose from, the odds of guessing correctly are 20%. If you can eliminate bad answer choices, those odds rise further!

• We know that it's tempting to battle questions to the end, especially if you "think" you can solve them. **Stubbornly hanging on, however, is a sure way to MANGLE your score**.

• Doing so wastes time (time that could be used to solve other problems) and is no more likely to result in a correct answer than guessing.

> So, if you find yourself stuck on a particular question, do yourself a favor: flag the question, then guess.

• If you can eliminate answer choices before doing so, great. Obeying the "2.5 minute rule" will help you save time for the questions at the end of the exam and avoid the debilitating panic that comes upon realizing that you've squandered your time.

5.   Don't work TOO QUICKLY.

• We know that time is a critical factor on the GRE and that the exam-makers don't give you much of it.

> **Working at a frenzied pace, however, will only result in one thing — careless errors. A lot of them.**

• The key to saving time is obeying the "2.5 minute rule" and learning the right way to solve each type of problem – not working at breakneck speeds.

 • If you know how to solve a problem, take the time to do so properly. You may not have time to triple check your work, but you do have time to work through any problem with care.

> **Watch out, however, for any question that you can solve in 10 seconds or fewer.**

• While there are plenty of GRE problems that can be solved in 10 seconds, exam-makers often design questions to take advantage of quick assumptions. Taking an extra 10 seconds to ensure that you haven't missed something is a great way to catch potential traps!

<u>**(14) Practice Tests**</u> – As you work through <u>Master Key to the GRE</u>, we strongly encourage you to take a practice exam every week or two.

• Success on the GRE is not just the byproduct of mastering its content — it also demands good test-taking skills.

> ➤ **Taking practice exams will help you build stamina and improve your time management.**

• Remember, the GRE takes nearly four hours to complete. Learning how to deal with the fatigue you'll encounter is part of the battle!

• The same is true of the pacing of the exam. If you don't master the speed at which you need to work, you can easily sabotage your score by working too quickly or too leisurely.

> ➤ Before you take the GRE, we encourage you to **take a minimum of SIX practice exams**.

• If you're like most test-takers, you'll need anywhere from six to eight practice exams to properly familiarize yourself with the GRE.

• For the first few — don't bother with the essays. As you begin your preparation, your time is better spent studying new material and reviewing what you've learned. Towards the end of your preparation, however, your practice exams should be full-blown dress rehearsals.

> ➤ **There are a number of different practice exams available online. Of these, only two are produced by the ETS, the company that designs the GRE.**

• At no cost, you can download the software that runs these exams from the following address: **http://www.ets.org/gre/revised_general/prepare/powerprep2/**.

• These exams have been designed to work on both Macs and PCs. As long as your computer's operating system and software are reasonably up to date, you should be able to use them on any computer.

> ➤ For additional exams, almost any of the available options will do. While they all have issues of one sort or another, most are reasonable facsimiles of the GRE.

• When taking such exams, however, please bear in mind that they are NOT the real thing. Some of their questions are unrealistic and their score predictions, though roughly accurate, are best taken with a grain of salt.

➢ Whenever you take a practice exam, it's important that you **make the experience as REALISTIC as possible**.

• Doing things you can't do on test day will only corrupt your practice results and prevent you from adopting helpful habits.

• If you can, take each exam in one sitting and resist the urge to pause the test or to use outside help. Likewise, refrain from drinking or eating during your tests. No coffee, no water, no snacks. Save these things for your 10-minute break between sections 3 and 4.

➢ Remember, you're preparing for a stressful "brain marathon" that's essentially 4-hours long. You'll need STAMINA to be successful.

• Figure out how much you need to eat and drink before your test. Figure out what to eat during your break. Identify the kind of foods that suit you best.

• The same goes for your bathroom habits. At the exam center, you can't pause the test to go to the bathroom. So, use your practice exams to learn how your eating habits affect your bodily needs! "Holding it in" for over an hour is a brutal way to take this test.

➢ As you take your practice exams, do your best to **stay off the "emotional rollercoaster"**. Don't get too high when things go well.

• And don't get too down if your scores don't shoot up instantly. Improving GRE scores is hard work.

• For some people, progress is a slow, steady crawl. For others, it's an uneven process, filled with periods of stagnation, occasional drops, and dramatic increases.

➢ However your exams may be going, keep grinding away! Stay focused on your goals and keep up the hard work.

• Test-takers who prepare like professionals — who keep an even keel, who do their assignments properly, and who commit to improving their weaknesses — ALWAYS achieve their goals in the end.

• As we tell our students, preparing for the GRE is like going to the gym. It may take you a while to get in shape, but ANYONE can do so if they put in the time and train properly.

> **After you complete each practice exam, go through it carefully and learn from your mistakes.**

• See whether you can identify any trends in your performance. Are you working too quickly and making careless errors? Are you struggling with the same topics repeatedly?

• Are you running out of time because you're violating the "2.5 minute rule"? Do you start off strong and then taper off as the test goes along? Does it take you half an hour to get "locked in" and then get better as you go?

> A lot of people believe they are "bad test-takers". This is nonsense. The reality is that people get questions wrong for tangible reasons.

• Analyzing your mistakes when the "game is real" will allow you to PINPOINT those reasons so you can ADDRESS them.

• To help you become a more "self-aware" test-taker, we encourage you to fill out the following table every time you complete an exam:

	Knew How to Solve	Didn't Know How to Solve
Correct	Bravo!	Luck
Incorrect	Carelessness?	**Expected**

> If you get a question wrong because you don't know how to solve it, see whether you can identify its TOPIC or notice any TRENDS.

• For example, you might notice that a lot of your mistakes involve Algebra. If so, that's a clear indication that you need to improve your Algebra skills.

• If you get a question wrong despite knowing how to solve it, see whether you can figure out how it happened. Did you misread the question? Did you write down information incorrectly? Did you make a silly math error?

> Mistakes such as these are often the result of RUSHING, which in turn is generally the byproduct of poor time management elsewhere.

• So keep track, to the best of your abilities, of whether you are finishing your sections too quickly or are making frantic efforts to finish because you're violating the "2.5 minute rule" too frequently. Both scenarios generally lead to a host of careless mistakes that will sabotage your progress.

Intro to Quantitative Reasoning

(15) Content Overview – The quantitative portion of the GRE is designed to measure your ability to think <u>smartly</u> about math — to find simple solutions to problems that seem complicated.

• The problems that you'll encounter may appear difficult or time-consuming, but there's ALWAYS a straightforward way to solve them.

> ➤ In terms of content, the GRE solely tests concepts that you learned in high school or use in everyday life.

• These concepts fall into four categories:

1. Arithmetic, Algebra, and Number Properties
2. Word Problems
3. Data Interpretation
4. Geometry

> ➤ You won't find any Calculus or Trigonometry on the GRE, nor will you find some of the more sophisticated forms of Algebra typically taught in an Algebra II course.

• That's because the emphasis of this exam is on your ability to reason.

• By limiting the content to the topics listed above, the GRE becomes less about "what you know" (everyone studied those topics in high school) and more about your ability to APPLY commonly known information and to think logically.

> ➤ This said, don't be fooled into thinking that GRE math can't be sophisticated. The exam demands that you know these topics EXTREMELY well.

• To be successful on the GRE, you'll need to relearn everything you learned about them (or were supposed to learn) back in high school.

• And, if you want to solve the most advanced questions, you'll need to learn a few intricacies that you almost surely were never taught.

➤ Based on our analysis of the official exam materials released to the public, roughly one-third of GRE questions focus on Arithmetic, Algebra, and Number Properties.

• Approximately 33% are Word Problems and a little more than a third involve Geometry or the interpretation of Charts and Graphs:

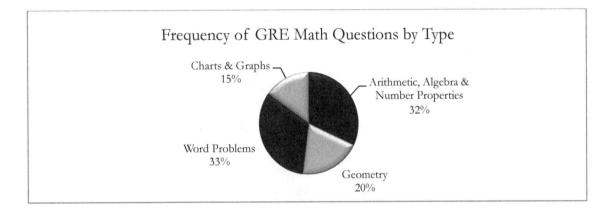

Frequency of GRE Math Questions by Type

Charts & Graphs 15%

Arithmetic, Algebra & Number Properties 32%

Word Problems 33%

Geometry 20%

• When viewing the diagram above, bear in mind that Word Problems and problems involving Geometry or Charts and Graphs often demand the use of Algebra and Arithmetic. Thus, in many ways, Algebra and Arithmetic are even more critical to your success than the diagram above suggests.

➤ Volume 1 of <u>Master Key to the GRE</u> is devoted to **Arithmetic & "Plan B" Strategies**.

• Here, you'll find discussion of such topics as:

Arithmetic Shortcuts	Strategies for "Smart Math"
Essential Number Lists	Strategies for Using the Answer Choices
Fractions	Number Picking Strategies
Decimals	Strategies for Guessing
Digit Problems	

➤ Volume 2 is dedicated to **Number Properties & Algebra**. Among the topics you'll find covered are:

Factors & Multiples	Exponents & Roots
Prime Factorization	The Properties of Evens & Odds
Number Line Problems	Algebra
Absolute Value	Functions, Sequences & Symbolism
Remainder Problems	

> Our discussion of **Word Problems** is divided between Volumes 3 and 4. Volume 3 focuses on topics such as:

Percents	Algebraic Word Problems
Mixtures	Age Problems
Alterations	Overlapping Sets
Ratios & Proportions	Exponential & Linear Growth
Rate Problems	

- Volume 4 examines **Statistics & Data Interpretation**.

> Among the various chapters of Volume 4, you'll find discussions of a wide range of topics, including:

Means, Medians & Modes	Probability
Weighed Averages	Combinatorics
Standard Deviation	Bar Graphs & Line Graphs
Quartiles & Boxplots	Pie Charts & Data Tables
Normal Distributions	Multi-Figure Data Sets
Equally Spaced Number Sets	

- Finally, Volume 5 is devoted to **Geometry**.

> Here, you'll find a detailed treatment of everything you may have been taught in high-school but have probably forgotten.

- The major topics include:

Lines & Angles	Rectangular Solids
Triangles	Cylinders
Quadrilaterals	Coordinate Geometry
Polygons	
Circles	

- If all of this seems intimidating, don't worry! We promise you: Master Key to the GRE will show you just how simple these concepts can be.

(16) Problem Solving Questions – Before we get started, let's take a few pages to discuss the ways in which the GRE formats its math questions.

• As you may recall, every GRE has two Quantitative Reasoning sections. Since each of these sections has 20 questions, your exam will feature a total of 40 math questions (that actually count).

   ➢ 25 of these will be "Problem Solving" questions and 15 will be "Quantitative Comparison" questions.

• If you've taken standardized tests before, Problem Solving questions will be familiar to you. Here's an example:

If $x + y > 14$ and $x = 2y + 8$, then which of the following must be true?

(A) $y < -3$ **(B)** $y < -2$ **(C)** $y = 0$ **(D)** $y > 2$ **(E)** $y > 4$

Answer. D. To answer questions in this format, you simply need to select the answer choice that represents the correct answer.

   ➢ Here, for example, we've been told that $x = 2y + 8$. Thus, we can rewrite $x + y > 14$ as follows, by substituting $2y + 8$ for x:

      Replace x with $2y + 8$

            ⟶ $(2y + 8) + y > 14$

• To simplify the Algebra, we can drop the parentheses and subtract 8 from both sides of the inequality. Doing so proves that the correct is (D), since:

$2y + 8 + y > 14$	Drop the parentheses.
$2y + y > 6$	Subtract 8 from both sides.
$3y > 6$	Add $2y + y$.
$y > 2$	Divide both sides by 3.

• If the math doesn't make sense here, don't worry! This question is simply intended to show you what a Problem Solving question looks like. The math behind it is covered in our book on Number Properties & Algebra.

(17) "Select One or More" Questions – From time to time, Problem Solving questions will prompt you to select one or more answer choices.

• On a typical exam, each quantitative section will contain (at most) one or two of these questions.

> ➤ "Select One or More" questions are easy to spot — they always ask you to "indicate all such values".

• What's more, **the answer choices are always in square boxes**. In regular Problem Solving questions, the answer choices are circled.

• According to the Official Guide to the GRE revised General Test, the directions for such questions are always as follows:

<u>Directions:</u> Select ONE or MORE answer choices according to the specific directions.

• If the question does not specify how many answer choices to select, you must select ALL that apply. The correct answer may be just one of the choices or as many as all of the choices. **There must, however, be at least one correct answer**.

> ➤ The exam-makers further specify that no credit is given unless you select all of the correct answers and no others. In other words, there is NO PARTIAL credit.

• Thus, if there are two correct answers, and you only select one, the GRE gives you zero credit. The same is true if there are three correct answers and you select four.

• Let's take a look at a sample question:

If $-2 \leq x \leq 8$ and $-4 \leq y \leq 3$, which of the following could represent the value of xy?

Indicate <u>all</u> such values.

$\boxed{A}$ -40 $\boxed{B}$ -32 $\boxed{C}$ 7 $\boxed{D}$ 15 $\boxed{E}$ 32

Answer: B, C, and D. Notice that there are two clues indicating that we may need to select more than one answer here.

- First, the question asks us to "indicate all such values". **Additionally, the answer choices are in boxes.**

  ➢ To answer this question, we first need to determine the range of possible values for xy.

- We can do so by identifying the greatest and smallest possible values for x and y.

- According to the problem, $-2 \leq x \leq 8$ and $-4 \leq y \leq 3$. Thus, the greatest and smallest values for each variable are:

$$x = -2 \text{ and } 8 \qquad\qquad y = -4 \text{ and } 3$$

  ➢ Next, we can **test all four combinations** of x times y to determine the largest and smallest values of xy.

- If x can be as small as -2 and as large as 8, and y can be as small as -3 and as large as 4, then those combinations would be:

Combo #1	Combo #2	Combo #3	Combo #4
$(-2)(-4) = 8$	$(-2)(3) = -6$	$(8)(-4) = -32$	$(8)(3) = 24$

  ➢ As we can see from these combinations, the greatest possible value of x times y is 24 and the smallest possible value is -32.

- Thus, the range of values for xy extends from -32 to 24. Algebraically, this can be stated as $-32 \leq xy \leq 24$.

- Since -32, 7, and 15 all fall within the range of value from -32 to 24, **we must select** $\boxed{\text{B}}$, $\boxed{\text{C}}$, **and** $\boxed{\text{D}}$, **and nothing more, to get credit for this question.** If we fail to select all three answer choices, or select a fourth, our response would be considered incorrect.

  ➢ Again, if the math doesn't make sense here, don't worry! This question is simply intended to show you what a "Select One or More" question looks like.

- The math behind it is covered in our book on Number Properties & Algebra.

(18) Numeric Entry Questions – On each of your quantitative sections, anywhere from one to three of your Problem Solving questions will ask you for a "Numeric Entry".

• Numeric Entry questions prompt you to **type a numeric answer into a box** below the problem.

> ➢ Such questions tend to be more difficult than other Problem Solving questions since you can't use the answer choices to determine whether you're on the right track.

• Further, it's almost impossible to guess the correct answer. With regular Problem Solving questions, you at least have a 1 in 5 chance of getting lucky.

• Let's take a look at a sample question:

When walking, a person takes 24 complete steps in 15 seconds. At this rate, how many steps does this person take in 5 seconds?

• There are several ways to solve a problem like this. Perhaps the easiest way is to set up a proportion:

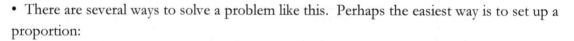

$$\frac{24 \text{ steps}}{15 \text{ seconds}} = \frac{x \text{ steps}}{5 \text{ seconds}}$$

• When comparing the bottoms of the two fractions, notice that "15 seconds" is exactly three times as large as "5 seconds".

> ➢ With proportions, the relationship between the tops of the fractions is the same as that between the bottoms.

• In other words, "24 steps" must be three times as large as "x steps", since "15 seconds" is three times as large as "5 seconds".

• Thus, $x = 8$, because 24 is three times as large as 8. To solve this problem, therefore, **we would need to type 8 into the numeric entry box** beneath the question.

> ➢ As with the previous sections, don't worry if the math doesn't make sense here! This question is simply intended to show you what a Numeric Entry question looks like.

• The math behind it is covered properly in our book on Word Problems.

(19) Quantitative Comparisons – The rest of your math questions will prompt you to compare two quantities.

• Such questions, commonly known as "Quantitative Comparisons", consist of two quantities, labeled Quantity A and Quantity B, and, in many cases, some additional information.

> ➢ Beneath the two quantities you'll find four answer choices, asking which of the two quantities is LARGER. The answer choices are always the SAME.

• **MEMORIZE them IMMEDIATELY.** 15 of your 40 math questions will be in this format. If you spend 10 seconds wading through the answer choices on each of these questions, you'll be wasting 2.5 minutes of your exam!

• Let's take a look at a sample problem:

$$xy \geq 1$$

Quantity A	**Quantity B**
xy	$(xy)^3$

(A) **Quantity A is greater.**
(B) **Quantity B is greater.**
(C) **The quantities are equal.**
(D) **The relationship cannot be determined from the information given.**

Answer: D. At the top of the problem, we are told that $xy \geq 1$. This means that xy can be any value equal to or greater than one.

> ➢ If $xy = 1$, notice that the quantities are equal, since $(1)^3 = 1 \times 1 \times 1 = 1$. If $xy = 2$, however, notice that Quantity B is greater than Quantity A, since $(2)^3 = 2 \times 2 \times 2 = 8$.

• Because the two quantities can be equal or can be different, we cannot determine which quantity is larger from the given information. The correct answer is therefore (D).

• Any time two quantities have an INCONSISTENT RELATIONSHIP — i.e. any time that A can be greater than or equal to B or that B can be greater than or equal to A — the relationship between the two quantities CANNOT be determined.

(20) Before You Get Started – If you've read through the preceding pages, you're ready to get started.

• Before you do, we'd like to offer you a last few bits of advice. We know that many people who take the GRE are not very comfortable with math.

➢ If you're one of them, you may have been told at an early age that you weren't a "math person" or that your brain "doesn't work that way".

• That's total nonsense. The truth is that EVERYONE can learn the sort of math required by the GRE.

• Yes, it may require hard work — especially if you haven't done math in over a decade. But you CAN do it. Don't let the idiotic assessment of a bad teacher or a misogynist prevent you from attaining your goals.

➢ As you begin to practice, **DON'T try to do everything in your head**. Scratch work is an IMPORTANT part of the problem solving process.

• Taking notes will SPEED you up and help you avoid careless errors.

• Make sure, however, that your writing is organized and legible. Sloppy handwriting is a sure path to careless errors. Writing the work for one problem atop the work for another problem is even worse. (Yes, some people do this.)

➢ Likewise, **make sure that your handwriting is appropriately sized**. If you can solve twenty problems on a single sheet of paper, your writing is too small.

• Yes, the GRE only provides you with a few sheets of unlined scratch paper, but you can always raise your hand to trade for new sheets BEFORE you run out.

• Conversely, if you're using one sheet of paper per question, write smaller. You shouldn't need to request paper frequently. Divide your sheets of scratch paper into six equal sections. With proper penmanship, you should be able to fit the work for any problem in one of the sections.

➢ When solving problems, **beware of crazy decimals or fractions**. If your scratch work involves something like $0.123 \times \frac{7}{13}$, you're doing something wrong.

• In general, the GRE tends to use "smart numbers" — numbers that are designed to yield simple results under the proper analysis.

- When the GRE uses exotic numbers, the exam is almost always testing your ability to identify patterns or relationships (e.g. $0.\overline{54} = \frac{5}{9}$) or to approximate.

  ➢ If you're worried about anxiety, preparing THOROUGHLY for the GRE is the best way to beat test-taking jitters.

- Nothing calms unsteady nerves more than seeing problems you KNOW how to solve because the content is EASY for you.

- You should also **set up a test date that allows you enough time to schedule a retake**, if necessary. (Remember, you can take the GRE every 21 days and up to 5 times a year.) Knowing that you'll have a second shot at the GRE can take the pressure off your first exam.

  ➢ On test day, bring food and water with you to the exam center. You'll be there for nearly five hours.

- Doing anything for that length of time is fatiguing. Eating a few nuts and a piece of fruit before your exam (and during your break) will help keep you sharp.

- Just be sure to steer clear of drinking too much water or consuming too much sugar or caffeine. You don't want to take multiple bathroom breaks while your exam is running or to crash during the final hour of your test.

  ➢ If you can, **get to the test center early**. Taking the GRE is stressful enough. You don't want to exacerbate that stress by running late.

- Plan to get there a half hour in advance. If you're commuting to an unfamiliar area, research the commute carefully and allot an additional 15 minutes (in case you get lost).

- Once inside (don't forget your ID and admissions ticket!), use the extra time to warm up with a few practice problems or to review your notes. Doing so will help get your brain "in gear" before your exam.

  ➢ Finally, **brace yourself for broken air-conditioners, sniffling neighbors, and unfriendly staffers**.

- Although test centers are generally well run, it's important to remember that there can be problems.

- As long as you dress in layers, however, and make use of the headphones or earplugs that are supplied with your exam, these issues shouldn't pose you any problems.

Chapter 2

Integer Properties

Integer Properties

To be discussed:

Fundamental Concepts

Whether you're aiming for a perfect score or a score closer to average, mastery of the following concepts is essential.

Rare or Advanced Concepts

The following concepts are either advanced or are tested only on rare occasions. If you don't need an elite math score, don't waste your time!

Practice Questions

There's no substitute for elbow grease. Practice your new skills to ensure that you internalize what you've studied.

Fundamental Concepts

(1) Introduction – The term "Integer Properties" designates a wide array of concepts, all of which involve the interplay of whole numbers (integers) or the analysis of their composition.

- For example, the following questions would all be considered Integer Properties questions:

"If x is odd and y is not, must xy^{xy} be even?"

"If $p^4 r^5 q^6 < 0$, is r positive or negative?"

"How many factors of 64 are multiples of 4?"

❯ Questions testing these concepts are frequently encountered on the GRE.

- In fact, questions involving Integer Properties appear more often than those involving Fractions, Decimals, Exponents, or Roots:

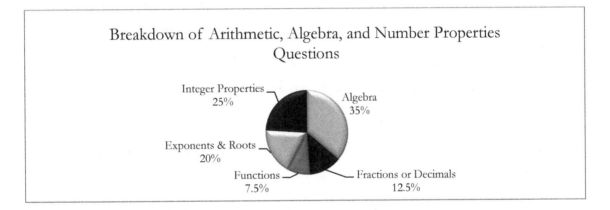

Breakdown of Arithmetic, Algebra, and Number Properties Questions

- Like most subjects tested by the GRE, the subject of Integer Properties likely contains some topics that are familiar to you and others that are not.

- Whatever the case may be, let's first make sure that you are comfortable with the subject's most basic concepts and terminology.

❯ To start, a **number line** is a picture of a straight line on which every point corresponds to a number and every number to a point.

- Numbers that correspond to points LEFT of zero are known as **negative numbers** and numbers that correspond to points RIGHT of zero are known as **positive numbers**.

➢ Although the image below only shows the numbers from –8 to 8, the line includes ALL numbers and continues forever in each direction:

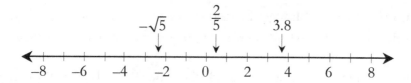

• Any point between two whole numbers corresponds to a decimal, or its fractional equivalent, and every point corresponds to a real number.

• **A real number is a number that is not imaginary**. Every positive and negative number is a real number, as is every whole number, fraction, and decimal.

➢ Thus, numbers such as –4, $\frac{3}{4}$, 2, and 3.8 are all considered real numbers, since each of these numbers can be found on the number line.

• Real numbers stand in contrast to imaginary numbers, which are numbers that do not exist. **An imaginary number can be defined as the square root of any negative number**.

• Such numbers are considered imaginary because it is impossible to square a number and obtain a negative product.

• For example, $\sqrt{-4}$ is an imaginary number, since no known number can be squared to obtain –4.

➢ In many cases, whole numbers are shown as specially-marked points that are evenly spaced on the line, as in the example at the top of the page.

• **Whole numbers are technically known as integers**. Thus, any number that contains no decimal or fractional part is commonly referred to as an integer.

• Positive whole numbers (1, 2, 3) and negative whole numbers (–1, –2, –3) are considered integers, since such numbers contain no decimal or fractional parts.

• Conversely, fractions ($-\frac{2}{3}, \frac{1}{2}, \frac{5}{4}$), mixed numerals ($-2\frac{1}{3}, 1\frac{2}{5}, 3\frac{4}{7}$), and decimals (–2.1, 0.2, 3.4) are not considered integers, since such numbers contain fractional or decimal parts.

➢ The term "**square of an integer**" simply refers to a specific integer that has been squared.

• For example, numbers such as 36, 81, 169, and 225 can all be referred to as "squares of an integer", since $36 = 6^2$, $81 = 9^2$, $169 = 13^2$, and $225 = 15^2$.

• Sometimes the square of an integer is referred to as a **perfect square**, since such numbers equal the square of a whole number. For example, 100 is considered a perfect square, since $100 = 10^2$.

• Conversely, 50 is not considered a perfect square. Although 50 equals the square of a number, that number is not an integer: $50 = (50\sqrt{2})^2$, and $50\sqrt{2}$ is not an integer.

➢ Finally, it is important to remember that **ZERO is considered an integer**.

• Even though it is the only number that is neither positive nor negative, it must <u>always</u> be counted as an integer.

• Likewise, although 0 is not considered positive or negative, it is considered EVEN (like 2, 4, and 6) as opposed to odd (like 1, 3, and 5).

• **When working with 0, always bear in mind that the number 0 has three <u>unique</u> properties**. If n is any number:

1. $n \pm 0 = n$.
2. $n \times 0 = 0$.
3. Division by 0 is impossible. Thus, $n \div 0 =$ undefined.

(2) Positives & Negatives – As you likely know, any number greater than zero is positive, and any number less than zero is negative.

• Perhaps less well known is that (i) zero is neither positive nor negative and that (ii) variables can represent positive, negative numbers, or zero.

> ➢ To solve problems that test your understanding of positive and negative numbers, you first need to know how to combine them.

• To **add or subtract** positive and negative numbers, simply remember that:

If both signs are the SAME, the result will <u>share</u> that sign	$7 + 8 = 15$ $-6 + (-2) = -8$ $-4 - 3 = -7$
If the signs are DIFFERENT, <u>subtract the negative</u> from the positive	$-6 + 8 = 2$ $9 + (-6) = 3$ $4 - 7 = -3$
Subtracting a NEGATIVE … is like adding a <u>positive</u>	$5 - (-6) = 5 + 6 = 11$ $-4 - (-3) = -4 + 3 = -1$

> ➢ Be careful, however, to avoid the following mistake:

Quantity A	**Quantity B**
$(9 - 4) - 3$	$9 - (4 - 3)$

Answer. B. Despite their appearance, these two quantities are not equal. Simplifying the information inside the parentheses proves that Quantity A = 2 and that Quantity B = 8:

Quantity A	Quantity B
$(\underline{9-4}) - 3 \;\rightarrow\; 5 - 3 = 2$	$9 - (\underline{4-3}) \;\rightarrow\; 9 - 1 = 8$

• Expressions such as $9 - (4 - 3)$ are often misunderstood as $9 - 4 - 3 = 2$. However, the notation indicates that we are subtracting BOTH 4 and –3 from 9. Thus, technically we are subtracting both elements within the parentheses, like so:

$$9 - (4 - 3) \;\rightarrow\; 9 - 4 - (-3) \;\rightarrow\; 9 - 4 + 3 = 8$$

• Thus, the correct answer is (B), since Quantity B is larger than Quantity A. (If you don't remember how the answer choices work for a Quantitative Comparison question, be sure to visit section ⟨19⟩ of the Introduction!)

- To **multiply or divide** positive and negative numbers, remember that:

TWO NEGATIVES …
equal a <u>positive</u>

$$-6 \times (-6) = 36$$
$$-8 \div (-2) = \frac{-8}{-2} = 4$$

One POSITIVE and one NEGATIVE …
equal a <u>negative</u>

$$5 \times (-6) = -30$$
$$6 \div (-3) = \frac{6}{-3} = -2$$

- In other words, when multiplying and dividing, two terms with the same sign will always be positive. Likewise, two terms with opposite signs will always be negative.

  ➢ This concept can be extended as follows: **when multiplying an EVEN number of negative terms, the product will be positive**.

- For example, $(-2) \times (-2) \times (-2) \times (-2) = 16$, since there are an even number of negative terms. Conversely, when multiplying an ODD number of negative terms, the product will be negative. Thus, $(-2) \times (-2) \times (-2) = -8$, as there are an odd number of negative terms.

- Note that **any term** (other than zero) **raised to an EVEN exponent must therefore be positive**, since an even exponent multiplies its base an <u>even</u> number of times. Hence, if $x \neq 0$ and $y \neq 0$, expressions such as x^2, y^4 and $(xy)^6$ must all be positive, as their exponents are even:

$$(-3)^2 = 9 \qquad (-2)^4 = 16 \qquad (-1 \times 2)^6 = 64$$

  ➢ When working with inequalities such as $x^2 y > 0$ or $x^4 y^2 z < 0$ (i.e. inequalities where the product of two or more variables is compared to <u>zero</u>), **you can always remove the even powered terms** to <u>SIMPLIFY</u> the expression.

- For example, we can rewrite the inequalities below as follows:

$$x^2 y > 0 \ \rightarrow \ y > 0 \qquad\qquad x^4 y^2 z < 0 \ \rightarrow \ z < 0 \qquad\qquad w^4 x^2 y^3 z^6 > 0 \ \rightarrow \ y^3 > 0$$

- The reason we can do this is simple: when combining positives and negatives, **only the negatives matter**. After all, a *positive* × a *negative* yields the same "sign" as a negative, and the same is true of a *positive* × a *positive* × a *negative*.

- Consider the following:

$$r^4s < 0$$
$$rs^2 > 0$$

Quantity A	**Quantity B**
r	s

Answer. A. The top inequality indicates that s is negative. Because r^4 has an even exponent, we can remove it from the statement, giving us: $r^4s < 0 \rightarrow s < 0$.

Likewise, the bottom inequality indicates that r is positive. Because s^2 has an even exponent, we can remove it from the statement, giving us: $rs^2 > 0 \rightarrow r > 0$. Since a positive number is always larger than a negative number, r must be larger than s.

> ➤ When working with variables, be sure to remember that variables can represent positive numbers, negative numbers, or zero.

• **It's easy to mistake a negative variable for a negative number**, or a positive variable for a positive number. Consider the following:

$$pq \neq 0$$

Quantity A	**Quantity B**
$-p(-q)$	0

Answer. D. We know that two negatives multiply to a positive, so $-p(-q) = pq$. However, **we don't know whether pq represents a positive or negative value**, since the variables can represent positive or negative numbers.

If p is positive and q is negative, pq would represent a negative value, since $pos \times neg = neg$. However, if p and q are both positive or both negative, pq would represent a positive value, since $neg \times neg = pos$ and $pos \times pos = pos$.

Because $-p(-q) = pq$, and pq can equal a positive or a negative value, the correct answer must be (D).

> ➤ Finally, you may find it helpful to **set up "If/Then" charts** for problems that seem advanced or overwhelming.

• "If/Then" charts will help you to determine which terms must be positive or negative and to keep track of their various combinations.

Sherpa
Prep

➤ You should also feel free to test simple numbers such as 2 or –3 if you feel that doing so might help you determine a particular outcome.

• Consider the following:

If $bc < 0$ and $ab > 0$, which of the following must be true?

Select all possible answers.

$\boxed{\text{A}}$ $ac < 0$ $\boxed{\text{B}}$ $abc > 0$ $\boxed{\text{C}}$ $abc^2 > 0$ $\boxed{\text{D}}$ $ab^2c < 0$ $\boxed{\text{E}}$ $-c < 0$

Answer. A, C, D. To solve this problem, let's first consider two scenarios: what happens if b is positive and what happens if b is negative. Why b? Because b is given in both statements.

$\boxed{\text{Scenario 1}}$: $b > 0$. According to the statement $bc < 0$, if b is positive, then c must be negative, since *pos* × *neg* = *neg*. However, according to the statement $ab > 0$, if b is positive, then a must be too, as *pos* × *pos* = *pos*. Thus, **if $b > 0$, then $c < 0$ and $a > 0$.**

$\boxed{\text{Scenario 2}}$: $b < 0$. According to the statement $bc < 0$, if b is negative, then c must be positive, since *neg* × *pos* = *neg*. However, according to the statement $ab > 0$, if b is negative, then a must be too, as *neg* × *neg* = *pos*. Thus, **if $b < 0$, then $c > 0$ and $a < 0$.**

• Let's also set up an "If/Then" chart to summarize these findings:

If	Then	And
b is +	c is −	a is +
b is −	c is +	a is −

$\boxed{\text{A}}$ $ac < 0$. True. The rows of our chart indicate that a and c have opposite signs. Therefore, ac must be negative, since *pos* × *neg* = *neg*.

$\boxed{\text{B}}$ $abc > 0$. False. The top row of our chart indicates that abc can be negative, since *pos* × *neg* × *pos* = *neg*.

$\boxed{\text{C}}$ $abc^2 > 0$. True. c^2 has an even exponent, so we can remove it from the inequality, leaving $ab > 0$. The question states that $ab > 0$, so ab must be positive.

$\boxed{\text{D}}$ $ab^2c < 0$. True. b^2 has an even exponent, so we can remove it from the inequality, leaving $ac < 0$. Our chart indicates that a and c have opposite signs, so ac must be negative.

$\boxed{\text{E}}$ $-c < 0$. False. According to our chart, c can be positive or a negative. If $c = -1$, then $-c = -(-1) = 1$, which is not less than 0.

Chapter 2: Integer Properties

<u>**(3) Absolute Value**</u> – As you likely know, a number line is simply a picture of a straight line on which every point corresponds to a number.

• Any point to the left of zero corresponds to a negative number, and any point to the right of zero corresponds to a positive number.

➢ What you may not know, or perhaps not know particularly well, is the concept of **absolute value**.

• You may recall that the absolute value of a number is indicated by **two vertical bars**. For example, the notation $|-4|$ indicates the absolute value of –4. You may also recall that absolute value brackets "**make a number positive**". Thus, $|-4| = 4$. Likewise, $|4| = 4$.

• But what exactly is absolute value? It's a measurement. It measures **the distance between zero and a particular number** on the number line. Thus, $|-4| = 4$ because –4 is "four steps from zero" on the number line.

➢ When working with absolute value, be sure to remember that **the absolute value of a number is NOT always positive**.

• Even though most people are taught that absolute value brackets "make a number positive," this is not 100% correct.

• After all, $|0| = 0$, since zero is "zero steps from zero" on the number line, and zero is neither positive nor negative. In other words, **the absolute value of a number is either positive or zero**. (Remember: distance cannot be negative!)

• Let's look at a sample problem involving absolute values:

What does the value of $|-3| + |8| + |-3 + 8| = ?$

(A) 22   (B) 16   (C) 10   (D) 5   (E) 0

Answer. B. To solve this problem, we first need to resolve each of the absolute value brackets separately:

$$|-3| = 3 \qquad |8| = 8 \qquad |-3 + 8| = |5| = 5$$

Since 3 + 8 + 5 = 16, the correct answer must be (B).

(4) **Number Line Problems** – Exam-makers can test your understanding of number lines in a variety of ways.

• The simplest number line problems typically ask you to determine **the distance between two points**. There are two ways you can do so.

  ➢ Perhaps the easiest way is to draw a number line and to **"count the steps"** between the two points.

• For example, the distance between –3 and 5 is 8, since the two numbers are clearly 8 "steps" apart:

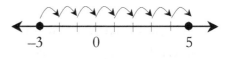

• The fastest way, however, is to **take the absolute value of their difference**. Thus, the distance between –4 and 5 must be 9, since their difference is –9, whose absolute value is 9:

$$|-4 - 5| = |-9| = 9$$

  ➢ Distance problems that involve **evenly spaced intervals**, however, are somewhat trickier.

• By "interval", we mean **the space between any two tick marks**. For example, the line segment to the right displays 5 tick marks and 4 intervals between them.

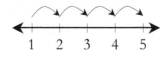

• To solve problems that involve evenly spaced intervals, you generally need to determine the length of the intervals. To do so, simply divide the distance between any two points by the number of intervals between them:

$$\frac{\textbf{Distance}}{\textbf{Number of Intervals}} = \textbf{Length of an Interval}$$

• For example, in the diagram to the right, the distance between 27 and 12 equals $|27 - 12| = 15$, and there are 5 intervals that separate the two points.

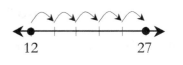

• Thus, the length of each interval must equal 3, since:

$$\frac{\text{Distance}}{\text{Number of Intervals}} = \frac{15}{5} = 3$$

➤ To get a better feel for solving problems involving evenly spaced intervals, consider the following:

The marks on the number line above are evenly spaced.

<u>Quantity A</u>   **<u>Quantity B</u>**

x **35**

Answer. B. To determine the value of x, we first need to determine the length of the intervals. The distance between 57 and 21 is 36, since $|57 - 21| = 36$, and there are 8 intervals that separate the two points. Thus, the length of the intervals must equal 4.5, as:

$$\frac{\text{Distance}}{\text{Number of Intervals}} = \frac{36}{8} = \frac{4(9)}{4(2)} = \frac{9}{2} = 4.5$$

Since x is 3 intervals to the right of 21, x must equal 34.5. After all, 3 intervals = 3×4.5, which equals 13.5, and $21 + 13.5 = 34.5$. Thus, Quantity B is larger than Quantity A.

➤ When working with intervals, you should always remember that **the number of tick marks will always be one greater than the number of intervals**.

• For example, 6 tick marks will always have 5 intervals between them, while 10 tick marks will always have 9 intervals between them.

• Advanced number line problems are often designed to take advantage of test-takers who are unaware of this. Consider the following:

Town X has planted 8 trees at 15-foot intervals along a straight street. What is the distance, in feet, between the first tree and the last tree?

(A) 90   (B) 100   (C) 105   (D) 120   (E) 135

Answer. C. Many test-takers assume the answer to this question is (D), since $8 \times 15 = 120$. However, this is incorrect. To understand why, visualize the 8 trees as a number line:

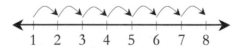

Between the 8 trees, there are 7 intervals. Since each interval is 15 feet long, the distance between the first and the eighth tree must be 105 feet, as $7 \times 15 = 105$.

➤ If a number line is labeled "**drawn to scale**", you can safely assume that any tick marks are evenly spaced.

• However, when working with "drawn to scale" problems, you also need to be sure that you **interpret every value as <u>precisely</u> as possible**.

• For example, in the number line to the right, values A, B, and C should be approximated as:

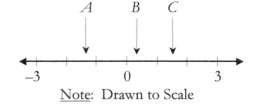

$A = -1.3$, $B = 0.3$, and $C = 1.5$

<u>Note</u>: Drawn to Scale

• If you were to approximate them more crudely, e.g. if you were to assume that $A = -1.5$ or $B = 0.5$, **you would answer some questions incorrectly**.

➤ Unless the number line is "drawn to scale", you CANNOT assume that tick marks are evenly spaced.

• Nor can you assume precise values from the way a diagram is drawn. **You can only assume basic truths.** For example, a tick mark between 0 and 1 can equal ANY value between 0 and 1, such as 0.01 or 0.99, but it cannot equal 0 or 1.

• Likewise, a tick mark to the RIGHT of another represents a LARGER value, since numbers get bigger as you move from left to right on a number line. Consider the following:

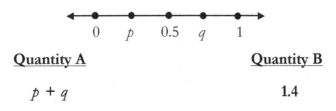

Quantity A	**Quantity B**
$p + q$	**1.4**

Answer: D. From the diagram, it's tempting to assume that $p + q$ equals a value less than 1.4, since p appears to equal 0.25 and q appears to equal 0.75. However, this is incorrect.

➤ Because the diagram has NOT been labeled "drawn to scale", p may equal ANY value between 0 and 0.5, and q may equal any value between 0.5 and 1.

• If $p = 0.25$ and $q = 0.75$, then $p + q = 1$, which is less than 1.4. However, if $p = 0.49$ and $q = 0.99$, then $p + q = 1.48$, which is larger than 1.4. Thus, the relationship between the two quantities cannot be determined, since $p + q$ can represent a value less than or greater than 1.4 (or can equal it).

> ➢ When working with multiple points, **take note whether the order of the points is given**.

• If the points have been drawn in a specific order, you can certainly trust that order. For example, in the diagram to the right, we know that $A < B < C$, as they've been drawn that way.

• However, **if the order of the points is not mentioned, you cannot assume a specific order**. You must consider EVERY possible arrangement. Consider the following:

Points A, B, and C lie on a straight line. The distance from A to B is 12, and the distance from A to C is 17.

<u>Quantity A</u>	<u>Quantity B</u>
The distance from B to C	5

Answer: D. If we assume that A, B, and C lie in the order A, B, C, then the distance from B to C would be 5, since the distance from A to B = 12 and that from A to C = 17:

However, the two quantities are not equal. Since **the problem does not state that A, B, and C lie in order**, we have to consider other possible arrangements, too.

If the order of the points were to be B, A, C, then the distance from B to C would be 29, since:

Since the distance from B to C can be 5 or 29, the answer must be (D): the relationship between the two quantities cannot be determined.

> ➢ Finally, when working with confusing or convoluted number line problems, we strongly encourage you to **label the intervals with variables**.

• Labeling the intervals will allow you to **set up simple equations**. These equations can then be plugged into one another to determine the values of the individual intervals.

➤ To get a better feel for how this strategy works, consider the following:

$$A \quad B \quad C \quad D \quad E$$

In the number line above, point B is the midpoint of AC and point D is the midpoint of CE. If BD has a length of 6, what is the length of AE?

(A) 11   (B) 12   (C) 13   (D) 14   (E) 15

• According to the problem, B is the midpoint of AC. Since a midpoint cuts a line segment in half, we know that AB and BC have the same length.

➤ We don't know what this length is, however, so let's set AB and $BC = x$.

• Next, since D is the midpoint of CE, let's set CD and $DE = y$. It's important that we don't use x for CD or DE, as we have no proof that either interval has the same length as AB or BC.

• In other words, our number line should now look like this:

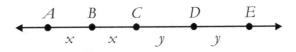

➤ The question states that BD has a length of 6. Since BD has the same length as $x + y$, we therefore know that $x + y = 6$.

• From the number line labeled above, we can see that AE has a length of $x + x + y + y$, a sum that adds to $2x + 2y$. This sum can further be simplified to $2(x + y)$. Since $x + y = 6$, AE must have a length of 12, as:

$$2(x + y) \rightarrow 2(6) = 12$$

• Thus, the correct answer is (B).

Chapter 2: Integer Properties

(5) Evens & Odds – Although the concept of even and odd numbers is a relatively simple one, problems involving even and odds can be surprisingly difficult for many test-takers.

• So, let's start by making sure you have a firm understanding of some fundamental information.

> ➤ As you likely know, an even number is an integer (whole number) that is divisible by 2. An odd number is an integer that is not.

• Put another way:

   Even numbers end in 0, 2, 4, 6, or 8   **Odd numbers** end in 1, 3, 5, 7, or 9

• What you may not know is that **zero is an even number**. Although it is not considered positive or negative, zero is considered even.

• You may also be unaware that all integers are either even or odd, **including negative integers**. Thus:

   –2, –4, and –6 are even numbers   –1, –3, and –5 are odd numbers

• Finally, **only integers are considered even or odd**. A decimal such as 12.35 would not be considered odd (or even), nor would a fraction such as $2\frac{1}{4}$.

> ➤ Most questions that involve even and odd numbers test your understanding of what happens to them when they are added, subtracted, or multiplied.

• In many cases, the rules for the addition, subtraction, and multiplication of even and odd numbers can be determined by **choosing numbers and testing them out**.

• For example, to determine the result of Odd + Odd, we can simply choose two odd numbers such as 3 and 5 and add them:

   Since 3 + 5 = 8, the sum of Odd + Odd = Even.

• Likewise, to determine the result of Odd × Even × Odd, we can choose numbers such as 3, 2, and 3 and multiply them.

   Since 3 × 2 × 3 = 18, the product of Odd × Even × Odd = Even.

Sherpa
Prep

> Choosing numbers can be an effective strategy for many problems involving evens and odds.

• Let's work through a practice problem together:

If x is an integer, which of the following must be an odd integer?

(A) $x^2 - x - 3$ **(B)** $x^2 - 6x + 4$ **(C)** $x^2 - 4x + 7$ **(D)** $x^2 + 5x + 4$ **(E)** $x^2 + 10x + 2$

Answer: A. To solve this problem, let's first pick an even number for x and test the results. To keep the arithmetic simple, let's make $x = 2$:

(A) $x^2 - x - 3 =$ Odd. $2^2 - 2 - 3 \rightarrow 4 - 2 - 3 = \boxed{-1}$

(B) $x^2 - 6x + 4 =$ Even. $2^2 - 6(2) + 4 \rightarrow 4 - 12 + 4 = \boxed{-4}$

(C) $x^2 - 4x + 7 =$ Odd. $2^2 - 4(2) + 7 \rightarrow 4 - 8 + 7 = \boxed{3}$

(D) $x^2 + 5x + 4 =$ Even. $2^2 + 5(2) + 4 \rightarrow 4 + 10 + 4 = \boxed{18}$

(E) $x^2 + 10x + 2 =$ Even. $2^2 + 10(2) + 2 \rightarrow 4 + 20 + 2 = \boxed{26}$

Since both (A) and (C) are odd when x is even, let's next test choices (A) and (C) further by picking an odd number for x. Let's make $x = 3$:

(A) $x^2 - x - 3 =$ Odd. $3^2 - 3 - 3 \rightarrow 9 - 3 - 3 = \boxed{3}$

(C) $x^2 - 4x + 7 =$ Even. $3^2 - 4(3) + 7 \rightarrow 9 - 12 + 7 = \boxed{4}$

As we've seen, (B), (D), and (E) are even when x is an even number. (C) is even when x is an odd number. Only answer choice (A) has been consistently odd.

> Picking numbers is a particularly effective strategy for even and odd problems involving **consecutive integers**.

• When picking, be sure to **choose two sets of consecutive integers**: one that begins with an odd number, such as 1, 2, 3, and one that begins with an even number, such as 2, 3, 4.

• Consider the following:

If a, b, c, and d are consecutive integers, which of the following expressions must be even?

Select all possible answers.

$\boxed{A}$ $a + b + c + d$ $\quad$ $\boxed{B}$ $a + b + c$ $\quad$ $\boxed{C}$ $ac - bd$

Answer: A only. With consecutive integers, it is best to pick two sets of integers: one set that begins with an odd number and one set that begins with an even. To solve this problem, let's first set a, b, c, $d = 1, 2, 3, 4$. Then let's set a, b, c, $d = 2, 3, 4, 5$:

$\boxed{A}$ $a + b + c + d =$ Even.	$1 + 2 + 3 + 4 = \boxed{10}$	$2 + 3 + 4 + 5 = \boxed{14}$
$\boxed{B}$ $a + b + c =$ Even or Odd.	$1 + 2 + 3 = \boxed{6}$	$2 + 3 + 4 = \boxed{9}$
$\boxed{C}$ $ac - bd =$ Odd.	$1(3) - 2(4) = \boxed{-5}$	$2(4) - 3(5) = \boxed{-7}$

Since $\boxed{B}$ is odd when a, b, c, $d = 2, 3, 4, 5$, and $\boxed{C}$ is odd no matter what numbers we choose, only $\boxed{A}$ is always even.

➤ Unfortunately, it can be difficult to solve **advanced** even and odd problems by testing numbers.

• To prepare for such problems, we encourage you to remember that **there are ONLY TWO WAYS to generate ODD** numbers through addition, subtraction, or multiplication:

1. **The addition or subtraction of one even number and one odd number.** Thus $2 + 3$, $5 - 2$, $6 - 3$, and $3 + 4$ all produce odd results.

2. **The multiplication of two odd numbers.** Hence 3×5, 7×1, and 9×11 all have odd products.

• **ALL other combinations will yield an EVEN result.**

➤ Thus, adding or subtracting two numbers that are the "same" (i.e. both odd or both even) will produce an even result: $3 + 5 = 8$ and $4 + 6 = 10$.

• Likewise, multiplying any number — or "string" of numbers — by an even will also produce an even result: $5 \times \boxed{6} = 30$ and $\boxed{2} \times 3 \times 5 \times 7 \times 9 = 1,890$.

• On a final note, we'd like to point out that questions involving the **division** of even and odd integers are extremely rare, since the division of integers often produces decimals (e.g. $9 \div 4 = 2.25$), which are neither even nor odd. In the unlikely event that your exam has a question with division, simply test numbers.

➤ When working with **ADVANCED** problems involving even and odd numbers, you may find it helpful to use "IF/THEN" charts.

• "If/Then" charts will help you to determine which variables must be odd or even and to keep track of their various combinations.

• You should also LOOK for information that hasn't been FACTORED.

➤ An unfactored statement or answer choice is almost always a huge clue that exam-makers are trying to HIDE something from you.

• Consider the following:

If m and n are integers and $m - n$ is even, which of the following must be even?

(A) n **(B)** mn **(C)** $m - 2n$ **(D)** $mn - n$ **(E)** $mn + 4m$

Answer. D. To solve this problem, let's first consider two scenarios: what happens if m is even and what happens if m is odd.

Scenario 1: m = Even. The problem states "$m - n$ is even". Therefore, if m is even, then n must also be even, as: Even – Even = Even.

Scenario 2: m = Odd. Since the problem states "$m - n$ is even", we know that if m is odd, then n must also be odd, as: Odd – Odd = Even.

• Let's also set up an "If/Then" chart to summarize these findings:

If	And If	Then
m = Even	$m - n$ = Even	n = Even
m = Odd	$m - n$ = Even	n = Odd

➤ From this, we can see that m and n are either BOTH even or BOTH odd.

• Next, let's look through the rest of the problem for any unfactored information. Skimming the answer choices reveals that (D) and (E) are suspicious, since each can be factored:

(D) $mn - n \rightarrow n(m - 1)$
(E) $mn + 4m \rightarrow m(n + 4)$

• In the case of answer choice (D), an "If/Then" chart reveals that $m - 1$ is even when n is odd and that $m - 1$ is odd when n is even, since:

If	And If	Then
n = odd	m = odd	$m - 1$ = even
n = even	m = even	$m - 1$ = odd

➢ In other words, if n and m are either both even or both odd, **then $m - 1$ is always the OPPOSITE of n.**

• Therefore, answer choice (D) is the correct answer, since $n(m - 1)$ must equal the product of ONE even number and ONE odd number, and Even × Odd = Even.

(6) Factors & Multiples – The most frequently encountered Integer Properties questions involve factors, multiples, and issues of divisibility.

• The **factors** of an integer are the <u>positive</u> integers that **divide evenly into** that integer. For example, the factors of 8 are 1, 2, 4, and 8, since all four numbers divide evenly into 8.

• Conversely, numbers such as 3 and 5 are not factors of 8, since each leaves a remainder when dividing into 8:

$$8 \div 3 = 2 \text{ remainder } 2 \qquad 8 \div 5 = 1 \text{ remainder } 3$$

> ➤ Fractions and decimals are NEVER considered factors.

• The same is true of **negative numbers**. Although numbers such as 1.5 and –3 divide evenly into 6, they are not factors of 6. The term factor only applies to positive integers.

• A synonym for the term factor is the term **divisor**. For example, 1, 2, 5, and 10 would all be considered divisors of 10, since each is a factor of 10.

> ➤ The **multiples** of an integer are the integers that can be **divided evenly by** that integer.

• For example, the multiples of 5 include integers such as 5, 10, 15, and 20, since each of these integers can be divided evenly by 5.

• **Multiples, unlike factors, may be negative**. Thus, the multiples of 5 include numbers such as –5, –10, and –15.

• **Zero is a multiple of every integer**, since zero is evenly divisible by every integer. Thus, $0 \div 1 = 0, 0 \div 2 = 0, 0 \div 3 = 0$, and so forth.

> ➤ It can be easy to confuse factors and multiples. In fact, remembering which is which is perhaps the chief difficulty for many test-takers.

• To keep them straight, simply remember that **factors are small. They are always less than or equal to a number.** Only multiples <u>can be</u> larger than a number.

• It can also be helpful to remember **the "M&M" rule**: every integer has "**More Multiples**" than factors. Thus, 8 only has four factors, but an infinite number of multiples:

1, 2, 4, and 8 ...–8, 0, 8, 16, 24...

➢ Most problems involving factors or multiples will test your ability to divide larger integers by smaller ones, and to do so quickly.

• In our book on <u>Arithmetic & "Plan B" Strategies</u>, we encouraged you to memorize a small list of rules commonly known as the "**Divisibility Rules**".

• As you may recall, these rules tell you whether an integer is divisible by the numbers from 1 to 10. Let's briefly review them:

➢ The rules for 5 and 10 are very simple.

Number	An integer is divisible by …
5	If it ends in a 0 or a 5.
10	If it ends in a 0.

• Thus, numbers such as 130 and 285 are divisible by 5, since they end in a 0 or a 5. Likewise, 170 is divisible by 10, since it ends in a 0.

➢ The rules for 2, 4, and 8 are similar to one another.

Number	An integer is divisible by …
2	If its <u>last</u> digit can be cut in half <u>once</u>.
4	If its last <u>two</u> digits can be cut in half <u>twice</u>.
8	If its last <u>three</u> digits can be cut in half <u>thrice</u>.

• Hence, 116 is divisible by 2, as its last digit can be cut in half once: $6 \rightarrow 3$. 228 is divisible by 4, as its last two digits can be cut in half twice: $28 \rightarrow 14 \rightarrow 7$. And 4,200 is divisible by 8, as its last three digits can be cut in half three times: $200 \rightarrow 100 \rightarrow 50 \rightarrow 25$.

➢ The rules for 3 and 9 are also similar to one another.

Number	An integer is divisible by …
3	If the sum of its digits is divisible by $\boxed{3}$.
9	If the sum of its digits is divisible by $\boxed{9}$.

• Thus, 381 is divisible by 3, since $3+8+1 = 12$, which is divisible by 3. Likewise, 738 is divisible by 9, since $7+3+8 = 18$, which is divisible by 9.

> Finally, the rule for 6 is a composite of the rules for 2 and 3, since 6 = 2 × 3.

Number	An integer is divisible by …
6	If it's divisible by ⬚2⬚ and ⬚3⬚.

• Hence, 108 is divisible by 6, since its last digit can be cut in half (the two rule) and the sum of its digits add to 9, which is divisible by 3 (the three rule).

> These rules can be tremendously helpful in solving problems involving factors or multiples.

• To get a sense of how, consider the following:

Which of the following numbers is both a factor of 108 and a multiple of 4?

Select all possible answers.

⬚A⬚ 3   ⬚B⬚ 4   ⬚C⬚ 6   ⬚D⬚ 8   ⬚E⬚ 9

Answer: B only. To solve this problem, let's first determine which of the answer choices are factors of 108. Remember, **a factor is a positive integer that divides evenly into a number of equal or larger size**.

⬚A⬚ 3 = Factor. 108 is divisible by 3 since the sum of its digits 1+0+8 = 9 is divisible by 3.
⬚B⬚ 4 = Factor. 108 is divisible by 4 since its last two digits can be cut in half twice:
      8 → 4 → 2.
⬚C⬚ 6 = Factor. 108 is divisible by 6 since it's divisible by 2 and by 3.
⬚D⬚ 8 = Not. 108 is not divisible by 8 since its last three digits cannot be cut in half three times: 108 → 54 → 27 → decimal.
⬚E⬚ 9 = Factor. 108 is divisible by 9 since the sum of its digits 1+0+8 = 9 is divisible by 9.

Thus, 3, 4, 6, and 9 are all factors of 108. Of these, however, only 4 is a multiple of 4.

Remember, **a multiple is a positive integer that can be evenly divided by a number of equal or smaller size.** Since 4 is evenly divisible by 4, but 3, 6, and 9 are not, the only correct answer is ⬚B⬚.

> ➤ If you need to determine whether a number is divisible by numbers not included in the divisibility rules, consider "chunking" the number.

• Remember, chunking is an alternative way of dividing numbers. It works by breaking numbers into "manageable chunks".

• For example, 224 is divisible by 7, since we can break 224 into 210 + 14, and each of these chunks is divisible by 7. Likewise 156 is divisible by 13, since we can break 156 into 130 + 26, and each of these chunks is divisible by 13.

> ➤ Let's work through another problem involving factors and multiples to see how chunking might come in handy.

• Consider the following:

Which of the following is a multiple of both 7 and 11?

(A) 105   (B) 121   (C) 132   (D) 147   (E) 154

• As you may recall from our book on <u>Arithmetic & "Plan B" Strategies</u>, the correct answer to "which of the following" questions is often (A) or (E).

> ➤ To save time, let's examine answer choice (A) first. If (A) is not correct, let's look at (E) next.

Answer (A): 105 is divisible by 7, since 105 = 70 + 35, and each of these chunks is divisible by 7. 105, however, is NOT divisible by 11: we can break it into 99 + 6, but one of these chunks is not divisible by 11.

• Thus, (A) is not the correct answer.

Answer (E): 154 is divisible by 7, since 154 = 140 + 14, and each of these chunks is divisible by 7. 154 is also divisible by 11: we can break it into 110 + 44, and each of these chunks is divisible by 11.

> ➤ Since 154 is divisible by both 7 and 11, answer choice (E) is a multiple of both 7 and 11.

• Thus, (E) must be the correct answer.

➢ From time to time, questions involving factors or multiples contain UNKNOWN NUMBERS.

• Here's an example:

If integer x is a multiple of both 3 and 7, which of the following must be true?

Select all such statements.

A x is an odd integer.   **B** x is not divisible by 9.   **C** x is divisible by 21.

• As you may recall from our book on <u>Arithmetic & "Plan B" Strategies</u>, the easiest way to solve problems that lack concrete values is to PICK NUMBERS.

➢ When picking, just be sure to respect any CONSTRAINTS within the problem.

• Here, for example, we can't pick just any value for x. Whatever we pick for x has to be a multiple of 3 and 7.

• A multiple of 3 is a number divisible by 3, and a multiple of 7 is a number divisible by 7. One number that is clearly divisible by both 3 and 7 is 21, the product of 3×7.

➢ However, 21 isn't the only number divisible by 3 and 7. When working with constraints, remember to ask yourself "**is there only one number that I can pick?**"

• If there are multiple numbers that satisfy the constraints of your problem, try to pick AT LEAST 3 examples.

• **If you pick just one, you may mislead yourself from time to time**. Other numbers that are divisible by 3 and 7 are 42 and 63, since $21 \times 2 = 42$ and $21 \times 3 = 63$.

➢ Of course, there are more numbers that are divisible by 3 and 7 (e.g. 21×4, 21×5, and so forth), but when picking numbers, 3 examples should be sufficient.

• Thus, if x can equal 42 or 63, **A** and **B** do not have to be true. If $x = 42$, then x can be an even number, and if $x = 63$, then x can be divisible by 9.

• Further, since "Select One or More Questions" must have at least one correct answer, C must be true. If C were false, we would have no correct answers.

(7) Identifying Factors – On occasion, you may need to identify the factors of an integer to solve a problem.

- To do so, first approximate the square root of that integer.

  ➢ Then **test the divisibility rules** for every integer less than (or equal to) that square root. Be sure to start with 1 and **stop when you reach the square root.**

- Every integer that goes into the original will come with a "**factor buddy**", a number with which it multiplies to equal the integer in question. That "buddy" will also be a factor.

- For example, 3 goes into 24 "eight times", so in the case of 24, 3 and 8 would be factor buddies. Likewise, 4 goes into 24 "six times", so 4 and 6 would be factor buddies.

  ➢ As you test the divisibility rules, jot down your "factor buddies" in a simple t-chart to keep your work organized.

- Once you reach the square root, you can stop testing: the "factor buddies" in your chart will be the factors of your integer.

- In the case of 48, the process would go as follows:

  ➢ The square root of 48 **is slightly less than 7** (since $7^2 = 49$), so we only need to "test" 48 with the divisibility rules from 1 through 6:

1	48
2	24
3	16
4	12
6	8

$1 \times 48 = 48$, so 1 and 48 are factor buddies.
$2 \times 24 = 48$, so 2 and 24 are factor buddies.
$3 \times 16 = 48$, so 3 and 16 are factor buddies.
$4 \times 12 = 48$, so 4 and 12 are factor buddies.
5 does not go into 48 : 48 does not end in 0 or 5.
$6 \times 8 = 48$, so 6 and 8 are factor buddies.

- Thus, the factors of 48 are 1, 2, 3, 4, 6, 8, 12, 16, 24, and 48, since those are the "factor buddies" in our t-chart.

  ➢ As you can see, identifying the factors of an integer involves a fair bit of arithmetic.

- If you have yet to do so, be sure to read through our book titled Arithmetic & "Plan B" Strategies. In particular, check out the sections on chunking, number tricks, and times tables. A firm grasp of that material will dramatically improve the speed of your calculations.

> ➤ Now that we've got a sense of how to identify the factors of an integer, let's take a look at a sample GRE question where you might find doing so helpful.

• Consider the following:

Quantity A	**Quantity B**
The sum of the odd factors of 72	**15**

Answer: B. The square root of 72 is greater than 8 (since $8^2 = 64$) but less than 9 (since $9^2 = 81$), so we only need to "test" 72 with the divisibility rules from 1 through 8.

$1 \times 72 = 72$, so 1 and 72 are factor buddies.
$2 \times 36 = 72$, so 2 and 36 are factor buddies.
$3 \times 24 = 72$, so 3 and 24 are factor buddies.
$4 \times 18 = 72$, so 4 and 18 are factor buddies.
| 5 does not go into 72 |: 72 does not end in 0 or 5.
$6 \times 12 = 72$, so 6 and 12 are factor buddies.
| 7 does not go into 72 |: $72 \div 7 = $ fraction.
$8 \times 9 = 72$, so 8 and 9 are factor buddies.

1	72
2	36
3	24
4	18
6	12
8	9

> ➤ Thus, the factors of 72 are 1, 2, 3, 4, 6, 8, 9, 12, 18, 24, 36, and 72.

• Since 1, 3, and 9 are the only odd factors of 72, and $1 + 3 + 9 = 13$, the sum of the odd factors of 72 is 13. Therefore, Quantity B is larger than Quantity A.

(8) Prime Numbers – A prime number is a positive integer that has exactly TWO <u>distinct</u> factors.

• For example, 5 is a prime number, since it has two factors: 1 and 5. Conversely, 9 is not a prime number, since it has three factors: 1, 3, and 9.

> ➤ There are two common MISCONCEPTIONS about prime numbers. The first is that 1 is a prime number.

• Because the only factor of 1 is itself, **1 is NOT a prime number**. Remember, prime numbers have exactly <u>two</u> distinct factors!

• The second misconception is that all prime numbers are odd. The number 2, however, is both even and prime, since it has exactly two factors: 1 and 2.

> ➤ When working with prime numbers, be sure to remember that **2 is the only EVEN prime number**.

• Many questions involving primes test this concept specifically. Consider the following:

If r and s are different prime numbers, which of the following must be true?

Select <u>all</u> possible answers.

$\boxed{A}$ rs **is an odd integer.** $\boxed{B}$ $r + s$ **is an even integer.** $\boxed{C}$ $\frac{r}{s}$ **is not an integer.**

• Statement $\boxed{A}$ does not have to be true, since either r or s can be 2, and 2 × any odd equals an even (e.g. 2 × 3 = 6).

> ➤ Statement $\boxed{B}$ does not have to be true either, since r or s can be 2, and 2 + any odd equals an odd (e.g. 2 + 3 = 5).

• Statement $\boxed{C}$, however, must be true, since every prime number can only be divided by 1 and itself. If r and s are both prime numbers, then r cannot be divided evenly by s.

• Thus, the correct answer is $\boxed{C}$ only.

Sherpa
Prep

➢ Many questions involving prime numbers require an immediate knowledge of the prime numbers under 30.

• To save time, **the prime numbers under 30 should be memorized**:

2, 3, 5, 7, 11, 13, 17, 19, 23, and 29

• Let's take a look at a particularly tricky sample problem involving common prime numbers:

**The product of all the prime numbers between 10 and 25 is closest
to what power of 10?**

(A) 10^4 (B) 10^5 (C) 10^6 (D) 10^7 (E) 10^8

Answer: C. The prime numbers between 10 and 25 are 11, 13, 17, 19, and 23. To get their product quickly and easily, we'll need to round them.

➢ Remember, **any problem that contains a phrase such as "closest to" or "approximately" <u>and</u> difficult numbers can be solved by rounding**.

• Since each of our primes can be rounded down to 10 or up to 20, we can approximate the question as:

$$10 \times 10 \times 20 \times 20 \times 20 = 8 \times 5 \text{ zeroes} = 800,000$$

• The closest power of 10 must therefore be 1,000,000, since 800,000 is closer to 1,000,000 than to 100,000.

➢ Finally, when working with powers of 10, remember that **the exponent will always tell you how many zeroes follow the 1**.

• $10^6 = 1,000,000$, since the exponent indicates the number will have six zeroes. Thus, (C) must be the correct answer.

➢ **To determine whether a large number is prime**, simply use the "identifying factors" technique discussed in the previous section.

• First, approximate its square root and then test the divisibility rules less than or equal to the square root to determine any factor buddies.

• In the case of 61, the process would go as follows:

➢ The square root of 61 **is slightly less than 8** (since $8^2 = 64$), so we only need to "test" 61 with the divisibility rules from 1 through 7.

→ $1 \times 61 = 61$, so 1 and 61 are factor buddies.
→ 2 does not go into 61: 61 is not even.
→ 3 does not go into 61: the sum of the digits of 61 are not divisible by 3.
→ 4 does not go into 61: the last two digits cannot be cut in half twice.
→ 5 does not go into 61: 61 does not end in 0 or 5.
→ 6 does not go into 61: 61 is not divisible by 2 or 3.
→ 7 does not go into 61: $61 \div 7 = $ fraction.

• Thus, 61 is a prime number, since it has only two factors: 1 and 61.

➢ There is also a **shortcut** for determining whether a number less than 100 is prime: simply test 2, 3, 5, and 7.

• Consider the following:

What is the sum of the prime numbers that are greater than 70 but less than 80?

(A) 144   (B) 150   (C) 152   (D) 223   (E) 300

Answer. D. The integers between 70 and 80 are 71, 72, 73, 74, 75, 76, 77, 78, and 79.

72, 74, 76, and 78 are divisible by 2: they're even.
75 is divisible by 5: it ends is a 5.
77 is divisible by 7: $7 \times 11 = 77$.

71 is not divisible by 2, 5, or 7, and the sum of its digits is not divisible by 3, so it must be prime. The same is true of 73 and 79. Thus, the correct answer is (D), since the sum of 71 + 73 + 79 = 223.

➢ Finally, there are two facts about prime numbers that most test-takers don't know.

• The first is that the **number of prime numbers is infinite**. Although prime numbers become rarer as numbers get larger, there is no limit at which numbers cease to be prime.

• The second is that the **square of any prime number has exactly 3 factors**. Thus:

$2^2 = 4$, whose factors are 1, 2, and 4. $3^2 = 9$, whose factors are 1, 3, and 9.

• Exam-makers **rarely** test these last two concepts.   If you don't need an elite math score, feel free to ignore them!

(9) Prime Factors – The prime factors of an integer are simply those factors that happen to be prime numbers.

- To illustrate the difference between a factor and a prime factor, consider the number 30. Although 1, 2, 3, 5, 6, 10, 15, and 30 are all factors of 30, some of these factors are prime numbers and some are not:

2, 3, and 5 are prime numbers   1, 6, 10, 15, and 30 are not

- Thus, 2, 3, and 5 would be considered the prime factors of 30, while 1, 6, 10, 15, and 30 would not.

  ➢ The best way to determine the prime factors of an integer is to create a **factor tree**, as shown below.

- To make a factor tree, first **split the number in question into any two factors that you can identify**. For example, if you wanted to determine the prime factors of 660, you might first split 660 into 66 × 10.

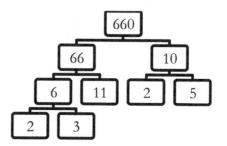

- **It does not matter which two you start with**. We've chosen 66 × 10, since it's usually faster to go with bigger numbers, but we also could have chosen 110 × 6 or 330 × 2.

  ➢ Then split each factor until every branch ends in a prime number. (Be sure to **split every branch that can be split**.)

- The collection of prime factors at the end of each branch will constitute the prime factors of your integer.

- For example, in the case of 660, the prime factors are 2, 2, 3, 5, and 11, since the dead ends of our tree are (from left to right) 2, 3, 11, 2, and 5.

➢ Of course, it is not always necessary to draw a tree diagram to determine the factors of an integer. Often, it is simply easier to break a number down one step at a time.

• For example, 42 can be broken down into 7×6, and 6 can be broken down into 2×3, so the prime factors of 42 are 2, 3, and 7.

• Likewise, 350 can be broken down into 35×10. Since 35 can be broken down into 7×5, and 10 can be broken down into 2×5, the prime factors of 350 are 2, 5, 5, and 7.

➢ To split an **unfamiliar number**, first try to divide it with one of the smaller prime numbers.

• For example, to split a number such as 237, you might try to divide it by 2, 3, or 5, and then proceed to progressively larger prime numbers if the smaller ones don't work. To get a sense of how this might work, consider the following:

<table>
<tr><th>Quantity A</th><th>Quantity B</th></tr>
<tr><td>The greatest prime factor of
$14^2 - 1$</td><td>13</td></tr>
</table>

Answer: C. To solve this problem, we first need to determine the value of $14^2 - 1$. If you've memorized your list of squares, you know that $14^2 = 196$. Thus, $14^2 - 1$ must equal 195.

➢ Next, we have to determine the prime factors of 195. To split such an **uncommon** number, let's first see whether it's divisible by any of the smaller primes: 2, 3, and 5.

• The last digit of 195 is a 5, so we know that it's divisible by 5. Using the chunking approach, we know that 195 can be broken into chunks of 150 and 45. Since $150 \div 5 = \boxed{30}$ and $45 \div 5 = \boxed{9}$, we know that $195 \div 5 = 39$.

• Further, we know that 39 is divisible by 3, since the sum of its digits is divisible by 3.

• 39 can be broken into chunks of 30 and 9. Thus, $39 \div 3 = 13$, as $30 \div 3 = \boxed{10}$ and $9 \div 3 = \boxed{3}$.

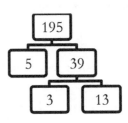

➢ Since the dead ends of our tree are (from left to right) 5, 3, and 13, the prime factors of 195 are 3, 5, and 13.

• 13 is the greatest of these prime factors, so the correct answer is (C).

(10) Remainders – Any number that is left over when one integer is not evenly divided by another is commonly known as a remainder.

• For example, 25 ÷ 6 has a remainder of 1, since 6 goes into 25 "four times" but leaves 1 "left over" when it does, as 6 × 4 only equals 24.

> ➤ Technically, the integer that gets divided is known as the **dividend** and the integer that does the dividing is known as the **divisor**.

• The resulting portion of the division that is not the remainder is known as the **quotient**.

• Algebraically, the relationship between the dividend, divisor, quotient, and remainder is most accurately expressed as follows:

$$\frac{x}{D} = Q + \frac{R}{D}$$

x = dividend, D = divisor, Q = quotient, and R = remainder

• If you know how to convert a fraction into a mixed numeral, you likely know this relationship already. For example, $\frac{25}{6} = 4\frac{1}{6}$, since 25 ÷ 6 = 4 plus a remainder of 1.

> ➤ While it may be unexpected, it is worth noting that any instance of division that has **a QUOTIENT of ZERO** can have a remainder.

• For example, **2 ÷ 7 has a remainder of 2**, even though it has quotient of 0, since 7 goes into 2 "zero times" but leaves 2 "left over" when it does. Likewise, **3 ÷ 8 has a remainder of 3**, since 8 goes into 3 "zero times" but leaves 3 "left over" when it does.

• It is also worth noting that if one number is divisible by another, then the **remainder is zero**. For example, 9 is divisible by 3, so 9 ÷ 3 has no remainder.

> ➤ In general, GRE remainder problems almost never involve concrete numbers, so the easiest way to solve them is to **pick numbers**.

• As with any problem that involves constraints, be sure to **pick at least 3 numbers** if multiple examples are possible. If you pick just one, you can easily mislead yourself.

➤ To start, let's a take a look at a sample problem that is fairly typical for the GRE.

• Consider the following:

n is a positive integer that is divisible by 7.

Quantity A	**Quantity B**
The remainder when n is divided by 14	**The remainder when n is divided by 21**

Answer. D. To solve this problem, let's first pick 3 numbers. If n is a positive integer divisible by 7, then n can equal values such as 7, 14, and 21, since:

$$7 \div 7 = 1 \qquad 14 \div 7 = 2 \qquad 21 \div 7 = 3$$

➤ If $n = 7$, the remainder for Quantity A would be 7, since 14 goes into 7 "zero times", leaving 7 "left over".

• Likewise, the remainder for Quantity B would also be 7, since 21 goes into 7 "zero times", leaving 7 "left over".

• Thus, if $n = 7$, Quantities A and B both have a remainder of 7.

➤ If $n = 14$, the remainder for Quantity A would be 0, since 14 goes into 14 "one time", leaving nothing "left over".

• The remainder for Quantity B, however, would be 14, since 21 goes into 14 "zero times", leaving 14 "left over".

• Thus, if $n = 14$, Quantity B has a larger remainder than Quantity A.

➤ Since the value of Quantity A can be equal to or less than the value of Quantity B, the two quantities have an inconsistent relationship.

• Therefore, the answer must be (D).

> ➤ To solve more difficult remainder problems, you generally need to **find several integers that produce a certain remainder** when divided by a specified divisor.

- For example, you may need to find several integers that leave a remainder of 4 when divided by 5, or several integers that leave a remainder of 3 when divided by 7.

- There are two ways to identify such integers.

> ➤ The nerdier way: first **rewrite the remainder formula** given at the start of this section by multiplying both sides of the equation by D:

$$x = DQ + R$$

x = dividend, D = divisor, Q = quotient, and R = remainder

- Then, **plug in your R and D.**

> ➤ In other words, we can express any integer that leaves a **remainder** of 4 when **divided** by 5 as $x = 5Q + 4$, since $R = 4$ and $D = 5$.

- Examples of such integers, therefore, include 9, 14, and 19, since:

    If $Q = 1$, then $x = 5(1) + 4 = 9$.
    If $Q = 2$, then $x = 5(2) + 4 = 14$.
    If $Q = 3$, then $x = 5(3) + 4 = 19$.

> ➤ The faster way is to **generate three multiples of your divisor**, and then to **add the remainder to each.**

- Thus, to find integers that leave a remainder of 4 when divided by 5, we simply need to **pick some multiples of 5** (such as 5, 10, 15) **and add 4 to each of them**:

$$5 + 4 = \boxed{9} \qquad 10 + 4 = \boxed{14} \qquad 15 + 4 = \boxed{19}$$

- Likewise, to find integers that leave a remainder of 3 when divided by 7, we simply need to **pick some multiples of 7** (such as 7, 14, 21) **and add 3 to each of them.**

$$7 + 3 = \boxed{10} \qquad 14 + 3 = \boxed{17} \qquad 21 + 3 = \boxed{24}$$

Sherpa
Prep

➢ Let's take a look at a more advanced GRE remainder problem.

• Consider the following:

When integer *n* is divided by 8, the remainder is 3.

Quantity A	**Quantity B**
The remainder when *n* is divided by 4	3

Answer. C. To solve this problem, we first need to find three integers that leave a remainder of 3 when divided by 8.

➢ To do this, let's get **three multiples of the divisor**, and then **add the remainder to each**:

$$8 + 3 = \boxed{11} \qquad 16 + 3 = \boxed{19} \qquad 24 + 3 = \boxed{27}$$

If *n* = **11**, the remainder when *n* is divided by 4 is 3, since 11 ÷ 4 = 2 rem. 3.
If *n* = **19**, the remainder when *n* is divided by 4 is also 3, since 19 ÷ 4 = 4 rem. 3.
If *n* = **27**, the remainder when *n* is divided by 4 is again 3, since 27 ÷ 4 = 6 rem. 3.

• Since each of our test numbers produced a remainder of 3 when divided by 4, it is clear that Quantity A must equal 3. Therefore, the correct answer is (C).

➢ Finally, it's worth pointing out that remainders are **NEVER negative** and **ALWAYS smaller than their divisors**.

• To understand why this is so, imagine dividing an integer by 3. If that integer were to equal 0, 1, or 2, the remainder would be 0, 1, and 2, respectively:

$$0 \div 3 = 0 \boxed{\text{no rem.}} \qquad 1 \div 3 = 0 \boxed{\text{rem. 1}} \qquad 2 \div 3 = 0 \boxed{\text{rem. 2}}$$

• And if that integer were to equal 3, 4, or 5, the remainder would **still** equal 0, 1, and 2, respectively:

$$3 \div 3 = 1 \boxed{\text{no rem.}} \qquad 4 \div 3 = 1 \boxed{\text{rem. 1}} \qquad 5 \div 3 = 1 \boxed{\text{rem. 2}}$$

• In fact, no matter what integer we choose, the remainder will never be negative and never equal to or greater than 3.

> ➤ Although **this concept is not commonly tested**, it can surface every now and then, particularly in more advanced questions.

- Consider the following:

If j, k, m, and n are all positive integers, and j has a remainder of 5 when divided by k and m has a remainder of 3 when divided by n, what is the least possible value of $k + n$?

(A) 6   (B) 7   (C) 8   (D) 10   (E) 12

Answer: D. If $j \div k$ has a remainder of 5, then k **must be 6 or larger**, since a divisor is always larger than its remainder.

> ➤ Likewise, if $m \div n$ has a remainder of 3, **then n must be 4 or larger**, since n must be an integer and, again, a divisor is always larger than its remainder.

- If k must be at least 6 and n must be at least 4, then the least possible value of $k + n = 10$, since $6 + 4 = 10$.

- Thus, (D) is the correct answer.

| Rare or Advanced Concepts |

(11) Difficult Divisibility – Every now and then exam-makers will design a divisibility question that cannot be solved with divisibility shortcuts or by picking numbers.

• Although such questions are rare, it's important that you be able to solve them if you need a perfect (or near perfect) math score.

➤ To get a sense of what a difficult divisibility question looks like, consider the following:

If x is the product of every odd integer from 3 to 13, which of the following is the smallest integer that is not a factor of x?

(A) 11 (B) 13 (C) 15 (D) 17 (E) 21

Answer. D. To answer a question like this, you simply need to understand one concept, which can be summarized as follows:

➤ One number is divisible by another if **ALL of the PRIME FACTORS of the divisor are contained** in the number being divided.

• For example, 42 is divisible by 6, since $6 = 2 \times 3$, and both a 2 and a 3 are contained in the prime factors of 42:

$$\frac{42}{6} = \frac{\boxed{2} \times \boxed{3} \times 7}{\boxed{2} \times \boxed{3}} = 7$$

• Likewise, 42 is a factor of 210, since $42 = 2 \times 3 \times 7$, and a 2, 3, and 7 are all contained in the prime factors of 210:

$$\frac{210}{42} = \frac{\boxed{2} \times 5 \times \boxed{3} \times \boxed{7}}{\boxed{2} \times \boxed{3} \times \boxed{7}} = 5$$

➤ Conversely, **if ALL the factors of the divisor are NOT contained** within the number being divided, the numbers are not divisible.

• For example, 20 is not divisible by 6, since $6 = 2 \times 3$, but only a 2 is contained in the prime factors of 20:

$$\frac{20}{6} = \frac{\boxed{2} \times 2 \times 5}{\boxed{2} \times 3} = \frac{10}{3}$$

- Likewise, 120 is not a multiple of 18, since $18 = 2 \times 3 \times 3$, but only a 2 and a 3 are contained in the prime factors of 120:

$$\frac{120}{18} = \frac{\boxed{2} \times 2 \times 2 \times \boxed{3} \times 5}{\boxed{2} \times \boxed{3} \times 3} = \frac{20}{3}$$

➤ To understand how this concept can help you solve difficult divisibility problems, let's look back at the question on the previous page.

- If x is the product of every odd integer from 3 to 13, then x equals:

$$x = 3 \times 5 \times 7 \times 9 \times 11 \times 13$$

- For a number to divide into x, therefore, **ALL of its PRIME FACTORS must be contained** within the product of $3 \times 5 \times 7 \times 9 \times 11 \times 13$.

➤ As such, we can solve this problem by working through the answer choices as follows:

(A) 11 must be a factor of x, since its only prime factor is 11 and x contains an 11:

$$x = 3 \times 5 \times 7 \times 9 \times \boxed{11} \times 13$$

(B) 13 must be a factor of x, since its only prime factor is 13 and x contains a 13:

$$x = 3 \times 5 \times 7 \times 9 \times 11 \times \boxed{13}$$

(C) 15 must be a factor of x, since its prime factors are 3×5 and x contains a 3 and a 5:

$$x = \boxed{3} \times \boxed{5} \times 7 \times 9 \times 11 \times 13$$

(D) 17 cannot be a factor of x, since its only prime factor is 17 and x does not contain a 17.

(E) 21 must be a factor of x, since its factors are 3×7 and x contains a 3 and a 7:

$$x = \boxed{3} \times 5 \times \boxed{7} \times 9 \times 11 \times 13$$

- Thus, the correct answer is (D), since 17 is the only answer choice whose prime factors are not contained in x, the number being divided.

➤ To ensure that you get the hang of solving advanced divisibility problems, let's work through two more examples together.

- Consider the following:

If $x!$ represents the product of all the integers from 1 to x, and 195 is a factor of $x!$, what is the least possible value of integer x?

(A) 5   (B) 7   (C) 11   (D) 13   (E) 15

Answer: D. Since the prime factorization of $195 = 5 \times 39 = 5 \times 3 \times 13$, and $x!$ is divisible by 195, the prime factors of $x!$ **must contain** a 3, 5, and 13.

$$\frac{x!}{195} = \frac{\boxed{x!}}{\boxed{3} \times \boxed{5} \times \boxed{13}}$$

• If x equals any value less than 13, x will NOT contain the factor 13. For example, if $x = 12$, then x only equals the product of every integer up to 12:

$$12! = 12 \times 11 \times 10 \times 9 \times 8 \times 7 \times 6 \times 5 \times 4 \times 3 \times 2 \times 1$$

➤ If $x = 13$, however, x **contains 13 as a factor**, since it equals the product of every integer up to 13:

$$13! = \boxed{13} \times 12 \times 11 \times 10 \times 9 \times 8 \times 7 \times 6 \times \boxed{5} \times 4 \times \boxed{3} \times 2 \times 1$$

• As such, the least possible value of x must be 13, since any factorial less than 13! will not contain 13 as a factor. The correct answer is therefore (D), since 13! also contains the factors 3 and 5.

What is the maximum value of m such that 2^m is a factor of 8!?

$$\boxed{}$$

Answer: 7. The notation 8! represents the product of every integer from 1 to 8:

$$8! = 8 \times 7 \times 6 \times 5 \times 4 \times 3 \times 2 \times 1$$

• Of these integers, 2, 4, 6, and 8 are multiples of 2. Since (i) $2 = \boxed{2} \times 1$, (ii) $4 = \boxed{2} \times \boxed{2}$, (iii) $6 = \boxed{2} \times 3$, and (iv) $8 = \boxed{2} \times \boxed{2} \times \boxed{2}$, the term 8! contains a total of seven 2's:

$$\frac{8!}{2^m} = \frac{\overbrace{\boxed{2} \times \boxed{2} \times \boxed{2}}^{8} \times 7 \times \overbrace{\boxed{2} \times 3}^{6} \times 5 \times \overbrace{\boxed{2} \times \boxed{2}}^{4} \times 3 \times \boxed{2}}{\boxed{2^m}}$$

• As such, 2^m can be no larger than 2^7, since a divisor with eight 2's would contain more 2's than the number being divided. The correct answer is therefore 7.

(12) GCFs and LCMs – The **greatest common factor (GCF)** of two or more integers is the largest factor shared by those integers.

• The **least common multiple (LCM)** of two or more integers is the smallest integer divisible by those integers.

• For example, the greatest common factor of 10 and 15 is 5, since 5 is the largest factor shared by 10 and 15. However, the lowest common multiple of 10 and 15 is 30, since 30 is the smallest integer divisible by both 10 and 15.

 ➤   When working with two small integers, it is usually possible to "spot" their GCF or LCM without much effort.

• For example, most people can easily see that 14 and 21 have a GCF of 7, or that 5 and 7 have an LCM of 35.

• When working with large integers or multiple integers, however, "spotting" a GCF or LCM can be quite difficult, if not impossible.

 ➤   To identify difficult GCF's or LCM's, determine the prime factorizations of each integer and **stack those factorizations in orderly rows** above one another.

• The rows will form easy-to-read "columns" that will help you determine both the GCF and LCM of any group of numbers:

The GCF will equal the product of **the factors <u>in common</u>** to each column.	The LCM will equal the product of of the <u>**largest factors**</u> found in each column.

• To get a better sense of how this works, let's get the GCF and LCM of 54, 72, and 90. As a first step, we'll want to **identify the prime factorizations** of each integer:

The prime factorization of 54 is $2^1 \times 3^3$, since $54 = 6 \times 9 = (2 \times 3) \times (3 \times 3)$.
The prime factorization of 72 is $2^3 \times 3^2$, since $72 = 8 \times 9 = (2 \times 2 \times 2) \times (3 \times 3)$.
The prime factorization of 90 is $2^1 \times 3^2 \times 5^1$, since $90 = 9 \times 10 = (3 \times 3) \times (2 \times 5)$.

➤ Next, let's **stack those factorizations in rows** above one another, as follows:

Factor:	2	3	5
54	2^1	3^3	
72	2^3	3^2	
90	2^2	3^2	5^1

• Finally, to determine the **GCF**, we'll need to identify the **factors in common** to each column. And to determine the **LCM**, we'll need to identify the **largest factors** in each column. (Remember, columns are vertical, rows are horizontal):

	factors in common	largest factors
"2 column":	2^1	2^3
"3 column":	3^2	3^3
"5 column":	nothing	5^1

• Thus, since the prime factorizations of 54, 72, and 90 all have a 2^1 and a 3^2 in common, the **GCF = $2^1 \times 3^2$ = 18**. And since 2^3, 3^3, and 5^1 are the largest factors in each column of our table, the **LCM** of 54, 72, and 90 equals **$2^3 \times 3^3 \times 5^1$ = 1,080**, since $8 \times 27 \times 5$ equals:

$$40 \times 27 = 4 \times 10 \times 27 = 4 \times 270 = 4 \times (250 + 20) = 1,000 + 80$$

➤ Like questions involving difficult divisibility, questions involving difficult GCF's and LCM's are RARE for the GRE.

• Still, if you're in need of a perfect quantitative score, it's worth the time to master this technique. The following questions will give you additional practice:

Which of the following equals the lowest common multiple of 24, 36, and 60 divided by their greatest common factor?

(A) 24   (B) 30   (C) 36   (D) 48   (E) 60

Answer. B. To determine the LCM and GCF of 24, 36, and 60, we first need to identify the prime factorizations of each integer:

The prime factorization of 24 is $2^3 \times 3^1$, since $24 = 8 \times 3 = (2 \times 2 \times 2) \times 3$.
The prime factorization of 36 is $2^2 \times 3^2$, since $36 = 4 \times 9 = (2 \times 2) \times (3 \times 3)$.
The prime factorization of 60 is $2^2 \times 3^1 \times 5^1$, since $60 = 4 \times 15 = (2 \times 2) \times (3 \times 5)$.

• Next, let's stack **those factorizations in columns.** The GCF will equal the product of **the factors <u>in common</u>** to each column.

- The LCM will equal the product of the **largest factors** in each column:

Factor:	2	3	5
24	2^3	3^1	
36	2^2	3^2	
60	2^2	3^1	5^1
GCF	2^2	3^1	
LCM	2^3	3^2	5^1

➢ Since the prime factors of 24, 36, and 60 all have two 2's and one 3 in common, their **GCF $= 2^2 \times 3 = 12$.**

- Likewise, 2^3, 3^2, and 5^1 are the largest factors in each column of our table, so the **LCM** of 24, 36, and 60 equals **$2^3 \times 3^2 \times 5^1 = 8 \times 9 \times 5 = 40 \times 9 = 360$.** Thus, the answer must be (B), since the LCM divided by the GCF $= 360 \div 12 = 30$.

If the least common multiple of 45 and x is 225, which of the following could equal x?

Select all possible values.

A 25   **B** 75   **C** 225

Answer: A, B, and C. To solve this problem, let's first identify the prime factorizations of 45 and the LCM, which is 225:

> The prime factorization of 45 is $3^2 \times 5^1$, since $45 = 9 \times 5 = (3 \times 3) \times 5$.
> The prime factorization of 225 is $3^2 \times 5^2$, since $225 = 15 \times 15 = (3 \times 5) \times (3 \times 5)$.

- Next, let's stack those factorizations in columns to see what we can determine about x:

Factor:	3	5
45	3^2	5^1
x	$? \leq 3^2$	$? = 5^2$
LCM	3^2	5^2

➢ According to our table, the LCM has a prime factorization of $3^2 \times 5^2$. Since **the LCM represents the largest factors in each column**, we can infer two things about x.

- First, x cannot have more than a 3^2 in its "3-column": anything larger would **exceed the LCM**. Second, x must have a 5^2 in its "5-column": the LCM demands a 5^2 from either 45 or x, and 45 only has a 5^1 in its "5-column".

- Therefore, x must consist of 5^2 and either 3^2, 3^1, or no 3's at all. As such, x can equal 225, 75, or 25, since x can equal $3^2 \times 5^2 = 225$, $3^1 \times 5^2 = 75$, or "no 3's" $\times 5^2 = 25$.

(13) Counting Factors – On extremely rare occasions, GRE questions will ask test-takers to determine the total number of factors for a particular integer.

• Earlier, we saw that the easiest way to **identify the factors** of an integer is to approximate the square root of that integer and to apply the factor rules for every integer equal to or less than the square root.

➤ This technique, however, is not a great way to determine **the total number of factors** for an integer.

• Imagine if the integer in question were 550. We would first have to approximate its square root and then try to divide it by every number from 1 to 23. No easy task!

• Fortunately, there is a very easy way to determine the total number of factors for any integer:

1. Determine the integer's prime factorization.
2. Add 1 to each exponent within that prime factorization.
3. Multiply the resulting sums.

• To get a better sense of how this works, let's determine the number of factors for 550. As a first step, we'll want to **identify its prime factorization**:

The prime factorization of 550 is $2^1 \times 5^2 \times 11^1$, since $550 = 10 \times 55 = (2 \times 5) \times (5 \times 11)$.

• Next, let's **add 1 to each of its exponents**. Since $2^1 \times 5^2 \times 11^1$ contains the exponents 1, 2, and 1, and adding 1 to each of these exponents yields the sums 2, 3, and 2.

• Finally, let's **multiply the resulting sums**. Since $2 \times 3 \times 2 = 12$, 550 has a total of 12 factors.

➤ Like questions involving difficult GCF's and LCM's, questions involving total factors are rare for the GRE.

• Still, they do appear every now and then. So if you're in need of a perfect quantitative score, it's worth the time to master this simple technique.

• Let's look at a sample question to get some additional practice:

Quantity A	Quantity B
The number of different positive divisors of 72	The number of different positive divisors of 150

Answer. C. To determine the number of factors for 72 and 150, we first need to **identify their prime factorizations**:

The prime factorization of 72 is $2^3 \times 3^2$, since $72 = 8 \times 9 = (2 \times 2 \times 2) \times (3 \times 3)$.
The prime factorization of 150 is $2^1 \times 3^1 \times 5^2$, since $150 = 10 \times 15 = (2 \times 5) \times (3 \times 5)$.

• Next, let's **add 1 to each of their exponents** and multiply the resulting sums.

➢ $2^3 \times 3^2$ contains the exponents 3 and 2, and adding 1 to each of these exponents yields the sums 4 and 3. Therefore, 72 has a total of 12 factors, since $4 \times 3 = 12$.

• Likewise, $2^1 \times 3^1 \times 5^2$ contains the exponents 1, 1, and 2, and adding 1 to each of these exponents yields the sums 2, 2, and 3. Therefore, 150 also has a total of 12 factors, since $2 \times 2 \times 3 = 12$.

• Since both quantities equal 12, the correct answer is (C).

➢ To understand why this technique works, let's look back at the number 72. As we saw, 72 has a prime factorization of $2^3 \times 3^2$.

• Thus, it's comprised of three 2's and two 3's. Any factor that goes into 72 must therefore be comprised of some combination of these 2's and/or these 3's.

• Note, for example, that any factor of 72 that you can think of is solely comprised of some combinations of 2's and/or 3's. Thus, $8 = 2^3$, $9 = 3^2$, $24 = 2^3 \times 3^1$, and $36 = 2^2 \times 3^2$.

Since any factor of 72 can contain as many as three 2's or no 2's at all, there are **4 ways** to choose the total number of 2's for a factor of 72.	Likewise, since any factor of 72 can contain as many as two 3's or no 3's at all, there are **3 ways** to choose the total number of 3's for a factor of 72.

• As you will learn in our book on <u>Statistics & Data Interpretation</u>, independent sets of options can always be multiplied to determine the total number of possible options.

• Since there are 4 ways we can choose 2's for any factor of 72, and 3 ways we can choose 3's, 72 has a total of $4 \times 3 = 12$ factors.

Practice Questions

(14) Problem Sets – The following questions have been arranged into three groups: fundamental, intermediate, and rare or advanced.

• Whether you're aiming for a perfect score or a score closer to average, mastery of the concepts in the FUNDAMENTAL questions is absolutely essential.

➢ As you might expect, the INTERMEDIATE questions are more difficult but are essential for test-takers who need an above-average score or higher.

• Finally, the RARE or ADVANCED questions test concepts that are very sophisticated or seldom encountered on the GRE. Mastery of such questions is required only if you need a math score above the 90th percentile.

• As always, if you find yourself confused, bogged down with busy work, or stuck, don't be afraid to fall back on your "Plan B" strategies!

➢ Remember, the "right way" to solve a problem is not always the fastest way, or the smartest.

Fundamental

1. If x is the largest prime number less than 22 and y is the smallest prime number greater than 14, then $xy =$

(A) 221   (B) 255   (C) 289   (D) 299   (E) 323

a, b, c, and d are negative integers.

Quantity A	Quantity B
2. The product of a, b, c, and d	The sum of a, b, c, and d

3. On a number line, x is the distance between the two points with coordinates –2 and 6, and y is the distance between the two points with coordinates –4 and –20. How much less is x than y?

(A) 8   (B) 12   (C) 16   (D) 24   (E) 32

4. Which of the following integers are multiples of both 3 and 4?

    Indicate all such integers.

Quantity A	Quantity B

5. The greatest prime factor of 500   The greatest prime factor of 65

Quantity A	Quantity B

6. $(-3)^8$ $(-4)^7$

7. Which of the following is NOT a divisor of 616?

    (A) 4   (B) 7   (C) 8   (D) 9   (E) 11

Quantity A	Quantity B

8. The number of prime numbers   The number of prime numbers
    between 30 and 40   between 60 and 70

9. Each of the following is the square of an integer EXCEPT

    (A) 49   (B) 64   (C) 121   (D) 169   (E) 252

    $x < 0, y < 0,$ and $z > 0.$

Quantity A	Quantity B

10. $xy + z$ $x + yz$

11. If p is any integer, o is an odd integer, and e is an even integer, which of the following must be an even integer?

    (A) $e + p$ (B) $o + p$ (C) $o + p^2$ (D) $e + 2p$ (E) $e + 3p$

Intermediate

12. If B is the midpoint of line segment AD and C is the midpoint of line segment BD, what is the value of $AB \div AC$?

(A) $\frac{3}{4}$ (B) $\frac{2}{3}$ (C) $\frac{1}{2}$ (D) $\frac{1}{3}$ (E) $\frac{1}{4}$

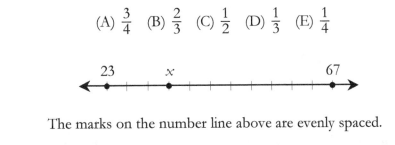

The marks on the number line above are evenly spaced.

	Quantity A	Quantity B
13.	x	34

14. If a, b, and c are consecutive positive integers and $a < b < c$, which of the following must be an odd integer?

(A) abc (B) $a + b + c$ (C) $a + bc$ (D) $a(b + c)$ (E) $(a + b)(b + c)$

n is an integer and the remainder when $2n$ is a divided by 8 is 0.

	Quantity A	Quantity B
15.	The remainder when n is divided by 8	0

16. If $M = (x - y) - z$ and $N = x - (y - z)$, then $M - N =$

(A) $2y$ (B) $2z$ (C) 0 (D) $-2y$ (E) $-2z$

	Quantity A	Quantity B
17.	The greatest even factor of 220 that is less than 110	The greatest odd factor of 220

18. If n is the number on the number line between 6 and 16 that is three times as far from 6 as from 16, then n is

$$\text{(A) } 9\tfrac{1}{2} \quad \text{(B) } 11 \quad \text{(C) } 12\tfrac{1}{2} \quad \text{(D) } 13\tfrac{1}{2} \quad \text{(E) } 14\tfrac{1}{3}$$

$$a^2bc^4 < 0$$
$$ab^4c^2 > 0$$

Quantity A	Quantity B

19. a b

20. If x is an integer divisible by 9 but not by 6, then which of the following CANNOT be an integer?

$$\text{(A) } \tfrac{x}{3} \quad \text{(B) } \tfrac{x}{5} \quad \text{(C) } \tfrac{x}{9} \quad \text{(D) } \tfrac{x}{12} \quad \text{(E) } \tfrac{x}{15}$$

21. How many positive integers are both multiples of 6 and factors of 84?

(A) Two   (B) Three   (C) Four   (D) Five   (E) Six

In the figure above, $PS = QT = 6$, $RS = 3(QR)$, and $PT = 8$.

Quantity A	Quantity B

22. QR $\dfrac{2}{3}$

23. If c and d are integers and $cd + d$ is odd, which of the following must be even?

(A) c (B) d (C) $c + d$ (D) $cd - d$ (E) $c^2 + d$

24. If x and y are both even integers, which of the following must be odd?

Indicate all such possibilities.

$$\boxed{A} \ xy^{xy} \quad \boxed{B} \ (x + 1)^y \quad \boxed{C} \ x^{(y + 1)}$$

25. A certain integer n is a multiple of both 7 and 9. Which of the following must be true?

    Indicate <u>all</u> such possibilities.

    $\boxed{A}$ n is an odd integer. $\boxed{B}$ n is equal to 63. $\boxed{C}$ n is a multiple of 21.

    q is a positive integer that is divisible by 10.

    <u>Quantity A</u>   <u>Quantity B</u>

26.   The remainder when q is divided   5
        by 4

27. If p equals any integer selected from the set $\{1, 3, 5, 7\}$ and q equals any integer selected from the set $\{1, 2, 4, 8\}$, which of the following must be an even integer?

    (A) pq (B) $p + q$ (C) $p - q$ (D) $p(q + 1)$ (E) $(p + 3)q$

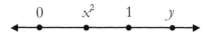

    <u>Quantity A</u>   <u>Quantity B</u>

28. x $\sqrt{y}$

29. If the remainder is 3 when the integer k is divided by 14, what is the remainder when k is divided by 7?

    (A) 1   (B) 2   (C) 3   (D) 5   (E) 6

30. If a and b are negative integers, which of the following must be true?

    Indicate <u>all</u> such statements.

    $\boxed{A}$ $ab > 0$ $\boxed{B}$ $b > b + a$ $\boxed{C}$ If $b < a$, then $b^2 > a^2$

Rare or Advanced

31.   If $-\frac{x}{11}$ is an odd integer, which of the following must be true?

(A) x is a negative number
(B) x is a positive number
(C) x is a prime number
(D) x is an odd integer
(E) x is an even integer

Set X contains every integer from 1 to 40. Three numbers are to be picked at random from set X.

	Quantity A	Quantity B
32.	The probability that the numbers multiply to an even.	The probability that the numbers multiply to an odd.

33.   If n is a non-negative integer with exactly two different factors greater than 1, then n must be

(A)   a prime
(B)   an even integer
(C)   a multiple of 3
(D)   the square of a prime
(E)   the square of an odd integer

34.   What is the least positive integer that is <u>not</u> a factor of 15! and is <u>not</u> a prime number?

(A) 22   (B) 24   (C) 26   (D) 32   (E) 34

35.   Parking meters are to be planted 20 feet apart along one side of a straight street 370 feet long. If the first meter is to be planted at one end of the street, how many meters are needed?

(A) 21   (B) 19   (C) $18\frac{1}{2}$ (D) 18   (E) 17

$$n = 5^2 \cdot 11^3$$

	Quantity A	Quantity B

36.   The number of distinct   12
             positive factors of n

37.   If n is a negative number such that $0 < |n| < q$, which of the following must also be negative numbers?

Indicate <u>all</u> such statements.

     $\boxed{\text{A}}$ $(n + q)^3$ $\boxed{\text{B}}$ $(q - n)^3$ $\boxed{\text{C}}$ $(n - q)^2$ $\boxed{\text{D}}$ $n^2 - q^2$ $\boxed{\text{E}}$ $q^2 - n^3$

38.   In a certain game, a red light flashes every 24 seconds, a blue light every 42 seconds, and a green light every 60 seconds. If all three lights flash together at a certain time, how many seconds later will all three lights flash together the next time?

         $\boxed{}$ seconds

(15) Solutions – Video solutions for each of the previous questions can be found on our website at **www.sherpaprep.com/videos**.

• BOOKMARK this address for future visits!

  ➤ To view the videos, you'll need the LOGIN and PASSWORD that you created upon registering your copy of Number Properties & Algebra.

• If you have yet to register your book yet, please go to **www.sherpaprep.com/activate** and enter your email address, last name, and shipping address.

• Be sure to provide the SAME last name and shipping address that you used to purchase your copy of Master Key to the GRE or to enroll in your GRE course with Sherpa Prep!

  ➤ When checking your answers, we encourage you to watch the solution for any problem that you answered INCORRECTLY

• The same goes for any problem that took you MORE than TWO MINUTES to solve.

• After digesting the explanation, REVISIT your mistake a couple of days later to ensure that the problem no longer poses issues to you.

  ➤ If you struggle to solve the problem a SECOND time, add it to your "LOG of ERRORS" and redo it every few weeks.

• Solving tricky questions MORE THAN ONCE is the best way to learn from your mistakes and to avoid similar difficulties on your actual exam.

Fundamental	Intermediate		Rare or Advanced
1. E	12. B	23. A	31. D
2. A	13. A	24. B	32. A
3. A	14. E	25. C	33. D
4. A, D, F	15. D	26. B	34. E
5. B	16. E	27. E	35. B
6. A	17. B	28. B	36. C
7. D	18. D	29. C	37. D
8. C	19. A	30. A, B, C	38. 840
9. E	20. D		
10. A	21. C		
11. D	22. A		

Chapter 3

Exponents

Exponents

To be discussed:

Fundamental Concepts

Whether you're aiming for a perfect score or a score closer to average, mastery of the following concepts is essential.

Rare or Advanced Concepts

The following concepts are either advanced or are tested only on rare occasions. If you don't need an elite math score, don't waste your time!

Review, Drills, and Practice Questions

There's no substitute for elbow grease. Practice your new skills to ensure that you internalize what you've studied.

Fundamental Concepts

(1) Introduction – Of all the topics tested by the GRE, perhaps none is more difficult to keep straight than that of exponents.

• For starters, exponents have a lot of rules.

• Worse still, problems that involve exponents often make use of 2 or 3 of the rules at the same time, making the rules **easy to confuse**.

> ➤ To keep them straight, we strongly encourage you to **review the rules every week**. If you only study exponents once, you may lose what you learn.

• Before examining those rules, let's first make sure that you have a solid understanding of some fundamental facts and concepts.

• First, any term raised to the 2nd power is known as a **square**, and any term raised to the 3rd power is known as a **cube**. Thus:

$$\text{The square of } 5 = 5^2 \qquad\qquad \text{The cube of } 5 = 5^3$$

• A **perfect square** is a number whose square root is a whole number, such as 25, 49, or 100. Similarly, a **perfect cube** is a number whose cube root is a whole number, such as 8, 27, or 64.

> ➤ When working with exponents, it can be tremendously helpful to have certain squares and cubes memorized.

• If you haven't done so already, **be sure to learn the following lists.**

• As you commit them to memory, do so **in both directions**. It's often more useful to know that $225 = 15^2$ or $64 = 4^3$ than it is to know that $15^2 = 225$ or $4^3 = 64$.

Squares		Cubes	
$10^2 = 100$	$15^2 = 225$	$1^3 = 1$	$5^3 = 125$
$11^2 = 121$	$20^2 = 400$	$2^3 = 8$	$6^3 = 216$
$12^2 = 144$	$25^2 = 625$	$3^3 = 27$	$10^3 = 1,000$
$13^2 = 169$	$30^2 = 900$	$4^3 = 64$	
$14^2 = 196$			

- And remember: **a square root is the opposite of a square** and a cube root is the opposite of a cube. Thus, if $25^2 = 625$ and $4^3 = 64$, then $\sqrt{625} = 25$ and $\sqrt[3]{64} = 4$.

  ➤ It can also be helpful to memorize certain powers of 2, 3, and 4, since GRE exponent problems often involve these powers.

- As with squares and cubes, be sure to **learn these lists in both directions.** It's just as useful to know that $4^3 = 64$ as it is to know that $64 = 4^3 = 2^6 = 8^2$.

Powers of Two, Three, & Four		
$2^1 = 2$	$3^1 = 3$	$4^1 = 4$
$2^2 = 4$	$3^2 = 9$	$4^2 = 16$
$2^3 = 8$	$3^3 = 27$	$4^3 = 64$
$2^4 = 16$	$3^4 = 81$	$4^4 = 256$
$2^5 = 32$	$3^5 = 243$	
$2^6 = 64$		

- When memorizing these powers, be sure to note that **$16 = 2^4$ and 4^2.** On occasion, exam-makers design questions testing this knowledge.

- Consider the following:

$$x^2 = 2^x$$

Quantity A	**Quantity B**
x	2

Answer: D. Because the statement $x^2 = 2^x$ is true when $x = 2$, it's easy to assume that the two quantities must be equal. However, Quantity A can also be larger than Quantity B, since the statement $x^2 = 2^x$ is also true when $x = 4$:

$$x^2 = 4^2 = 16 \qquad\qquad 2^x = 2^4 = 16$$

Since the two quantities can be equal, or Quantity A can be greater than Quantity B, the correct answer is (D).

➤ Beware of exponent problems containing variables with **even exponents**.

• Exam-makers love to design questions involving even exponents, since it's easy to forget that **a variable with an even exponent typically has two solutions**: one positive and one negative.

• For example, if $x^2 = 25$, then $x = 5$ or -5, since:

$$5^2 = 5 \times 5 = 25 \qquad\qquad (-5)^2 = -5 \times -5 = 25$$

• Thankfully, variables with **odd exponents** are easy: they only have one solution. For example, if $x^3 = 27$, then $x = 3$ only, since $(-3)^3 = -3 \times -3 \times -3 = -27$. Likewise, if $x^3 = -8$, then $x = -2$ only, since $2 \times 2 \times 2 = 8$.

➤ **Zero** raised to any power equals zero (save for 0^0, which is indeterminate), and **one** raised to any power equals one:

$$0^3 = 0 \times 0 \times 0 = 0 \qquad\qquad 1^4 = 1 \times 1 \times 1 \times 1 = 1$$

• If raised to an even exponent, **negative one** equals positive one. If raised to an odd exponent, however, it equals negative one:

$$(-1)^2 = -1 \times -1 = 1 \qquad\qquad (-1)^3 = -1 \times -1 \times -1 = -1$$

• Thus, **if $x^2 = x^4$, then x can equal -1, 0, or 1**. But if $x^2 = x^3$, then x can equal 0 or 1, but not -1, since $(-1)^2$ does not equal $(-1)^3$.

➤ Finally, when working with exponents, **watch out for numbers between zero and one**.

• As you know, squaring or cubing numbers **greater than one** makes them larger:

$$2^3 = 2 \times 2 \times 2 = 8 \qquad \left(\frac{3}{2}\right)^2 = \frac{3}{2} \times \frac{3}{2} = \frac{9}{4} = 2.25$$

• As we saw in the Fractions and Decimals chapters of our book on <u>Arithmetic & "Plan B" Strategies</u>, however, the opposite is true of fractions and decimals between zero and one.

• **The more we multiply numbers between zero and one**, the smaller they get:

$$\left(\frac{1}{2}\right)^3 = \frac{1}{2} \times \frac{1}{2} \times \frac{1}{2} = \frac{1}{8} \qquad\qquad (0.8)^2 = 0.8 \times 0.8 = 0.64$$

(2) Bases vs. Coefficients – As you know, an exponent is a superscript number to the right of a term, indicating how many times that term is to be multiplied by itself.

- Thus, notations such as 5^4, y^3, and $(3n)^2$ are simply shorthand representations for:

$$5^4 = 5 \times 5 \times 5 \times 5 \qquad y^3 = y \times y \times y \qquad (3n)^2 = 3n \times 3n$$

- What you may not know is that the term to which an exponent is attached is known as the **base**, and any term situated before the base is known as a **coefficient**.

    ➢ When working with exponents, you MUST be able to distinguish the base of an expression from its coefficient.

- This distinction is important because **the exponent only applies to the base**. The exponent does **NOT** apply to the co-efficient.

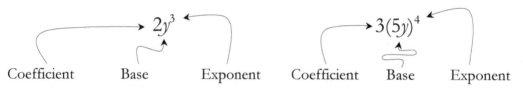

| Coefficient | Base | Exponent | Coefficient | Base | Exponent |

- For example, $2y^3$ has a base y and a coefficient 2, and thus equals $2 \times y \times y \times y$. Likewise, $3(5y)^4$ has a base $5y$ and a coefficient 3, and thus equals $3 \times 5y \times 5y \times 5y \times 5y$.

    ➢ Notice that **parentheses are used to indicate which elements belong to the base** — if the base has more than one element.

- For example, the notation $(2n)^3$ indicates a base of $2n$, while the notation $2n^3$ indicates a base of n and a coefficient 2.

- In other words, in the case of $(2n)^3$, $2n$ is cubed, but **in the case of $2n^3$, ONLY the n is cubed**:

$$(2n)^3 = 2n \times 2n \times 2n = 8n^3 \qquad\qquad 2n^3 = 2 \times n \times n \times n$$

    ➢ The distinction between base and coefficient is a VITAL one.

- As you will see, several exponent rules are easily misconstrued when this distinction is confused.

- Further, exam-makers are aware that some test-takers do not understand the difference between expressions such as $2n^3$ and $(2n)^3$ and design questions to exploit the confusion.

• Consider the following:

$$n = 2$$

Quantity A

$5n^2$

Quantity B

100

Answer. B. It's easy to assume that the quantities are equal, since $5 \times 2 = 10$, and $10^2 = 100$. However, the notation $5n^2$ represents $5 \times n^2$, since the base is n and 5 is just a coefficient.

• If Quantity A were written $(5n)^2$, the base would be $5n$ and Quantity A would equal $5n \times 5n = 10 \times 10 = 100$. However, $5n^2 = 5 \times n^2$, so Quantity A = 20 and the correct answer is (B):

$$5n^2 = 5 \times 2^2 = 5 \times 4 = 20$$

➤ Exam-makers occasionally combine questions involving bases vs. coefficients with questions about positives and negatives:

• Let's take a look at one more sample problem:

Quantity A

-3^4

Quantity B

$(-3)^4$

Answer. B. As with the question above, it's tempting to assume that the two quantities are equal, since **multiplying an EVEN number of negative terms produces a positive product**.

➤ However, the notation -3^4 stands for -1×3^4, since the **base is 3 and the negative sign is just a coefficient**.

• Thus, Quantity A = −81:

$$-1 \times 3^4 = -1 \times 81 = -81$$

• In contrast, Quantity B = 81, since **the parentheses indicate that the negative sign is part of the base**. Thus:

$$(-3)^4 = (-3) \times (-3) \times (-3) \times (-3) = 81$$

• Since Quantity A = −81 and Quantity B = 81, the correct answer is therefore (B).

(3) Resolving Parentheses – When working with exponent expressions, it's normally useful to get rid of any parentheses.

- In general, there are two ways to do so. The first way is to **write out the expression longhand**.

- For example, we can remove the parentheses from expressions such as $(3n)^4$ and $(2 \times 3)^2$ by writing them out as follows:

$$(3n)^4 = 3n \times 3n \times 3n \times 3n = 81n^4 \qquad (2 \times 3)^2 = (2 \times 3)(2 \times 3) = 6 \times 6 = 36$$

➤ The faster way is to **distribute the exponent to EVERY term within the parentheses**.

- Going forward, we will call this ⊡ **The Distribution Shortcut** ⊡.

- For example, we can also remove the parentheses from $(3n)^4$ and $(2 \times 3)^2$ by distributing their exponents as follows:

$$(3n)^4 = 3^4 \times n^4 = 81n^4 \qquad (2 \times 3)^2 = 2^2 \times 3^2 = 4 \times 9 = 36$$

➤ To understand why this shortcut works, consider an expression such as $(4n)^2$.

- Its parentheses indicate a base of $4n$, so we know that $(4n)^2 = 4n \times 4n$. The notation $4n \times 4n$ is shorthand for $4 \times n \times 4 \times n$, which in turn equals $4^2 \times n^2$. In other words:

$$(4n)^2 = 4n \times 4n = 4 \times n \times 4 \times n = 4^2 \times n^2$$

➤ But BEWARE: **the distribution shortcut only works for SIMPLE expressions**.

- As you may recall from our book on <u>Arithmetic & "Plan B" Strategies</u>, a **simple expression** contains no addition or subtraction. A **complex expression** does.

- For example, $(xy)^2$ would be considered a simple expression, and $(x + y)^2$ would be considered complex, since:

<u>SIMPLE</u>   <u>COMPLEX</u>

$(xy)^2$ and has no addition (or subtraction) $(x + y)^2$ has addition (or subtraction)

➤ To resolve the parentheses of a complex expression, you have to **combine the terms** within the parentheses before distributing the exponent:

$$(3 + 4)^2 = (7)^2 = 49$$

- To understand why you CANNOT use the shortcut with a complex expression, consider $(1 + 4)^3$. According to its parentheses, $(1 + 4)^3$ has a base of $1 + 4$, so we know that:

$$(1 + 4)^3 = (1 + 4)(1 + 4)(1 + 4) = (5)(5)(5) = 125$$

- If we were to distribute the exponent throughout the parentheses, **we would incorrectly get 65** instead of 125:

$$(1 + 4)^3 \neq 1^3 + 4^3, \text{ since } 1^3 + 4^3 = 1 + 64 = 65$$

➤ If the terms within the parentheses cannot be combined, **the parentheses must be written out longhand**:

- To understand why, let's take a look at $(x + y)^2$.

- According to its parentheses, $(x + y)^2$ has a base of $x + y$. Written out, $(x + y)^2$ therefore equals $(x + y)(x + y)$, which in turn equals $x^2 + 2xy + y^2$.

INCORRECT	CORRECT
$(x + y)^2 = x^2 + y^2$	$(x + y)^2 = (x + y)(x + y) = x^2 + 2xy + y^2$

(If you don't recall this sort of Algebra, you'll find it covered in the
FOIL section of our chapter on Algebra!)

- In other words, if $(x + y)(x + y) = x^2 + 2xy + y^2$ when properly multiplied, then $(x + y)^2$ CANNOT equal $x^2 + y^2$.

➤ This last point is an important one, since many test-takers mistakenly assume that $(x + y)^2 = x^2 + y^2$.

- In fact, it is one of the **most common mistakes** made by GRE test-takers.

- And, of course, if test-takers commonly mistake something, you can bet that exam-makers frequently design questions to test it.

(4) Raising Powers to a Power – Raising something with an exponent to yet another exponent is commonly known as "raising a power to a power".

- Expressions such as $(x^3)^4$ and $(2^4)^2$ would both be considered "powers raised to a power", since both expressions have **exponents inside and outside** their parentheses.

  ➢ To raise a power to a power, simply **multiply the exponents**.

- For example, $(x^3)^4 = x^{12}$, since $3 \times 4 = 12$. Likewise, $(2^4)^2 = 2^8 = 256$, since $4 \times 2 = 8$.

- To understand why, consider $(2^3)^2$. We know that $(2^3)^2 = 2^3 \times 2^3$. We also know that $2^3 = 2 \times 2 \times 2$. Therefore, $2^3 \times 2^3 = 2 \times 2 \times 2 \times 2 \times 2 \times 2$, which equals 2^6. In other words:

$$(2^3)^2 = 2^3 \times 2^3 = 2 \times 2 \times 2 \times 2 \times 2 \times 2 = 2^6$$

- Let's run through a few difficult examples to be sure you have the hang of it:

$$(x^3)^y = x^{3 \times y} = x^{3y} \qquad (5^a)^b = 5^{a \times b} = 5^{ab} \qquad (4^n)^n = 4^{n \times n} = 4^{n^2}$$

  ➢ When working with SIMPLE expressions, be sure to distribute the outside exponent to EVERY term within the expression.

- **It's easy to miss items in the front of parentheses,** since your eye tends to focus on the side-by-side exponents at the back:

<u>INCORRECT</u>

$$(2x^2)^3 = 2x^6$$

<u>CORRECT</u>

$$(2x^2)^3 = 2^3 x^6 = 8x^6$$

- If your expression is COMPLEX, remember: you need to **combine the terms** within the parentheses **before multiplying** the exponents:

$$(3^2 - 2^2)^2 = (9 - 4)^2 = 5^2 = 25 \qquad (9x^2 - 2x^2)^2 = (7x^2)^2 = 7^2 x^2 = 49x^4$$

- And if the terms cannot be combined, you have to write out the expression longhand:

<u>INCORRECT</u>

$$(3^2 + x^2)^2 = 3^4 + x^4$$

<u>CORRECT</u>

$$(3^2 + x^2)^2 = (3^2 + x^2)(3^2 + x^2)$$

(5) Multiplication & Division: Same Bases – Exponent expressions can be multiplied or divided if they have the SAME BASE.

• For example, we can multiply or divide 3^4 and 3^2, since they each have a base of 3, but we cannot multiply or divide 2^2 and 3^5, since their bases are different.

 ➢ To **multiply** terms with the SAME BASE, simply **add their exponents**.

• For example, $3^4 \times 3^2 = 3^6$, since $3^{4+2} = 3^6$. Likewise, $n^2 \times n^3 \times n^4 = n^9$, since $n^{2+3+4} = n^9$.

• To understand why we can add the exponents, consider $2^2 \times 2^3$. We know that $2^2 = 2 \times 2$ and that $2^3 = 2 \times 2 \times 2$. Thus $2^2 \times 2^3 = 2 \times 2 \ \times \ 2 \times 2 \times 2$, which equals 2^5. In other words:

$$2^2 \times 2^3 = 2 \times 2 \times 2 \times 2 \times 2 = 2^5$$

• Let's run through a few difficult examples to be sure you have the hang of it:

$$5^4 \times 5^{-2} = 5^{4+(-2)} = 5^2 \qquad 7^x \times 7^{2x} = 7^{x+2x} = 7^{3x} \qquad n^4 \times n^{-2} \times n^{-2} = n^{4+(-2)+(-2)} = n^0$$

 ➢ When multiplying with the same base, be sure that you **NEVER multiply the bases**.

• Although you should feel free to multiply any coefficients you come across, you have to leave the bases alone:

Leave the BASES alone   Multiply the COEFFICIENTS

$$5^5 \times 5^5 = 5^{10} \qquad\qquad 5n^4 \times 5n^2 = 25n^6$$

• To understand why, think back to the multiplication of $2^2 \times 2^3$. Written out, $2^2 \times 2^3$ equals $2 \times 2 \times 2 \times 2 \times 2$, which is a collection of 2's. Specifically, it's five of them. That's why $2^2 \times 2^3$ equals 2^5.

WRONG   CORRECT

$$2^2 \times 2^3 = 4^5 \qquad\qquad\qquad 2^2 \times 2^3 = 2^5$$

• Conversely, notice that $2 \times 2 \times 2 \times 2 \times 2$ is not a collection of 4's, even though some of the terms may multiply to 4.

• Put another way, $4^5 = 4 \times 4 \times 4 \times 4 \times 4$, which certainly doesn't equal $2 \times 2 \times 2 \times 2 \times 2$.

> ➤ To **divide** terms with the SAME BASE, simply **subtract their exponents**.

- For example, $\dfrac{3^4}{3^2} = 3^2$, since $3^{4-2} = 3^2$. Likewise, $\dfrac{n^9}{n^6} = n^3$, since $n^{9-6} = n^3$.

- To understand why we can subtract the exponents, consider the division of $\dfrac{2^4}{2^2}$. Written out, we can simplify it as follows:

$$\frac{2^4}{2^2} = \frac{2 \times 2 \times 2 \times 2}{2 \times 2} = \frac{2 \times 2 \times \cancel{2} \times \cancel{2}}{\cancel{2} \times \cancel{2}} = 2 \times 2 = 2^2$$

- Since $\dfrac{2^4}{2^2}$ and 2^{4-2} both equal 2^2, we can therefore say that $\dfrac{2^4}{2^2} = 2^{4-2} = 2^2$.

- Again, let's run through a few difficult examples to be sure you have the hang of it:

$$\frac{5^4}{5^{-2}} = 5^{4-(-2)} = 5^6 \qquad \frac{7^x}{7^{2x}} = 7^{x-2x} = 7^{-x} \qquad \frac{x^n}{x^{n-1}} = x^{n-(n-1)} = x^{n-n+1} = x^1$$

> ➤ As with multiplication, be sure **to leave the bases alone** when using division.

- Although you should feel free to divide any coefficients you come across, you have to leave the bases alone:

<table>
<tr><td>Leave the BASES alone</td><td>Divide the COEFFICIENTS</td></tr>
<tr><td>$\dfrac{10^8}{10^3} = 10^5$</td><td>$\dfrac{8x^6}{2x^3} = 4x^3$</td></tr>
</table>

- When working with coefficients, however, be sure to note that the coefficients of different bases can be multiplied, even if the exponents cannot be added:

$$4x^2 \times 7y^5 = 28x^2y^5 \qquad\qquad 5(3)^4 \times 2(7)^5 = 10(3)^4(7)^5$$

- And, of course, the same goes for division. You can divide the coefficients, even if you can't subtract the exponents:

$$\frac{8a^4}{12b^2} = \frac{2a^4}{3b^2} \qquad\qquad \frac{10(4)^5}{2(3)^2} = \frac{5(4)^5}{(3)^2}$$

(6) Negative Exponents: Flip the Base – In the previous section, you may have noticed several equations containing negative exponents.

- If you're like many test-takers, you may have wondered "what the heck is this?" In short, a negative exponent is the opposite of a positive exponent:

> A positive exponent tells us how many times to **multiply** by something.

> A negative exponent tells us how many times to **divide** by something.

- For example, $3^1 = 1 \times 3$, so $3^{-1} = 1 \div 3$. Likewise $3^2 = 1 \times 3^2$, so $3^{-2} = 1 \div 3^2$.

  ➢ Because, however, $1 \div 3 = \frac{1}{3}$ and $1 \div 3^2 = \frac{1}{3^2}$, it is generally easier to think of negative exponents like this: $x^{-n} = \frac{1}{x^n}$.

- We like to call this relationship "flipping the base". **You can make any exponent positive by taking the reciprocal of its base** (i.e. "flipping the base" upside down):

$$5^{-3} = \frac{1}{5^3} = \frac{1}{125} \qquad n^{-4} = \frac{1}{n^4} \qquad \left(\frac{2}{3}\right)^{-2} = \left(\frac{3}{2}\right)^2 = \frac{9}{4}$$

  ➢ Note, by the way, that if you find a negative exponent on the bottom of a fraction, you can **flip its base to the top**, like this:

$$\frac{1}{3^{-2}} = 3^2 = 9 \qquad \frac{1}{n^{-4}} = n^4 \qquad \frac{1}{(x^2)^{-3}} = (x^2)^3 = x^6$$

- Likewise, if you find a fraction with negative exponents on both top <u>and</u> bottom, you can flip the top base to the bottom and the bottom base to the top, like this:

$$\frac{3^{-1}}{4^{-1}} = \frac{4^1}{3^1} = \frac{4}{3} \qquad \frac{a^{-10}}{b^{-5}} = \frac{b^5}{a^{10}} \qquad \frac{2^{-3}}{5^{-2}} = \frac{5^2}{2^3} = \frac{25}{8}$$

  ➢ When working with coefficients, however, **just be sure that you only flip the base!**

- Remember, coefficients are not attached to the exponent and thus should not be flipped. **Only the bases move**, and they take their exponents with them:

<u>WRONG</u>

$$2x^{-3} = \frac{1}{2x^3}$$

<u>CORRECT</u>

$$2x^{-3} = \frac{2}{x^3}$$

(7) The Powers of Zero & One – Any term raised to the zero power equals one, save for zero itself.

$$n^0 = 1 \qquad\qquad \left(\frac{2}{3}\right)^0 = 1 \qquad\qquad 3^0 = 1$$

- To understand why, let's think back to our division rule in which we subtract the exponents. According to that rule, any power divided by itself should yield a power of zero:

$$2^1 \div 2^1 = 2^{1-1} = 2^0 \qquad 3^4 \div 3^4 = 3^{4-4} = 3^0 \qquad x^n \div x^n = x^{n-n} = x^0$$

- However, any power divided by itself also yields one: $2^1 \div 2^1 = 1$, $x^3 \div x^3 = 1$, and so forth. Therefore, since any power divided by itself equals both a power of zero and 1, the two must be equal. In other words:

$$\frac{x^n}{x^n} = 1 \text{ and } \frac{x^n}{x^n} = x^{n-n} = x^0, \text{ thus } x^0 = 1$$

  ➢ There is one exception to this rule: **0^0 is considered indeterminate.**

- 0^0 is considered indeterminate, since $0^1 \div 0^1 = 0^{1-1} = 0^0$, and some scholars believe that $0 \div 0 = 1$, while others believe that anything divided by zero is **undefined**.

- Fortunately, the GRE will NEVER ask you about 0^0. However, it will expect you to understand the difference between the following:

$$(-2)^0 = 1 \qquad\qquad -2^0 = -1$$

- The reason that -2^0 does NOT equal 1, is that the **negative sign is a coefficient**: it is not part of the base. In other words:

$$-2^0 = -1 \times 2^0 = -1 \times 1 = -1$$

  ➢ Any term raised to the **first power** equals itself.

$$2^1 = 2 \qquad \left(\frac{2}{3}\right)^1 = \frac{2}{3} \qquad (-5)^1 = -5 \qquad 0^1 = 0$$

- The converse of this is also true: **any term without an exponent** equals itself to the 1st power. For example, $5 = 5^1$. When working with exponents, we strongly encourage you to **write down the "one"**. Doing so can make all the difference:

$$2 \times 2^4 = 2^1 \times 2^4 = 2^{1+4} = 2^5 \qquad\qquad x^4 \div x = x^4 \div x^1 = x^{4-1} = x^3$$

(8) Addition & Subtraction: Factor – Of all the exponent rules, perhaps none cause more confusion (or are tested more frequently) than those involving addition and subtraction.

- The good news is that the core idea is relatively simple.

  ➢ To add or subtract exponent expressions **you have to FACTOR** them.

- The term factoring refers to the "splitting" of a complex expression into simpler terms that multiply to the original.

- For example, each term in the expression $2x + 6y$ has a factor of 2, so we can factor $2x + 6y$ as $2(x + 3y)$, since:

$$2(x + 3y) = 2x + 6y$$

  ➢ The bad news is that factoring can be tricky. To factor more intimidating expressions, there are two questions you have to ask yourself:

  1. What is the **largest element** in common to all of my terms?
  2. What do I have to multiply with that common element to **recreate the original** expression?

- For example, imagine that you needed to factor $12n^3 + 4n^2 + 8n$. To start, you would need to identify the largest element in common to $12n^3$, $4n^2$, and $8n$.

  ➢ Since each of these terms is both a multiple of 4 (4, 8, 12) and contains at least one n (n, n^2, and n^3), that element must be $4n$.

- Next, you would need to multiply $4n$ by $3n^2 + n + 2$ to recreate $12n^3 + 4n^2 + 8n$:

$$12n^3 + 4n^2 + 8n$$

$$4n \times \boxed{3n^2} = 12n^3 \qquad 4n \times \boxed{n} = 4n^2 \qquad 4n \times \boxed{2} = 8n$$

- In other words, $12n^3 + 4n^2 + 8n$ can be factored as $4n(3n^2 + n + 2)$, since:

$$4n(3n^2 + n + 2) \;\rightarrow\; 4n(3n^2) + 4n(n) + 4n(2) \;\rightarrow\; 12n^3 + 4n^2 + 8n$$

➤ With exponents, factoring generally involves the multiplication rule in which you ADD the exponents.

- For example, $10^4 + 10^5 + 10^6$ can be factored as $10^4(10^0 + 10^1 + 10^2)$, since:

$$10^4 \times \boxed{10^0} = 10^{4+0} = 10^4 \qquad 10^4 \times \boxed{10^1} = 10^{4+1} = 10^5 \qquad 10^4 \times \boxed{10^2} = 10^{4+2} = 10^6$$

- And since $10^0 + 10^1 + 10^2 = 1 + 10 + 100 = 111$, the expression $10^4 + 10^5 + 10^6$ ultimately equals $10^4(111)$:

$$10^4 + 10^5 + 10^6 = 10^4(10^0 + 10^1 + 10^2) = 10^4(1 + 10 + 100) = 10^4(111)$$

➤ Let's run through a few difficult examples to make sure that you've got the hang of it:

$$x^2 + x^5 = x^2(x^0 + x^3) = x^2(1 + x^3) \qquad 3^6 - 3^4 = 3^4(3^2 - 3^0) = 3^4(9 - 1) = 81(8)$$

$$2^{29} - 2^{28} = 2^{28}(2^1 - 2^0) = 2^{28}(1) = 2^{28} \qquad 6^6 + 6^7 - 6^8 = 6^6(6^0 + 6^1 - 6^2) = 6^6(-29)$$

- Let's also take a look at a tricky sample problem:

Quantity A	**Quantity B**
9^{10}	$9^9 + 3 \cdot 9^9 + 6 \cdot 9^9$

Answer: B. To add or subtract exponent expressions, **we have to factor** them. Since $9^9, 3 \cdot 9^9$, and $6 \cdot 9^9$ have a common factor of 9^9, we can initially factor Quantity B as follows:

$$9^9 + 3 \cdot 9^9 + 6 \cdot 9^9 = 9^9(9^0 + 3 \cdot 9^0 + 6 \cdot 9^0)$$

Further, since $9^0 = 1$, we can add the terms within the parentheses to 10:

$$9^9(9^0 + 3 \cdot 9^0 + 6 \cdot 9^0) = 9^9(1 + 3 \cdot 1 + 6 \cdot 1) = 9^9(10)$$

Since Quantity A $= 9^{10}$, which equals $9^9 \times 9^1$, and Quantity B $= 9^9 \times 10$, Quantity B must be larger than Quantity A: $9^9 \times 10$ is larger than $9^9 \times 9$.

➤ When subtracting exponent expressions, watch out for **the DIFFERENCE between two SQUARES**.

• The difference between two squares can only be determined through a special sort of factoring, which can be summarized as follows:

$$\underline{\text{Difference Between Squares:}} \quad x^2 - y^2 = (x+y)(x-y)$$

• To understand how this works, imagine that you needed the difference between 17^2 and 13^2.

• Rather than squaring both 17 and 13, and then subtracting the smaller term, you could also get this difference by rewriting the squares as follows:

$$17^2 - 13^2 = (17 + 13)(17 - 13) = (30)(4) = 120$$

➤ Thus, **$101^2 - 99^2$ may LOOK like it should equal 2^2, but it does not.** It actually equals 400, since we can factor it as follows:

$$101^2 - 99^2 = (101 + 99)(101 - 99) = (200)(2) = 400$$

• The formula for the difference between squares is an important one.

• You will see it resurface in our chapter on Algebra and in our book on <u>Geometry</u>. We encourage you to memorize it immediately: it's a prominent **shortcut** for many GRE problems.

➤ On a final note, keep an eye out for **like terms**.

• Like terms are terms with **the same base** and **the same exponent**. For example, $6x^3$ and $2x^3$ are like terms, since they have the same base and exponent.

• Conversely, x^2 and x^3 are not like terms, since they have different exponents. The same goes for x^3 and 5^3, which have different bases.

➤ Although like terms can be factored, they are more easily combined through simple addition and subtraction.

• Thus:

$$x^2 + x^2 + x^2 = 3x^2 \qquad 6y^3 - 2y^3 = 4y^3 \qquad 5^3 + 5^3 + 5^3 = 3(5^3)$$

➢ To ensure that you've got it, let's work through a fairly tricky sample problem together.

• Consider the following:

$4^4 + 4^4 + 4^4 + 4^4$ equals which of the following?

(A) 4^5 (B) 8^4 (C) 16^4 (D) 4^{16} (E) 16^{16}

Answer: A. Because the terms above are like terms, we can combine them through addition:

$$4^4 + 4^4 + 4^4 + 4^4 = 4(4^4)$$

➢ Further, since $4 = 4^1$, we can rewrite $4(4^4)$ as $4^1(4^4)$. Thus, the correct answer is (A), since:

$$4(4^4) = 4^1(4^4) = 4^{1+4} = 4^5$$

• Alternatively, we can factor $4^4 + 4^4 + 4^4 + 4^4$, since each term has a 4^4 in common, although doing so would involve a bit more work:

$$4^4 + 4^4 + 4^4 + 4^4 = 4^4(4^0 + 4^0 + 4^0 + 4^0) = 4^4(1 + 1 + 1 + 1) = 4^4(4)$$

(9) Multiplication & Division: Same Exponents – Earlier, we saw that terms with the SAME BASE can be multiplied by adding their exponents.

- However, terms with the SAME EXPONENT can also be multiplied.

  ➤ To do so, simply **multiply their bases.**

- For example $2^4 \times 5^4 = 10^4$, since $2 \times 5 = 10$. Likewise, $n^8 \times p^8 = (np)^8$, since $n \times p = np$.

- To understand why this is so, consider $2^4 \times 5^4$. We know that $10^4 = (2 \times 5)^4$, since 10 equals 2×5. We also know that $(2 \times 5)^4 = 2^4 \times 5^4$, thanks to the **distribution shortcut** we learned earlier. Therefore $10^4 = 2^4 \times 5^4$, since:

$$10^4 = (2 \times 5)^4 = 2^4 \times 5^4$$

- Let's run through a few more examples to make sure that you've got the hang of it:

$$2^2 \times 3^2 = 6^2 \qquad 5^4 \times 4^4 = 20^4 \qquad a^4 \times b^4 = (ab)^4$$

  ➤ When multiplying with the same exponent, **LEAVE the exponents ALONE.**

- It's always easy to confuse what's supposed to change and what needs to remain the same:

INCORRECT	CORRECT
$2^5 \times 3^5 = 6^{10}$ or 6^{25}	$2^5 \times 3^5 = 6^5$

- An easy way to keep it straight: whatever's the SAME has to remain the SAME. Here, the initial exponents are the same ($2^5 \times 3^5$), so the exponent remains the same (6^5).

  ➤ To **divide** terms with the same exponent, simply **divide their bases.**

- For example, $\dfrac{10^4}{2^4} = 5^4$, since $10 \div 2 = 5$. Likewise, $\dfrac{x^3}{y^3} = \left(\dfrac{x}{y}\right)^3$, since $x \div y = \dfrac{x}{y}$.

- To understand why this is so, consider $10^4 \div 2^4$. We know that $5^4 = (10 \div 2)^4$, since $10 \div 2 = 5$. We also know that $(10 \div 2)^4 = 10^4 \div 2^4$ because of the **distribution shortcut**. Thus, $10^4 \div 2^4 = 5^4$, since:

$$5^4 = (10 \div 2)^4 = 10^4 \div 2^4$$

- Again, let's run through a few more examples to make sure that you've got the hang of it:

$$9^4 \div 3^4 = 3^4 \qquad 15^3 \div 3^3 = 5^3 \qquad 14^x \div 2^x = 7^x$$

(10) Break Down the Bases! – You now know every exponent rule tested by the GRE.

• However, if you want to solve some of the more difficult GRE exponent problems, there's still one more thing that you should know.

    ➢ When working with exponents, it's often helpful to **break down the bases** to their PRIME FACTORS.

• Exam-makers often mask simple relationships with complicated bases.

• Breaking down those bases to their prime factors typically exposes these relationships, making it easy to solve scary-looking problems.

    ➢ To break a base into its prime factors, first put the base in parentheses. Then split it into progressively smaller numbers.

• Once your numbers are **as small as they can get,** use the distribution shortcut to distribute the original exponent to <u>each</u> term within the parentheses.

• Let's take a look at a few examples:

$$15^{25} = (3 \times 5)^{25} = 3^{25} \times 5^{25} \qquad 77^{10} = (7 \times 11)^{10} = 7^{10} \times 11^{10}$$

$$8^{12} = (2 \times 2 \times 2)^{12} = (2^3)^{12} = 2^{3 \times 12} = 2^{36} \qquad 12^{12} = (4 \times 3)^{12} = (2^2 \times 3^1)^{12} = 2^{24} \times 3^{12}$$

• To get a better sense of how all this can help you, let's take a look at a couple of sample problems:

<table>
<tr><td align="center"><u>Quantity A</u></td><td align="center"><u>Quantity B</u></td></tr>
<tr><td align="center">16^6</td><td align="center">8^8</td></tr>
</table>

Answer: C. To compare 16^6 to 8^8, we only need to break down the bases to their prime factors. Since $16 = 2 \times 2 \times 2 \times 2 = 2^4$ and $8 = 2 \times 2 \times 2 = 2^3$, the two quantities must be equal, as:

$$16^6 = (2^4)^6 = 2^{24} \qquad\qquad 8^8 = (2^3)^8 = 2^{24}$$

• This one is more difficult:

Which of the following is equal to $\dfrac{10^{13}}{2^6 \times 5^4}$?

(A) $2^3 \times 5^3$ **(B)** $2^7 \times 5^3$ **(C)** $2^7 \times 5^7$ **(D)** $2^7 \times 5^9$ **(E)** $2^9 \times 5^9$

Answer: D. To start, let's break down 10^{13}:

$$10^{13} = (2 \times 5)^{13} = 2^{13} \times 5^{13}, \text{ therefore } \frac{10^{13}}{2^6 \times 5^4} = \frac{2^{13} \times 5^{13}}{2^6 \times 5^4}$$

Next, let's divide the twos and then the fives:

$$\frac{2^{13}}{2^6} = 2^{13-6} = 2^7 \qquad\qquad \frac{5^{13}}{5^4} = 5^{13-4} = 5^9$$

Since we're left with $2^7 \times 5^9$, the correct answer must be (D).

➤ If you're ever UNSURE of how to attack an exponent problem, particularly one with **large bases or exponents**, splitting the bases is usually a smart first move.

• It may not always be the correct approach, but it usually is. Let's take a look at one last example, one a little bit trickier than the first two:

If 32 goes into 6^{20} exactly n times, what is the value of n?

(A) 2^{15} **(B)** $\left(2^{15}\right)\left(3^{20}\right)$ **(C)** 6^{15} **(D)** $\left(2^{18}\right)\left(3^{18}\right)$ **(E)** 10^{15}

Answer: B. To answer a question like this, it can be helpful to express its information in the form of a fraction. It can also be helpful to express 32 as 2^5:

$$\frac{6^{20}}{2^5} = n, \text{ what is } n?$$

Remember, if you're ever unsure about how to attack an exponent question, particularly one with very **large bases or exponents**, splitting the bases is usually a smart first move.

In this case, $6^{20} = (2 \times 3)^{20} = 2^{20} \times 3^{20}$, so we can rephrase our question as follows:

$$\frac{2^{20} \times 3^{20}}{2^5} = n$$

Finally, since $2^{20} \div 2^5 = 2^{20-5} = 2^{15}$, the correct answer must be (B), as:

$$\frac{2^{20} \times 3^{20}}{2^5} = \frac{2^{20}}{2^5} \times \frac{3^{20}}{1} = 2^{15} \times 3^{20} = n$$

(11) Exponent Equations – Any equation in which a variable occurs in the exponent is commonly known as an exponent(ial) equation.

• For example, $2^{2x-1} = 16$ would be considered an exponent equation, since 2^{2x-1} has a variable in its exponent. Conversely, $(x + 2)^3 = 27$ would not, since its exponent lacks a variable.

> ➤ To solve problems involving exponent equations, you simply need to **make the bases the same**.

• Once the bases on BOTH sides of an equation are the same, they can be ignored, allowing you to **set their exponents equal** to solve for x.

• Thus, in the case of $2^{2x-1} = 8$, x must equal 2, since $8 = 2^3$:

$2^{2x-1} = 2^3$	Make the bases the same.
$2x - 1 = 3$	Set the exponents equal.
$2x = 4$, so $x = 2$	Add 1 to both sides, solve for x.

> ➤ In most cases, you will need to **break down one (or both) of your bases** to make them the same.

• Let's look at a slightly harder question.

$$9^{4x} = 27^{2x+2}$$

Quantity A	**Quantity B**
x^x	**36**

Answer: B. Our equation has exponents in its variables, so we need to **make their bases the same**. Since 9 and 27 are both powers of 3, we can break them down as follows: $9 = 3^2$ and $27 = 3^3$. Doing so allows us to solve the equation in the following manner:

$(3^2)^{4x} = (3^3)^{2x+2}$	Make the bases the same.
$3^{8x} = 3^{6x+6}$	Raise the powers to powers.
$8x = 6x + 6$	Set the exponents equal.
$2x = 6$, so $x = 3$	Subtract $6x$ from both sides, solve for x.

If $x = 3$, then $x^x = 3^3 = 27$. Thus, the correct answer must be (B), since Quantity B is larger than Quantity A.

➢ Any inequality in which a variable occurs in the exponent is commonly known as an **exponent(ial) inequality**.

• Exponent inequalities work just like exponent equations. To solve them, you first need to make their bases the same.

• Let's look at a couple of sample problems:

$$n > 0, \text{ and } 625^{n} < 5^{1-n}$$

Quantity A	**Quantity B**
$\sqrt{n}$	n

Answer. A. Our inequality has exponents in its variables, so we need to **make their bases the same**. Since $625 = 5^{4}$, we can solve the inequality in the following manner:

$(5^{4})^{n} < 5^{1-n}$	Make the bases the same.
$5^{4n} < 5^{1-n}$	Raise the power to a power.
$4n < 1 - n$	Set the exponents equal.
$5n < 1$, so $n < 1/5$	Add n to both sides, solve for n.

If n is less than 1/5 but greater than 0, then $\sqrt{n}$ must be greater than n, since **the square root of a value between 0 and 1 is larger than the original value**. (Thus $\sqrt{0.5} \approx 0.71$.) Therefore, (A) must be the correct answer.

Chapter 3: Exponents

Rare or Advanced Concepts

---

(12) Powers of Ten – As you may recall, any number that consists of nothing but tens is commonly known as a "power of ten".

• You may also recall that multiplying a number by a power of ten slides its decimal point to the right and that dividing a number by a power of ten slides its decimal to the left.

➢ What you may not know, however, is that questions involving decimals and powers of ten can get dramatically harder once other exponents are added to the mix.

• In general, there are two sorts of questions involving decimals, exponents, and powers of ten, both of which are EXTREMELY rare.

• The FIRST will ask you to determine **how many CONSECUTIVE ZEROES** a number has to the left or right of its decimal point.

• The important thing to understand, when dealing with such questions, is that **zeroes come from "10"s**.

➢ To determine the number of consecutive zeroes that an integer has to the LEFT of its decimal point, count the number of "10"s it contains.

• For example, the product of $2,000 \times 70$ has 4 zeroes to the left of its decimal point, since $2,000 = 2 \times 10 \times 10 \times 10$, and so contains three "10"s, while $70 = 7 \times 10$, and so contains one "10". Thus, $2,000 \times 70 = 140,000$.

• In more difficult cases, you will need to multiply "2"s and "5"s into "10"s. Since $10 = 2 \times 5$, **the number of "10"s will be dependent on the number of "2 × 5"s.**

• Let's take a look at a sample question:

If $k = 2^6 \times 5^{10}$ is expressed as an integer, how many zeroes will k have between its decimal point and its first non-zero digit?

(A) 6 (B) 7 (C) 8 (D) 9 (E) 10

Answer: A. If k were expressed an integer, it would have 6 zeroes between its decimal point and its first non-zero digit, since $2^6 \times 5^{10}$ contains **six "2 × 5"s**, giving it six "10"s:

$$k = 2^6 \times 5^{10} = 2^6 \times 5^6 \times 5^4 = 10^6 \times 5^4 = 1,000,000 \times 625 = 625,000,000$$

> ➢ To determine the number of consecutive zeroes that a number has to the RIGHT of its decimal point, first count the number of "10"s in its denominator.

- Then determine the product of any numbers that do not produce a "10".

If the product is:	The product will add:
Less than 10	ZERO "10"s
Between 10 and 100	ONE "10"
Between 100 and 1,000	TWO "10"s

- And so forth. Let's take a look at another sample question:

$$g = \frac{1}{2^6 \times 5^7 \times 7}$$

If g is expressed as a decimal, how many zeroes will g have between its decimal point and the first non-zero digit to the right of its decimal point?

Answer: 7. Since $2^6 \times 5^7 \times 7 = 2^6 \times 5^6 \times 5^1 \times 7 = 10^6 \times 35 = 35,000,000$, g contains <u>six</u> "10"s in its denominator.

There are also two numbers in the denominator of g that do not produce a "10": namely, the 7 and the extra 5. Since $7 \times 5 = 35$, and 35 is **between 10 and 100**, the 7×5 contribute <u>one more</u> "10".

Thus, the denominator of g has a total of seven "10"s, so g will have 7 zeroes to the right of its decimal point:

$$\frac{1}{2^6 \times 5^7 \times 7} = \frac{1}{2^6 \times 5^6 \times 5^1 \times 7} = \frac{1}{10^6 \times 35} = \frac{1}{35,000,000} = 0.00000002857...$$

- The <u>OTHER</u> sort of question involving decimals, exponents, and powers of ten will ask you to determine **the number of NON-ZERO digits** within a decimal.

> ➢ To solve such questions, first CONVERT the "10"s in the denominator to 10^{-n}.

- Then **express the remaining fraction as a decimal**. (Use a calculator if necessary.) The non-zero digits of that decimal will be the non-zero digits you are looking for.

- To get a better sense of what we mean by all this, consider the following:

$$x = \frac{1}{2^{11} \times 5^8}$$

If x is expressed as a decimal, how many non-zero digits will the decimal have?

(A) One (B) Three (C) Four (D) Six (E) Eight

Answer: B. Since $2^{11} \times 5^8 = 2^3 \times 2^8 \times 5^8 = 2^3 \times 10^8$, x contains eight "10"s in its denominator.

To determine the number of non-zero digits in x, first convert the eight "10"s to 10^{-8}. Then use the fraction-to-decimal "conversion list" to express $\frac{1}{8}$ as a decimal:

$$x = \frac{1}{2^3 \times 10^8} = \frac{1}{2^3} \times 10^{-8} = \frac{1}{8} \times 10^{-8} = 0.125 \times 10^{-8}$$

Since 10^{-8} will simply shift the decimal point of 0.125 eight places to the left, x has a total of three non-zero digits: 125. Thus, (B) is the correct answer.

• Here's a slightly harder example:

$$n = \frac{1}{2^{10} \times 5^{16}}$$

Quantity A	**Quantity B**
If n is expressed as a decimal, the number of non-zero digits that n contains	4

Answer: B. Since $2^{10} \times 5^{16} = 2^{10} \times 5^{10} \times 5^6 = 10^{10} \times 5^6$, n contains ten "10"s in its denominator.

To determine the number of non-zero digits in n, first convert the ten "10"s to 10^{-10}. Then express $\frac{1}{5^6}$ as a decimal. To avoid the calculator, you can convert $\frac{1}{5^6}$ to $(0.2)^6$:

$$n = \frac{1}{5^6 \times 10^{10}} = \frac{1}{5^6} \times 10^{-10} = \left(\frac{1}{5}\right)^6 \times 10^{-10} = (0.2)^6 \times 10^{-10} = 0.000064 \times 10^{-10}$$

Since 10^{-10} will simply shift the decimal point of 0.000064 ten places to the left, n has a total of two non-zero digits: 64. Thus, Quantity B is larger than Quantity A, so the correct answer is (B).

(13) Equivalent Answers – Every now and then, the GRE will play a fairly crafty trick on unsuspecting test-takers.

- It will **rephrase a perfectly acceptable answer** into an unexpected format.

  ➢ As you've seen by now, a single exponent expression can generally be stated in multiple ways.

- For example, $2^4 \times 2^4$ equals 2^8 if we add its exponents, but $2^4 \times 2^4$ can also equal 4^4 if we multiply its bases. Further, $2^8 = \dfrac{1}{2^{-8}}$ and $4^4 = \dfrac{1}{4^{-4}}$, so we can say:

$$2^4 \times 2^4 = 4^4 \text{ or } (2^2)^4 \text{ or } 2^8 \text{ or } \frac{1}{2^{-8}} \text{ or } \frac{1}{4^{-4}}$$

- Exam-makers occasionally use **equivalent answers** to make exponent problems harder.

  ➢ In the vast majority of cases, the GRE prefers equivalents with **small bases** and positive exponents.

- Consider the following:

If $x = 3^2$, then $x^x =$

(A) 3^4 (B) 3^8 (C) 3^{12} (D) 3^{18} (E) 3^{24}

Answer. D. If $x = 3^2$, then $x = 9$. Thus, $x^x = 9^9$. However, the correct answer is (D), since:

$$9^9 = (3^2)^9 = 3^{18}$$

  ➢ In more difficult cases, however, the exam may unexpectedly **combine powers** to create equivalents with larger bases.

- This is especially common for powers of two and five, which combine to form powers of ten. Consider the following:

If $5^n = 625$, then $(2^{n+2})(5^{n+1}) =$

(A) 10^4 (B) $2(10^6)$ (C) $5(10^6)$ (D) $2(10^5)$ (E) $5(10^5)$

Answer. D. If $5^n = 625$, then $n = 4$. Therefore $(2^{n+2})(5^{n+1}) = (2^6)(5^5)$. However, (D) is the correct answer, since $(2^6)(5^5)$ can be rephrased as $2(10^5)$:

$$(2^6)(5^5) = (2^1 \times 2^5) \times 5^5 = 2^1 \times (2^5 \times 5^5) = 2^1 \times 10^5$$

Review and Drills

(14) Common Exponent Mistakes – Below are some of the most common exponent mistakes.

• **See if you can figure out what's wrong in the left column** before you check out the correct answer in the right column.

➤ If you find yourself making any of these errors, put the mistake on a note card and review it on a frequent basis.

• The rules of exponents are easy to confuse. If you only study them once, you may lose what you learn.

Incorrect	Correct
If $x^2 = 16$, then $x = 4$	If $x^2 = 16$, then $x = \pm 4$
$(x + y)^2 = x^2 + y^2$	$(x + y)^2 = (x + y)(x + y) = x^2 + 2xy + y^2$
$n^2 \times n^3 = n^6$	$n^2 \times n^3 = n^{2+3} = n^5$
$(x^2)^3 = x^5$	$(x^2)^3 = x^{2 \times 3} = x^6$
$(2x^3)^4 = 2x^{12}$	$(2x^3)^4 = 2^4 x^{12} = 16x^{12}$
$5^4 \times 5^8 = 25^{12}$	$5^4 \times 5^8 = 5^{12}$
If $x = 3$, then $4x^2 = 12^2 = 144$	If $x = 3$, then $4x^2 = 4(3)^2 = 4(9) = 36$
$x^2 + x^3 = x^5$	$x^2 + x^3 = x^2(x^0 + x^1) = x^2(1 + x)$
$-7^0 = 1$	$-7^0 = -1 \times 7^0 = -1 \times 1 = -1$
If $x = -4$, then $x^2 = -4^2 = -16$	If $x = -4$, then $x^2 = (-4)^2 = 16$
$5 \times 5^x = 25^x$	$5 \times 5^x = 5^1 \times 5^x = 5^{x+1}$
$3^x + 3^x + 3^x = 3^{3x}$	$3^x + 3^x + 3^x = 3(3^x) = 3^1(3^x) = 3^{x+1}$
$3^4 \times 4^2 = (3 \times 4)^{4+2} = 12^6$	$3^4 \times 4^2 = 81 \times 16 = 1{,}296$

(15) Drills – The following drills have been broken down into three levels: fundamental, intermediate, and advanced.

• Simplify the following expressions as much as possible. Solutions can be found on the following page.

Fundamental

1. $\dfrac{x^6}{x^4}$

2. $(3^4)^5$

3. $(r^3)(r^{-3})$

4. $(x^n)^n$

5. $n(n^2)(n^3)$

6. $\dfrac{x^{-4}}{y^{-5}}$

7. $7^3(3)^3$

8. $8^3 \times 4^6$

Intermediate

9. $\dfrac{8^3}{2^3} - 2^6$

10. $4^7 - 4^8 + 4^9$

11. $3^3 + 3^3 + 3^3$

12. $23^2 - 22^2 + 21^2 - 20^2$

13. $(8^3)^4$

14. $12^3 \times 3^3$

Advanced

15. $(2^n + 2^n)(3^n + 3^n + 3^n)$

16. $\dfrac{3^{x+y}}{3^{x-y}}$

17. $\left(\dfrac{1}{2}\right)^{-6}\left(\dfrac{1}{4}\right)^{-4}\left(\dfrac{1}{8}\right)^{-2}$

18. $\dfrac{1}{2^{12}} + \dfrac{1}{2^{13}} + \dfrac{1}{2^{13}}$

Solutions

1. When dividing by the same base, subtract the exponents:

$$\frac{x^6}{x^4} = x^{6-4} = x^2$$

2. To raise a power to a power, multiply the exponents:

$$(3^4)^5 = 3^{4 \times 5} = 3^{20}$$

3. When multiplying by the same base, add the exponents (but leave the bases alone):

$$\text{If } r \neq 0: \ (r^3)(r^{-3}) = r^{3+(-3)} = r^0 = 1 \qquad \text{If } r = 0: \ r^0 = 0^0 = \text{undefined}$$

4. To raise a power to a power, multiply the exponents:

$$(x^n)^n = x^{n \times n} = x^{n^2}$$

5. Any term without an exponent equals itself to the first power, so $n = n^1$:

$$n(n^2)(n^3) = n^1 \times n^2 \times n^3 = n^{1+2+3} = n^6$$

6. If you have a fraction with negative exponents on both top and bottom, have them trade places. Flip the top base to the bottom and the bottom base to the top:

$$\frac{x^{-4}}{y^{-5}} = \frac{y^5}{x^4}$$

7. When multiplying terms with the same exponent, multiply the bases (but leave the exponent alone):

$$7^3(3)^3 = (7 \times 3)^3 = 21^3$$

8. Break down your bases to give terms the same base:

$$8^3 \times 4^6 = (2^3)^3 \times (2^2)^6 = 2^9 \times 2^{12} = 2^{9+12} = 2^{21}$$

9. When dividing terms with the same exponent, divide the bases (but leave the exponent alone):

$$\frac{8^3}{2^3} - 2^6 = \left(\frac{8}{2}\right)^3 - 2^6 = 4^3 - 2^6 = (2^2)^3 - 2^6 = 2^6 - 2^6 = 0$$

10. To add or subtract exponent expressions you have to **factor** them:

$$4^7 - 4^8 + 4^9 = 4^7(4^0 - 4^1 + 4^2) = 4^7(1 - 4 + 16) = 4^7(13)$$

11. Only **like terms** can be added or subtracted:

$$3^3 + 3^3 + 3^3 = 3(3^3) = 3^1(3^3) = 3^4 = 81$$

12. The difference between squares should be factored as follows: $x^2 - y^2 = (x + y)(x - y)$

$$(23^2 - 22^2) + (21^2 - 20^2)$$
$$(23 + 22)(23 - 22) + (21 + 20)(21 - 20)$$
$$(45)(1) + (41)(1) = 86$$

13. Break down your bases to their prime factors:

$$(8^3)^4 = 8^{12} = (2^3)^{12} = 2^{36}$$

14. Be sure to distribute exponents to **each** term within parentheses:

$$12^3 \times 3^3 = 36^3 = (4 \times 9)^3 = (2^2 \times 3^2)^3 = 2^6 \times 3^6 \text{ or } 6^6$$

15. Remember to combine **like terms** and that any term without an exponent equals itself to the first power:

$$(2^n + 2^n)(3^n + 3^n + 3^n) = 2(2^n) \times 3(3^n) = 2^1(2^n) \times 3^1(3^n) = 2^{n+1} \times 3^{n+1} \text{ or } 6^{n+1}$$

16. When dividing terms with the same base, subtract your exponents (no matter how complex they may look)!

$$\frac{3^{x+y}}{3^{x-y}} = 3^{x+y-(x-y)} = 3^{x+y-x+y} = 3^{2y}$$

17. To make an exponent positive, remember to "flip its base":

$$\left(\frac{1}{2}\right)^{-6}\left(\frac{1}{4}\right)^{-4}\left(\frac{1}{8}\right)^{-2} = (2)^6(4)^4(8)^2 = (2)^6\left(2^2\right)^4\left(2^3\right)^2 = (2)^6(2)^8(2)^6 = 2^{6+8+6} = 2^{20}$$

18. To add fractions, simply give them a common denominator:

$$\frac{1}{2^{12}} + \frac{1}{2^{13}} + \frac{1}{2^{13}} = \frac{2^1(1)}{2^1(2^{12})} + \frac{1}{2^{13}} + \frac{1}{2^{13}} = \frac{2}{2^{13}} + \frac{1}{2^{13}} + \frac{1}{2^{13}} = \frac{4}{2^{13}} = \frac{2^2}{2^{13}} = 2^{-11} = \frac{1}{2^{11}}$$

(16) Cheat Sheet: Rules of Exponents – In the table below, you will find a shorthand listing of every exponent rule tested by the GRE.

Exponent Rule	Example With Variables	Example With Numbers
Resolving Parentheses: *Simple vs. Complex*	*Simple:* $(xy)^2 = x^2y^2$ *Complex:* $(x + y)^2 = (x + y)(x + y)$	$(3x)^2 = 3^2x^2 = 9x^2$ $(4 + 9)^2 = (13)^2 = 169$
Powers to Powers	$(w^4)^3 = w^{4 \times 3} = w^{12}$	$(2^3)^3 = 2^{3 \times 3} = 2^9$
Multiplication: *Same Base*	$n^3 \times n^3 = n^{3+3} = n^6$	$3^5 \times 3^5 = 3^{5+5} = 3^{10}$
Division: *Same Base*	$x^8 \div x^3 = x^{8-3} = x^5$	$5^8 \div 5^3 = 5^{8-3} = 5^5$
Negative Exponents: *Flip the Base*	$x^{-2} = \dfrac{1}{x^2}$ and $\dfrac{1}{x^{-2}} = x^2$	$5^{-2} = \dfrac{1}{5^2}$ and $\dfrac{1}{5^{-2}} = 5^2$
Powers of 0	$x^0 = 1$ and $(-x)^0 = 1$ if $x \neq 0$	$(-7)^0 = 1$ and $-7^0 = -1$
Powers of 1	$x(x^4) = x^1(x^4) = x^5$	$3^4 \div 3 = 3^4 \div 3^1 = 3^3$
Addition/Subtraction: *Factor*	$x^2 + x^3 = x^2(x^0 + x^1) = x^2(1 + x)$	$2^6 - 2^5 = 2^5(2^1 - 2^0) = 2^5(1) = 2^5$
Difference of Squares	$x^2 - y^2 = (x + y)(x - y)$	$101^2 - 99^2 = (101 + 99)(101 - 99)$
Multiplication: *Same Exponent*	$f^4 \times g^4 = (fg)^4$	$2^7 \times 5^7 = (2 \times 5)^7 = 10^7$
Multiplication: *Same Base, Same Exponent*	$n^5 \times n^5 = n^{10}$ or $(n^2)^5$	$2^3 \times 2^3 = 2^6$ or 4^3
Division: *Same Exponent*	$a^7 \div b^7 = \left(\dfrac{a}{b}\right)^7$	$12^4 \div 6^4 = (12 \div 6)^4 = 2^4$
Complicated Bases: *Break Them Down*	N/A	$12^7 = (2^2 \times 3^1)^7 = 2^{14} \times 3^7$
Exponent Equations: *Make Bases the Same, Set the Exponents Equal*	$x^{a+4} = x^{8-3a}$ $a + 4 = 8 - 3a$	$8^2 = 2^x \rightarrow (2^3)^2 = 2^x$ $6 = x$

(17) Problem Sets – The following questions have been arranged into three groups: fundamental, intermediate, and rare or advanced.

• Whether you're aiming for a perfect score or a score closer to average, mastery of the concepts in the FUNDAMENTAL questions is absolutely essential.

➤ As you might expect, the INTERMEDIATE questions are more difficult but are essential for test-takers who need an above-average score or higher.

• Finally, the RARE or ADVANCED questions test concepts that are very sophisticated or seldom encountered on the GRE. Mastery of such questions is required only if you need a math score above the 90th percentile.

• As always, if you find yourself confused, bogged down with busy work, or stuck, don't be afraid to fall back on your "Plan B" strategies!

Fundamental

Quantity A	Quantity B
4^x	5^x

1.

2. If $n = 2^{(r-3)^2}$ and $r = 5$, then $n =$

(A) 8 (B) 16 (C) 32 (D) 64 (E) 128

$$x^2 = 65$$

Quantity A	Quantity B
x	8

3.

4. If $27^{4x-2} = 9^{5x}$, what is the value of x?

(A) 0 (B) 1 (C) 2 (D) 3 (E) 4

	Quantity A	Quantity B
5.	50^3	3^{50}

6. If $k \neq 0$, which of the following is equivalent to $\dfrac{k(k^3)^2}{k^2}$?

$\quad$ (A) k^2 $\quad$ (B) k^3 $\quad$ (C) k^4 $\quad$ (D) k^5 $\quad$ (E) k^6

x and a are positive numbers, and a is a multiple of 5.

	Quantity A	Quantity B
7.	$\dfrac{x^a}{x^5}$	$x^{\frac{a}{5}}$

8. $10,001^2 - 9,999^2 =$

$\quad$ (A) 4 $\quad$ (B) 10 $\quad$ (C) $2^4 \times 5^4$ $\quad$ (D) 4×10^4 $\quad$ (E) 10^8

	Quantity A	Quantity B
9.	$\dfrac{15^6}{3^4}$	$3^2 \cdot 5^6$

$$(8)(16)(32) = 2^{x+y}$$

	Quantity A	Quantity B
10.	The average (arithmetic mean) of x and y	6

Intermediate

11. $\dfrac{\left(24^2\right)\left(15^3\right)}{\left(30^5\right)} =$

(A) $\dfrac{2}{25}$ (B) $\dfrac{3}{15}$ (C) $\dfrac{4}{5}$ (D) $\dfrac{10}{3}$ (E) $\dfrac{25}{6}$

$$x(x^{-2})(x^4) = 64$$

Quantity A	Quantity
x^2	2^x

12.

13. If $(6 \times 10^3)(5 \times 10^2)(7 \times 10^4) = 2.1 \times 10^n$, then $n =$

(A) 60 (B) 32 (C) 30 (D) 11 (E) 9

Quantity A	Quantity B
$9^{22} - 9^{21}$	$9^{21}(8)$

14.

15. $\dfrac{24^2 - 16^2}{8^2} =$

(A) 1 (B) 3 (C) 4 (D) 5 (E) 8

Quantity A	Quantity B
$\dfrac{77^7}{7^{77}}$	$\dfrac{11^7}{7^{70}}$

16.

17. If $\dfrac{27^{3x-2}}{3^{2x+1}} \geq 1$, then $x =$

(A) $x \leq -3$ (B) $x \geq -1$ (C) $x \geq 1$ (D) $x \leq 3$ (E) $x = 3$

	Quantity A	Quantity B
18.	$(0.41)^3(0.41)^4$	$(0.41)^8$

19. What is the least integer x such that $\dfrac{1}{3^x} < 0.01$?

(A) 5 (B) 6 (C) 7 (D) 50 (E) 51

$$x < 0 < y$$

	Quantity A	Quantity B
20.	x^{-6}	y^{-3}

21. If $n = 2^2$, then $2n^{2n}$ equals

(A) 2^8 (B) 2^{16} (C) 2^{17} (D) 2^{24} (E) 2^{27}

$$2^n = 32$$

	Quantity A	Quantity B
22.	$\dfrac{3^{2n}}{27^{n-1}}$	$\dfrac{1}{9}$

23. $\dfrac{5^4(5^8 + 5^8)}{5^6} =$

(A) $2(5^4)$ (B) $2(5^6)$ (C) 5^8 (D) $2(5^8)$ (E) 5^{10}

	Quantity A	Quantity B
24.	$\dfrac{3^{26} - 3^{24}}{2^3}$	3^{24}

25. If $m = 5^n$, then $m^2 =$

(A) 10^n (B) 5^{2n} (C) 5^{n^2} (D) 10^{n^2} (E) 25^{n^2}

Rare or Advanced

26. If $\frac{1}{3^a} + \frac{1}{3^a} + \frac{1}{3^a} = \frac{1}{3^b}$, then b expressed in terms of a is

(A) $\frac{a}{3}$ (B) $a-1$ (C) $a+1$ (D) $3a$ (E) a^3

27. The number 10^{15} is divisible by all of the following EXCEPT

(A) 500   (B) 250   (C) 64   (D) 32   (E) 6

$$p = 2^9 \times 5^5.$$
r is an integer.
10^r is a factor of p.

Quantity A	Quantity B
28. The greatest possible value of 10^r	100,000

29. If $\left(\frac{1}{9}\right)^{3n} = \frac{1}{3} \times 3^n$, then $n =$

(A) 3^{-2} (B) 7^{-1} (C) 3^{-1} (D) $3(7^{-1})$ (E) $2(3^{-1})$

$$2^{-x} + 2^{-x} > 1$$

Quantity A	Quantity B
30. x^2	1

31. What is the greatest positive integer x such that 3^x is a factor of 18^{12}?

(A) 12   (B) 15   (C) 21   (D) 24   (E) 72

$$n = 7^8 - 7^9 + 7^{10}$$

	Quantity A	Quantity B
32.	The greatest prime factor of n	11

$$n = \frac{1}{(2^8)(5^{12})}$$

	Quantity A	Quantity B
33.	If n is expressed as a terminating decimal, the number of nonzero digits that n has.	3

(18) **Solutions** – Video solutions for each of the previous questions can be found on our website at **www.sherpaprep.com/videos**.

• BOOKMARK this address for future visits!

> ➢ To view the videos, you'll need the LOGIN and PASSWORD that you created upon registering your copy of Number Properties & Algebra.

• If you have yet to register your book yet, please go to **www.sherpaprep.com/activate** and enter your email address, last name, and shipping address.

• Be sure to provide the SAME last name and shipping address that you used to purchase your copy of Master Key to the GRE or to enroll in your GRE course with Sherpa Prep!

> ➢ When checking your answers, we encourage you to watch the solution for any problem that you answered INCORRECTLY

• The same goes for any problem that took you MORE than TWO MINUTES to solve.

• After digesting the explanation, REVISIT your mistake a couple of days later to ensure that the problem no longer poses issues to you.

> ➢ If you struggle to solve the problem a SECOND time, add it to your "LOG of ERRORS" and redo it every few weeks.

• Solving tricky questions MORE THAN ONCE is the best way to learn from your mistakes and to avoid similar difficulties on your actual exam.

Fundamental	Intermediate		Rare or Advanced
1. D	11. A	21. C	26. B
2. B	12. C	22. C	27. E
3. D	13. D	23. B	28. C
4. D	14. C	24. C	29. B
5. B	15. D	25. B	30. D
6. D	16. C		31. D
7. D	17. C		32. A
8. D	18. A		33. B
9. C	19. A		
10. C	20. D		

Chapter 4

Roots

Roots

To be discussed:

Fundamental Concepts

Whether you're aiming for a perfect score or a score closer to average, mastery of the following concepts is essential.

Rare or Advanced Concepts

The following concepts are either advanced or tested only on rare occasions. If you don't need an elite math score, don't waste your time!

Drills, Review, and Practice Questions

There's no substitute for elbow grease. Practice your new skills to ensure that you internalize what you've studied.

> ## Fundamental Concepts

(1) Introduction – Although roots and exponents are mirror images of one another, roots are a lot easier to work with on the GRE than are exponents.

• For starters, the GRE doesn't require test-takers to understand that roots are fractional exponents, so there are relatively few rules to learn about roots.

• What's more, the rules that the GRE does test are pretty simple, so they're fairly easy to keep straight.

> ➢ Still, roots can be intimidating, so let's make sure that you have a solid understanding of some fundamental concepts before examining those rules.

• First, the square root of a number is simply any value that, when squared, gives the original number. For example, 7 is a square root of 49 since $7^2 = 7 \times 7 = 49$.

• In other words, **a root is basically the opposite of an exponent**. Since the square of 5 is 25, therefore 5 is a square root of 25:

The **square** of $5 = 5^2 = 25$ A **square root** of $25 = 5$

• Like squares, square roots can be dangerous, since positive numbers always have TWO square roots: one positive and one negative. For example, 25 has square roots of 5 and –5, since 5^2 and $(-5)^2$ both equal 25.

> ➢ Square roots are typically signified by the symbol $\sqrt{}$, which is known as a radical.

• Thus, the notation $\sqrt{4}$ signifies the square root of 4.

• It is a widespread misconception that the square root symbol denotes both the positive and negative roots of a number. Actually, the radical symbol **ONLY denotes the POSITIVE** root (or non-negative root) of a number.

• The **negative root** of a number is indicated by a **negative radical**. In other words, 2 and –2 may both be square roots of 4, but the notation $\sqrt{4}$ only signifies 2:

$\sqrt{4}$ ONLY equals 2 $-\sqrt{4}$ equals –2

➢ On rare occasions, exam-makers may test your knowledge of cube roots, which are signified by the symbol $\sqrt[3]{}$.

• Like squares and square roots, cubes and cube roots are also opposites. Since the cube of 2 is 8, 2 is therefore the cube root of 8:

$$\text{The }\textbf{cube}\text{ of }2 = 2^3 = 8 \qquad\qquad \text{The }\textbf{cube root}\text{ of }8 = \sqrt[3]{8} = 2$$

• Unlike square roots, however, cube roots only have ONE answer.

A positive number always has a positive cube root, and a negative number always has a negative cube root. For example, $\sqrt[3]{8} = 2$, but not –2, since:

$$2 \times 2 \times 2 = 8 \qquad\qquad -2 \times -2 \times -2 \neq 8$$

➢ When working with roots, it can be tremendously helpful to have certain values memorized.

• In our discussion of Exponents, we encouraged you to memorize certain squares, cubes, and special powers. Those values will help you just as much with roots.

• For roots, we also encourage you to **memorize the decimal values of the square roots from $\sqrt{1}$ to $\sqrt{10}$**. As mentioned in our book on <u>Arithmetic & "Plan B Strategies"</u>, knowing these values will not only save you time, but can prevent you from making silly mistakes.

$$\sqrt{1} = 1 \qquad \sqrt{2} \approx 1.4 \qquad \sqrt{3} \approx 1.7 \qquad \sqrt{4} = 2 \qquad \sqrt{5} \approx 2.2$$
$$\sqrt{6} \approx 2.4 \qquad \sqrt{7} \approx 2.6 \qquad \sqrt{8} \approx 2.8 \qquad \sqrt{9} = 3 \qquad \sqrt{10} \approx 3.2$$

• An easy way to commit these values to memory is to remember that values larger than $\sqrt{4}$ **increase in increments of 0.2**, and values smaller than $\sqrt{4}$ **decrease in increments of 0.3**.

Greater than $\sqrt{4}$: Add 0.2	Less than $\sqrt{4}$: Subtract 0.3
$\sqrt{4} = 2$	$\sqrt{4} = 2$
$\sqrt{5} \approx 2.2$	$\sqrt{3} \approx 1.7$
$\sqrt{6} \approx 2.4$	$\sqrt{2} \approx 1.4$
$\sqrt{7} \approx 2.6$	
$\sqrt{8} \approx 2.8$	
$\sqrt{9} = 3$	
$\sqrt{10} \approx 3.2$	

- Do note that this pattern doesn't hold forever. For example, $\sqrt{11}$ is closer to 3.5 than to 3.4 and $\sqrt{1}$ does not equal 1.1. The rule only holds for the square roots from 2 to 10.

  ➤ If you need to determine the value of a larger root, simply **find the perfect squares** that it lies between and then approximate.

- For example, $\sqrt{52}$ roughly equals 7.2 (or something similar), since $\sqrt{52}$ lies between $\sqrt{49} = 7$ and $\sqrt{64} = 8$, and is much closer to $\sqrt{49}$ on the number line than to $\sqrt{64}$:

- If you need to, you can also use the onscreen calculator to approximate square roots. Be aware, however, that **the calculator cannot approximate cube roots**.

- To determine the value of a cube root, therefore, you'll need to identify the perfect cubes that it lies between and approximate.

- For example, $\sqrt[3]{80}$ approximately equals 4.3 (or something similar), since $\sqrt[3]{80}$ lies between $\sqrt[3]{64} = 4$ and $\sqrt[3]{125} = 5$, and is somewhat closer to $\sqrt[3]{64}$ than to $\sqrt[3]{125}$:

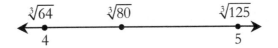

  ➤ Finally, it's important to remember that ANY SQUARE ROOT × ITSELF equals the value under the radical.

- For example, $\sqrt{4} \times \sqrt{4} = 4$. Likewise, $\left(\sqrt{12}\right)^2 = \sqrt{12} \times \sqrt{12} = 12$. This property also holds true for variables. Thus:

$$\sqrt{n} \times \sqrt{n} = n \qquad\qquad \left(\sqrt{s}\right)^2 = \sqrt{s} \times \sqrt{s} = s$$

- In fact, we can extend the principle to cube roots as well. The only difference: **a cube root must be cubed** to equal the number under the radical. Thus:

$$\sqrt[3]{8} \times \sqrt[3]{8} \times \sqrt[3]{8} = 8 \qquad\qquad \left(\sqrt[3]{n}\right)^3 = \sqrt[3]{n} \times \sqrt[3]{n} \times \sqrt[3]{n} = n$$

(2) Multiplying and Dividing Roots – Of all the rules involving roots, the most fundamental is that involving multiplication and division.

- It's also the easiest.

  ➢ To multiply two or more square roots, simply **place the multiplication within a SINGLE root.**

- For example, $\sqrt{12} \times \sqrt{3}$ can be expressed as $\sqrt{12 \times 3}$. Likewise, $\sqrt{5} \times \sqrt{20}$ can be expressed as $\sqrt{5 \times 20}$. In other words:

$$\sqrt{12} \times \sqrt{3} = \sqrt{12 \times 3} = \sqrt{36} = 6 \qquad \sqrt{5} \times \sqrt{20} = \sqrt{5 \times 20} = \sqrt{100} = 10$$

- Similarly, **to divide two roots**, simply place the division within a single root. Thus, $\sqrt{24} \div \sqrt{6}$ can be expressed as $\sqrt{24 \div 6}$. Likewise, $\sqrt{72} \div \sqrt{8}$ can be expressed as $\sqrt{72 \div 8}$:

$$\frac{\sqrt{24}}{\sqrt{6}} = \sqrt{\frac{24}{6}} = \sqrt{4} = 2 \qquad \frac{\sqrt{72}}{\sqrt{8}} = \sqrt{\frac{72}{8}} = \sqrt{9} = 3$$

  ➢ In fact, you can extend this technique to any situation involving the multiplication or division of roots.

- For example, you can use it to multiply a string of roots together:

$$\sqrt{3} \times \sqrt{4} \times \sqrt{2} \times \sqrt{6} = \sqrt{3 \times 4 \times 2 \times 6} = \sqrt{12 \times 12} = \sqrt{144} = 12$$

- You can also use it to solve expressions containing **both multiplication and division**:

$$\frac{\sqrt{12} \times \sqrt{21}}{\sqrt{7}} = \sqrt{\frac{12 \times 21}{7}} = \sqrt{\frac{12 \times 3 \times \cancel{7}}{\cancel{7}}} = \sqrt{12 \times 3} = \sqrt{36} = 6$$

  ➢ Finally, this principle can also be applied in REVERSE.

- If you have multiplication or division **WITHIN a root**, that root can be broken down into SEPARATE roots that are then multiplied or divided. Thus:

$$\sqrt{\frac{4}{9}} = \frac{\sqrt{4}}{\sqrt{9}} = \frac{2}{3} \qquad \sqrt{\frac{9}{16}} = \frac{\sqrt{9}}{\sqrt{16}} = \frac{3}{4}$$

$$\sqrt{16 \times 9} = \sqrt{16} \times \sqrt{9} = 4 \times 3 = 12 \qquad \sqrt{25 \times 36} = \sqrt{25} \times \sqrt{36} = 5 \times 6 = 30$$

(3) Simplifying Roots – In the previous section, we only saw expressions that resulted in perfect squares.

- Unfortunately, not every problem involving roots ends up with tidy whole numbers. Sometimes roots are messy and must be simplified.

  ➤ A square root can be simplified if one (or more) of its factors is a **perfect square** – numbers whose square roots are whole numbers, such as 4, 25, 49, or 100.

- For example, numbers such as $\sqrt{33}$ and $\sqrt{70}$ cannot be simplified, since neither has factors that are perfect squares:

$$\sqrt{33} = \sqrt{3 \times 11} = \sqrt{3} \times \sqrt{11} \qquad \sqrt{70} = \sqrt{2 \times 5 \times 7} = \sqrt{2} \times \sqrt{5} \times \sqrt{7}$$

- Numbers such as $\sqrt{18}$ and $\sqrt{24}$, however, can be simplified, since both have factors that are perfect squares:

$$\sqrt{18} = \sqrt{9 \times 2} = \sqrt{9} \times \sqrt{2} = 3\sqrt{2} \qquad \sqrt{24} = \sqrt{4 \times 6} = \sqrt{4} \times \sqrt{6} = 2\sqrt{6}$$

  ➤ Unfortunately, it is not always easy to know whether a number has a perfect square for a factor, particularly when working with large or unfamiliar numbers.

- To simplify more difficult square roots, first **break the number into its prime factors**. Then **replace any "pairs"** that you find inside the radical with the same number outside the radical.

- To get a sense of how this works, let's simplify $\sqrt{150}$.

- Because $150 = 15 \times 10 = 3 \times 5 \times 5 \times 2$, we know that $\sqrt{150} = \sqrt{3 \times 5 \times 5 \times 2}$. If we replace the pair of "5"s inside the radical with a 5 outside the radical, we get:

$$\sqrt{150} = \sqrt{3 \times \underbrace{5 \times 5}_{\text{pair}} \times 2} = 5\sqrt{3 \times 2} = 5\sqrt{6}$$

  ➤ With some numbers, you may find two (or more) "pairs". In such cases, simply **replace both pairs** with numbers outside the radical and multiply.

- Let's simplify $\sqrt{180}$.

- Because $180 = 3 \times 60 = 3 \times 15 \times 4$, we know that $\sqrt{180} = \sqrt{3 \times 3 \times 5 \times 2 \times 2}$. If we replace the pair of "3"s and the pair of "2"s with a 3 and a 2 outside the radical, we get:

$$\sqrt{180} = \sqrt{\underbrace{3 \times 3}_{pair} \times 5 \times \underbrace{2 \times 2}_{pair}} = (3 \times 2)\sqrt{5} = 6\sqrt{5}$$

  ➤ To understand why this technique works, consider $\sqrt{108}$.

- Because $108 = 9 \times 12 = 9 \times 4 \times 3$, we know that $\sqrt{108} = \sqrt{3 \times 3 \times 2 \times 2 \times 3}$. This, in turn, equals $\sqrt{3} \times \sqrt{3} \times \sqrt{2} \times \sqrt{2} \times \sqrt{3}$, since a root containing multiplication or division can be broken into SEPARATE roots.

- We also know that $\sqrt{3} \times \sqrt{3} = 3$ and that $\sqrt{2} \times \sqrt{2} = 2$, since any SQUARE ROOT × ITSELF equals the value under its radical. In other words:

$$\sqrt{108} = \underbrace{\sqrt{3} \times \sqrt{3}} \times \underbrace{\sqrt{2} \times \sqrt{2}} \times \sqrt{3} = 3 \times 2 \times \sqrt{3} = 6 \times \sqrt{3}$$

- Finally, since the notation $6\sqrt{3}$ is shorthand for $6 \times \sqrt{3}$, we can say that $\sqrt{108} = 6\sqrt{3}$.

  ➤ In the unlikely event that you need **to simplify a cube root**, the process works the same way.

- The only difference: simply pull out "triplets" instead of "pairs". For example, the cube root of 24 is $2 \times \sqrt[3]{3}$, since 24 contains three "2"s:

$$\sqrt[3]{24} = \sqrt[3]{8 \times 3} = \sqrt[3]{\underbrace{2 \times 2 \times 2}_{triplet} \times 3} = 2 \times \sqrt[3]{3} = 2\sqrt[3]{3}$$

  ➤ Going forward, we encourage you to break down numbers and to pull out pairs when **multiplying square roots**.

- It's a lot easier to simplify expressions such as $\sqrt{22} \times \sqrt{33}$ if you break down the numbers before multiplying:

<table>
<tr><td>WAY too SLOW</td><td>FAST and EASY</td></tr>
<tr><td>$\sqrt{22} \times \sqrt{33} = \sqrt{22 \times 33} = \sqrt{726}$</td><td>$\sqrt{22 \times 33} = \sqrt{2 \times 11 \times 3 \times 11} = 11\sqrt{6}$</td></tr>
</table>

(4) Working With Coefficients – Any number directly before a radical is known as a coefficient.

- For example, $5\sqrt{2}$ has a coefficient of 5.

- As we have seen, notation such as $5\sqrt{2}$ is shorthand for $5 \times \sqrt{2}$. In other words, a coefficient is simply a number that multiplies the root it precedes.

  ➤ To multiply roots with coefficients, **multiply the roots and coefficients separately**.

- For example, $5\sqrt{2} \times 5\sqrt{2} = 50$, since the notation is shorthand for $5 \times \sqrt{2} \times 5 \times \sqrt{2}$, which can be rearranged as follows:

$$\underbrace{5 \times 5}_{\text{coefficients}} \times \underbrace{\sqrt{2} \times \sqrt{2}}_{\text{roots}} = 25 \times 2 = 50$$

- Likewise, $4\sqrt{2} \times 2\sqrt{3} = 8\sqrt{6}$, since $4 \times 2 = 8$ and $\sqrt{2} \times \sqrt{3} = \sqrt{6}$.

  ➤ Roots with coefficients can be divided in the same manner.

- Hence, $8\sqrt{24} \div 16\sqrt{6} = 1$, since:

$$\frac{8\sqrt{24}}{16\sqrt{6}} = \underbrace{\frac{8}{16}}_{\text{coefficients}} \times \underbrace{\sqrt{\frac{24}{6}}}_{\text{roots}} = \frac{1}{2} \times \sqrt{4} = \frac{1}{2} \times 2 = 1$$

  ➤ A root without a number before its radical has a **coefficient of 1**.

- Thus, $3\sqrt{3} \times \sqrt{2} = 3\sqrt{6}$, since $3 \times 1 = 3$ and $\sqrt{3} \times \sqrt{2} = \sqrt{6}$. Likewise, $4\sqrt{15} \div \sqrt{3} = 4\sqrt{5}$, since:

$$\frac{4\sqrt{15}}{\sqrt{3}} = \frac{4}{1} \times \sqrt{\frac{15}{3}} = 4 \times \sqrt{5} = 4\sqrt{5}$$

  ➤ Finally, when simplifying a root with a coefficient, be sure to **multiply the coefficient with any "pair"** you place outside the radical.

- For example, $2\sqrt{50} = 10\sqrt{2}$, since:

$$2\sqrt{50} = 2\sqrt{\underbrace{5 \times 5}_{\text{pair}} \times 2} = (2 \times 5)\sqrt{2} = 10\sqrt{2}$$

(5) Adding and Subtracting Roots – The rule for adding and subtracting roots is the last of the major rules for roots.

- It's also pretty straightforward.

  ➢ Roots with the SAME radical CAN be added or subtracted by combining their coefficients.

- For example, $4\sqrt{3} + 3\sqrt{3} = 7\sqrt{3}$, since $4\sqrt{3}$ and $3\sqrt{3}$ share a radical of 3. Similarly:

$$9\sqrt{5} - 6\sqrt{5} = 3\sqrt{5} \qquad \sqrt{10} + \sqrt{10} = 2\sqrt{10} \qquad 4\sqrt{11} - 3\sqrt{11} = \sqrt{11}$$

- Roots with DIFFERENT radicals CANNOT be added or subtracted. Thus, $\mathbf{4\sqrt{3} + 3\sqrt{2}}$ **cannot be combined**, since $4\sqrt{3}$ has a radical of 3 while $3\sqrt{2}$ has a radical of 2.

  ➢ Roots with different radicals, however, can be combined through approximation.

- Hence, $4\sqrt{3} + 3\sqrt{2}$ roughly equals 11, since $\sqrt{3} \approx 1.7$ and $\sqrt{2} \approx 1.4$:

$$4(1.7) + 3(1.4) = 6.8 + 4.2 = 11$$

- Tip : As you will see, **many root problems cannot be solved without approximation**: particularly those designed to take advantage of common test-taker misunderstandings. Don't be afraid to approximate.

  ➢ When adding or subtracting roots, however, be sure to **SIMPLIFY the roots** (if possible) before approximating them.

- While approximation is often a great strategy, roots with different radicals can end up with the same radical, once simplified.

- Consider the following:

Quantity A	**Quantity B**
$\sqrt{20} + \sqrt{45}$	$6\sqrt{5}$

Answer: B. Simplifying $\sqrt{20}$ and $\sqrt{45}$ shows that Quantity A = $5\sqrt{5}$, proving that Quantity B is greater than Quantity A:

$$\sqrt{20} + \sqrt{45} = \sqrt{\underbrace{2 \times 2}_{pair} \times 5} + \sqrt{\underbrace{3 \times 3}_{pair} \times 5} = 2\sqrt{5} + 3\sqrt{5} = 5\sqrt{5}$$

(6) Common Root Mistakes – Many GRE problems involving roots are designed to take advantage of common test-taker misunderstandings.

• Below, you'll find three classic root mistakes. If you fall for any of them, we encourage you to put the mistake on a note card and to review it several times before taking your exam.

➢ $\boxed{\text{Mistake \#1}}$: SPLITTING roots that contain ADDITION or SUBTRACTION.

• Earlier, we saw that roots containing multiplication or division can be separated into smaller roots.

➢ **This property cannot be extended to roots containing addition or subtraction**.

• As with complex fractions, we have to carry out the addition or subtraction within a "complex" root before we can split it apart. Consider the following:

Quantity A	**Quantity B**
$\sqrt{100 + 64}$	18

➢ Although we may be tempted to break down Quantity A into $\sqrt{100} + \sqrt{64}$, we cannot: roots with addition or subtractions cannot be split into smaller roots.

• To solve this problem, we first need to carry out the addition in Quantity A:

$$\sqrt{100 + 64} = \sqrt{164}$$

• Since $13^2 = 169$, we know that $\sqrt{169} = 13$. Thus, whatever the precise value of Quantity A, it must be less than 13, because $\sqrt{164}$ is less than $\sqrt{169}$. Therefore, the correct answer is (B), since 18 is larger than 13.

> ➤ ☐Mistake #2☐: ADDING roots with DIFFERENT radicals.

- As we saw in the previous section, roots with different radicals cannot be added. The only way to combine such roots is through **approximation**. Consider the following:

Quantity A	Quantity B
$\sqrt{40} + \sqrt{60}$	$\sqrt{100}$

- Although we may be tempted to answer (C), the two quantities are not equal.

> ➤ Two roots with different radicals cannot be added, so $\sqrt{40} + \sqrt{60} \neq \sqrt{100}$. The only way to add such roots is to approximate their values.

- Because $\sqrt{40}$ is larger than $\sqrt{36} = 6$ but smaller than $\sqrt{49} = 7$, we know that $\sqrt{40}$ equals a value between 6 and 7. Similarly, $\sqrt{60}$ is larger than $\sqrt{49} = 7$ but smaller than $\sqrt{64} = 8$, so $\sqrt{60}$ must equal a value between 7 and 8.

- A number bigger than 6 plus a number bigger than 7 equals a number bigger than 13. Thus, the correct answer must be (A), since Quantity B equals 10.

> ➤ ☐Mistake #3☐: CONFUSING COEFFICIENTS with independent numbers.

- From time to time, exam-makers will design questions intended to mislead test-takers into confusing an independent number with a coefficient. Consider the following:

Quantity A	Quantity B
$2 + 4\sqrt{5}$	$6\sqrt{5}$

- Despite its appearance, $2 + 4\sqrt{5}$ does not add to $6\sqrt{5}$. It may look as though we should add the 2 + 4, but we cannot.

> ➤ The reason that we cannot add the 2 + 4 is that the **4 is the coefficient** of $4\sqrt{5}$ and the **2 is an independent number**.

- If the 2 and the 4 were both part of the coefficient, parentheses would enclose them as follows: $(2 + 4)\sqrt{5}$.

- To compare these two quantities, we need to **approximate their values**. Since $\sqrt{5} \approx 2.2$, Quantity A roughly equals 2 + 4(2.2) = 2 + 8.8 = 10.8. Similarly, Quantity B roughly equals 6(2.2) = 6(2) + 6(0.2) = 12 + 1.2 = 13.2, so the correct answer must be (B).

(7) Comparing Roots – On the GRE, the vast majority of questions involving roots are Quantitative Comparison questions.

• Since many of these questions require the comparison of two roots, it's important that you be able to compare roots quickly.

➢ Fortunately, there is a very easy way to do so. To compare two roots, simply **SQUARE THEM**.

• As you know, any SQUARE ROOT × ITSELF = the value under its radical. By squaring both quantities, you'll **eliminate their roots**, making the two quantities easier to compare. Consider the following:

Quantity A	**Quantity B**
$\sqrt{\dfrac{7}{3}}$	$\dfrac{1}{3}\sqrt{14}$

Answer. A. To make this comparison easier, let's square both quantities. Since any SQUARE ROOT × ITSELF equals the value under its radical, Quantity A squared equals $\frac{7}{3}$:

$$\left(\sqrt{\frac{7}{3}}\right)^2 = \sqrt{\frac{7}{3}} \times \sqrt{\frac{7}{3}} = \frac{7}{3}$$

➢ Quantity B is a touch harder. When squaring a quantity, be sure to **put parentheses around the entire quantity** in order to remind yourself to square everything within the quantity.

• Thus, the square of Quantity B equals $\frac{14}{9}$, as:

$$\left(\frac{1}{3}\sqrt{14}\right)^2 = \left(\frac{1}{3}\right)^2 \times \left(\sqrt{14}\right)^2 = \frac{1}{9} \times 14 = \frac{14}{9}$$

• Since $\frac{7}{3} = 2\frac{1}{3}$ and $\frac{14}{9} = 1\frac{5}{9}$, Quantity A is larger than Quantity B. The correct answer is therefore (A).

➢ This shortcut is particularly effective for comparing quantities involving ROOTS WITHIN ROOTS.

• To get rid of a root within a root, **keep squaring both sides until all the roots are gone**.

- Consider the following:

Quantity A	**Quantity B**
$\sqrt{\dfrac{1}{2}}$	$\sqrt{\sqrt{\dfrac{1}{4}}}$

Answer: C. As with the previous problem, we can make this question easier by squaring both quantities.

> Since any SQUARE ROOT × ITSELF equals the value under its radical, doing so gives us:

$$\left(\sqrt{\dfrac{1}{2}}\right)^2 = \sqrt{\dfrac{1}{2}} \times \sqrt{\dfrac{1}{2}} = \dfrac{1}{2} \qquad \left(\sqrt{\sqrt{\dfrac{1}{4}}}\right)^2 = \sqrt{\sqrt{\dfrac{1}{4}}} \times \sqrt{\sqrt{\dfrac{1}{4}}} = \sqrt{\dfrac{1}{4}}$$

- However, Quantity B still has a root, so let's square both sides again to get rid of it:

$$\left(\dfrac{1}{2}\right)^2 = \dfrac{1}{2} \times \dfrac{1}{2} = \dfrac{1}{4} \qquad \left(\sqrt{\dfrac{1}{4}}\right)^2 = \sqrt{\dfrac{1}{4}} \times \sqrt{\dfrac{1}{4}} = \dfrac{1}{4}$$

- Thus, the correct answer is (C), since both quantities equal $\dfrac{1}{4}$ when squared a second time.

> Exactly why this technique works will be discussed when we cover Algebra. Until then, simply be aware that **this technique only works for POSITIVE values.**

- Thankfully, the GRE appears to use positive roots exclusively. However, **be careful of squaring VARIABLES**, since variables can represent negative <u>or</u> positive values. Consider the following:

$$n^2 = \dfrac{1}{4}$$

Quantity A	**Quantity B**
n	$\sqrt{\dfrac{1}{4}}$

Answer: D. Although squaring both quantities makes them equal, the answer here is not (C):

$$n^2 = \dfrac{1}{4} \qquad \sqrt{\dfrac{1}{4}} \times \sqrt{\dfrac{1}{4}} = \dfrac{1}{4}$$

- If $n^2 = \dfrac{1}{4}$, then n can equal $\sqrt{\dfrac{1}{4}}$ or $-\sqrt{\dfrac{1}{4}}$, so the correct answer must be (D).

Rare or Advanced Concepts

(8) Irrational Fractions and Conjugates – Every now and then, GRE problems involve fractions with square roots in their denominators.

• For reasons that need not be discussed here, math nerds consider such fractions "irrational" and in need of simplification.

> To simplify an irrational fraction, you must multiply the top and bottom of the fraction **by whatever makes the radical disappear.**

• Once the denominator is free of square roots, the fraction is considered simplified.

• In most cases, you can rid a denominator of its square root by multiplying the fraction by the **SAME SQUARE ROOT**. In other words, to rid a denominator of a $\sqrt{3}$, multiply the fraction's top and bottom by $\sqrt{3}$. To rid one of a $\sqrt{5}$, multiply top and bottom by $\sqrt{5}$:

$$\frac{2}{\sqrt{3}} = \frac{2}{\sqrt{3}} \times \frac{\sqrt{3}}{\sqrt{3}} = \frac{2\sqrt{3}}{3} \qquad\qquad \frac{4}{\sqrt{5}} = \frac{4}{\sqrt{5}} \times \frac{\sqrt{5}}{\sqrt{5}} = \frac{4\sqrt{5}}{5}$$

> This operation is, of course, simply a cosmetic one.

• Multiplying a fraction by $\dfrac{\sqrt{3}}{\sqrt{3}}$ or $\dfrac{\sqrt{5}}{\sqrt{5}}$ doesn't change its value, since $\dfrac{\sqrt{3}}{\sqrt{3}} = 1$ and $\dfrac{\sqrt{5}}{\sqrt{5}} = 1$.

• It merely "removes the root" from the denominator by replacing the original fraction with a fraction of equivalent value. Let's take a look at a sample question:

$$\text{If } x = \frac{\frac{1}{2}}{\sqrt{\frac{1}{2}}}, \text{ which of the following is equal to } x?$$

(A) $\dfrac{1}{2}$ (B) $\sqrt{\dfrac{1}{2}}$ (C) $2\sqrt{\dfrac{1}{2}}$ (E) $2\sqrt{2}$ (E) $4\sqrt{\dfrac{1}{2}}$

Answer. B. To simplify x, we have to multiply it as follows:

$$\frac{\frac{1}{2}}{\sqrt{\frac{1}{2}}} \;\rightarrow\; \frac{\frac{1}{2}}{\sqrt{\frac{1}{2}}} \times \boxed{\frac{\sqrt{\frac{1}{2}}}{\sqrt{\frac{1}{2}}}} \;\rightarrow\; \frac{\cancel{\frac{1}{2}}\sqrt{\frac{1}{2}}}{\cancel{\frac{1}{2}}} = \sqrt{\frac{1}{2}}$$

> ➢ Unfortunately, irrational fractions with **"complex" denominators** – denominators containing addition or subtraction – cannot be simplified in the same manner.

- The only way to simplify such fractions is to multiply them by their CONJUGATES. The conjugate of an expression is formed by **switching its plus or minus sign**. For example:

$$1 + \sqrt{2} \text{ has the conjugate } 1 - \sqrt{2} \qquad\qquad 5 - \sqrt{2} \text{ has the conjugate } 5 + \sqrt{2}$$

- In other words, to simplify an expression such as $\dfrac{5}{2 + \sqrt{3}}$, we need to multiply its top and bottom by $2 - \sqrt{3}$ as follows:

$$\frac{5}{2 + \sqrt{3}} \;\rightarrow\; \frac{5}{2 + \sqrt{3}} \times \boxed{\frac{2 - \sqrt{3}}{2 - \sqrt{3}}} \;=\; \frac{5(2 - \sqrt{3})}{(2 + \sqrt{3})(2 - \sqrt{3})}$$

> ➢ Mathematically, the difficulty of conjugation can be reduced by **factoring the difference between perfect squares**.

- As you will learn in the "FOIL" Identities section of our chapter on Algebra, the difference between squares can be stated as:

$$x^2 - y^2 = (x + y)(x - y)$$

- In other words, $\dfrac{5(2 - \sqrt{3})}{(2 + \sqrt{3})(2 - \sqrt{3})}$ can be simplified by rewriting its denominator as:

$$\underbrace{(2 + \sqrt{3})(2 - \sqrt{3})}_{(x+y)(x-y)} = \underbrace{(2)^2 - (\sqrt{3})^2}_{x^2 - y^2}$$

> ➢ Thus, $\dfrac{5}{2 + \sqrt{3}} = 5(2 - \sqrt{3})$, since:

$$\frac{5}{2 + \sqrt{3}} \;\rightarrow\; \frac{5}{2 + \sqrt{3}} \times \boxed{\frac{2 - \sqrt{3}}{2 - \sqrt{3}}} \;=\; \frac{5(2 - \sqrt{3})}{(2)^2 - (\sqrt{3})^2} \;=\; \frac{5(2 - \sqrt{3})}{4 - 3} \;=\; 5(2 - \sqrt{3})$$

- Likewise, the expression $\dfrac{7}{\sqrt{8} - 3} = -7(\sqrt{8} + 3)$, since:

$$\frac{7}{\sqrt{8} - 3} \;\rightarrow\; \frac{7}{\sqrt{8} - 3} \times \boxed{\frac{\sqrt{8} + 3}{\sqrt{8} + 3}} \;=\; \frac{7(\sqrt{8} + 3)}{(\sqrt{8})^2 - (3)^2} \;=\; \frac{7(\sqrt{8} + 3)}{8 - 9} \;=\; -7(\sqrt{8} + 3)$$

(9) Factoring "Complex" Roots – Every now and then, exam-makers design problems with roots that are difficult to simplify by conventional methods.

- For example, imagine that you needed to simplify $\sqrt{16(4) + 32(16)}$.

- While you could certainly multiply 16×4, add 32×16, and reduce $\sqrt{576}$, doing so could prove time consuming.

  ➢ Fortunately, there's a fast way to simplify "complex" roots such as this. You just have to **factor them**.

- The key to factoring complex roots **is to look for perfect squares** – numbers such as 4, 9, 16, 25, or 36 – that are mutual to both terms under the radical.

- For example, $\sqrt{16(4) + 32(16)}$ can be factored to $\sqrt{16(4 + 32)}$, since 16 is common to both $16(4)$ and $32(16)$. In other words, $\sqrt{16(4) + 32(16)}$ simply equals 24, as:

$$\sqrt{16(4 + 32)} = \sqrt{16(36)} = \sqrt{16} \times \sqrt{36} = 4 \times 6 = 24$$

  ➢ Let's work through a more difficult example together:

Which of the following is equal to $\sqrt{50(13) + 10(15)}$?

(A) $20\sqrt{2}$ **(B)** $18\sqrt{3}$ **(C)** $16\sqrt{5}$ **(D)** $21\sqrt{5}$ **(E)** $24\sqrt{3}$

Answer. A. At first glance, there appear to be no perfect squares in common to $50(13)$ and $10(15)$.

- However, if we break these terms down to $25 \times 2 \times 13$ and $2 \times 5 \times 5 \times 3$, respectively, we can rewrite them as $25(26)$ and $25(6)$.

  ➢ Since $25(26)$ and $25(6)$ share a factor of 25, we can therefore factor $\sqrt{50(13) + 10(15)}$ as follows:

$$\sqrt{25(26 + 6)} = \sqrt{25(32)} = \sqrt{25} \times \sqrt{32} = 5 \times 4\sqrt{2} = 20\sqrt{2}$$

- Thus, (A) is the correct answer.

(10) Taking the Root of a Decimal – On rare occasions, it is necessary to take the square root (or cube root) of a decimal to solve a GRE problem.

• With square roots, the easiest way to do so is to ask yourself the following question:

"WHAT × WHAT equals the value under the radical?"

• For example, the square root of 0.04 must be 0.2, since $0.2 \times 0.2 = 0.04$. Likewise, the square root of 0.0081 must be 0.09, since $0.09 \times 0.09 = 0.0081$.

• With cube roots, the question simply becomes "WHAT CUBED?" equals the value under the radical. For example, the cube root of 0.027 must be 0.3, since $0.3 \times 0.3 \times 0.3 = 0.027$.

➢ If you find this sort of approach difficult, there is a second way to determine the root of a decimal.

• Its only drawback is that it requires a bit of memorization. To start, use the formula below to determine the number of decimal places in the answer:

Decimals Places of Answer × "Root Number" = Decimals Places of Radical

• Then **ignore the decimal point** within the radical and "take the root" of that value. When combined, these two pieces of information will give you your answer.

➢ To get a sense of how all this works, consider the following:

$\sqrt[3]{0.000064}$ is equal to which of the following?

(A) 0.4   (B) 0.02   (C) 0.04   (D) 0.002   (E) 0.004

Answer: C. $\sqrt[3]{0.000064}$ has a "root number" of 3, because it is a cube root, and the radical has 6 decimal places. Thus, **our answer must have 2 decimal places**, since:

Decimals Places of Answer × "Root Number" = Decimals Places of Radical
$$??? \times 3 = 6$$
decimal places of answer = 2

Further, if we ignore the decimal in $\sqrt[3]{0.000064}$, **our root must have a value of 4**, since $\sqrt[3]{64} = 4$. Therefore, the correct answer is (C), since our answer must have two decimal places and a value of 4.

(11) Roots as Exponents – The GRE will never directly test your ability to convert roots into exponents.

- Every now and then, however, there are problems where doing so can come in handy.

  ➢ To express a root as an exponent, simply **let a square root = an exponent to the $\frac{1}{2}$ power**, let a cube root = an exponent to the $\frac{1}{3}$ power, and so forth.

- For example:

$$\sqrt{4} = 4^{\frac{1}{2}} \qquad \sqrt[3]{8} = 8^{\frac{1}{3}} \qquad \sqrt[4]{16} = 16^{\frac{1}{4}}$$

- To get a sense of how converting a root into an exponent might help you, consider the following:

Which of the following is equal to $\sqrt{16^8}$?

(A) 2^4 (B) 2^8 (C) 2^{10} (D) 2^{12} (E) 2^{16}

Answer: E. To solve this problem, let's first convert $\sqrt{16^8}$ to $(16^8)^{\frac{1}{2}}$. Next, we'll need to raise the power to a power as follows:

$$(16^8)^{\frac{1}{2}} = 16^{8 \times \frac{1}{2}} = 16^4$$

Finally, since 16^4 can be broken down as $(2^4)^4$, the correct answer must be (E), as:

$$(2^4)^4 = 2^{4 \times 4} = 2^{16}$$

  ➢ Let's also take a look at the following to ensure that you've got it:

If $n > 0$, then $\sqrt[3]{0.027n^{12}} =$

(A) $0.003n^3$ (B) $0.03n^3$ (C) $0.03n^4$ (D) $0.3n^3$ (E) $0.3n^4$

Answer: E. As a first step, let's split $\sqrt[3]{0.027n^{12}}$ to $\sqrt[3]{0.027} \times \sqrt[3]{n^{12}}$. Next, let's simplify $\sqrt[3]{n^{12}}$ as follows:

$$\sqrt[3]{n^{12}} = (n^{12})^{\frac{1}{3}} = n^{12 \times \frac{1}{3}} = n^4$$

Finally, since $0.3 \times 0.3 \times 0.3 = 0.027$, $\sqrt[3]{0.027}$ must equal 0.3. Thus, (E) must be correct, as:

$$\sqrt[3]{0.027n^{12}} = \sqrt[3]{0.027} \times \sqrt[3]{n^{12}} = 0.3 \times (n^{12})^{\frac{1}{3}} = 0.3n^4$$

Review and Drills

---

(12) Drills – The following drills have been broken down into three levels: fundamental, intermediate, and advanced.

- Simplify the following expressions as much as possible. Solutions can be found on the following page.

Fundamental

1. $\sqrt{108}$

2. $\sqrt{6} \times \sqrt{15}$

3. $\dfrac{10\sqrt{12}}{2\sqrt{3}}$

4. $4\sqrt{3} \times 4\sqrt{3}$

5. $\sqrt{\dfrac{16}{36}}$

6. $\dfrac{\sqrt{14} \times \sqrt{21}}{\sqrt{6}}$

7. $\sqrt{48} - \sqrt{27}$

8. $5\sqrt{2} + 4\sqrt{3}$

Intermediate

9. $\left(\dfrac{1}{2}\sqrt{12}\right)^2$

10. $\sqrt[3]{64 - 8}$

11. $\left(\sqrt{8} + \sqrt{8}\right)^2$

12. $(\sqrt{7} + \sqrt{3})(\sqrt{7} - \sqrt{3})$

13. $\dfrac{12\sqrt{6}}{\sqrt{10}}$

Advanced

14. $\dfrac{1}{4 + \sqrt{15}}$

15. $\sqrt{9(18) + 27(6)}$

$$\boxed{\text{Solutions}}$$

1. When simplifying a root, **break the number into prime factors**. Then **replace any "pairs"** that you find inside the radical with the same number outside the radical.

$$\sqrt{108} = \sqrt{9 \times 12} = \sqrt{\underbrace{3 \times 3}_{\text{pair}} \times \underbrace{2 \times 2}_{\text{pair}} \times 3} = (3 \times 2)\sqrt{3} = 6\sqrt{3}$$

2. When multiplying roots, **put the multiplication under a single radical**. Then break down the numbers and pull out any "pairs":

$$\sqrt{6} \times \sqrt{15} = \sqrt{6 \times 15} = \sqrt{2 \times \underbrace{3 \times 3}_{\text{pair}} \times 5} = 3\sqrt{10}$$

3. When dividing roots, **put the division under a single radical**. Coefficients can be divided separately:

$$\frac{10\sqrt{12}}{2\sqrt{3}} = \frac{10}{2} \times \frac{\sqrt{12}}{\sqrt{3}} = 5 \times \sqrt{\frac{12}{3}} = 5 \times \sqrt{4} = 5 \times 2 = 10$$

4. As with division, coefficients and roots can be multiplied separately:

$$4\sqrt{3} \times 4\sqrt{3} = \underbrace{4 \times 4}_{\text{coefficients}} \times \underbrace{\sqrt{3} \times \sqrt{3}}_{\text{roots}} = 16 \times 3 = 48$$

5. Division within a single root can be **split into smaller roots**:

$$\sqrt{\frac{16}{36}} = \frac{\sqrt{16}}{\sqrt{36}} = \frac{4}{6} = \frac{2}{3}$$

6. When multiplying and dividing roots, you can put both operations under a single radical:

$$\frac{\sqrt{14} \times \sqrt{21}}{\sqrt{6}} = \sqrt{\frac{14 \times 21}{6}} = \sqrt{\frac{\cancel{2} \times 7 \times \cancel{3} \times 7}{\cancel{2} \times \cancel{3}}} = \sqrt{7 \times 7} = \sqrt{7} \times \sqrt{7} = 7$$

7. To add or subtract roots, **both terms must have the same radical**. Be sure to simplify your roots whenever possible:

$$\sqrt{48} - \sqrt{27} = \sqrt{6 \times 8} - \sqrt{9 \times 3} = \sqrt{3 \times \underbrace{2 \times 2}_{\text{pair}} \times \underbrace{2 \times 2}_{\text{pair}}} - \sqrt{\underbrace{3 \times 3}_{\text{pair}} \times 3} = 4\sqrt{3} - 3\sqrt{3} = 1\sqrt{3} = \sqrt{3}$$

8. The only way to add **roots with different radicals** is through approximation:

$$5\sqrt{2} + 4\sqrt{3} \approx 5(1.4) + 4(1.7) = 7 + 6.8 = 13.8$$

9. When squaring parentheses, be sure to **square the entire parentheses**:

$$\left(\frac{1}{2}\sqrt{12}\right)^2 = \underbrace{\left(\frac{1}{2}\right)^2 \times \left(\sqrt{12}\right)^2}_{\text{distribute the exponent}} = \frac{1}{4} \times 12 = 3$$

10. Only roots with multiplication or division can be split into smaller roots. **When simplifying cubes, be sure to remove any "triplets"**:

$$\sqrt[3]{64-8} = \sqrt[3]{56} = \sqrt[3]{8 \times 7} = \sqrt[3]{8 \times 7} = \sqrt[3]{\underbrace{2 \times 2 \times 2}_{\text{triplet}} \times 7} = 2 \times \sqrt[3]{7}$$

11. Roots with the same radical can be added by combining their coefficients:

$$\left(\sqrt{8} + \sqrt{8}\right)^2 = \left(1\sqrt{8} + 1\sqrt{8}\right)^2 = \left(2\sqrt{8}\right)^2 = (2)^2 \times \left(\sqrt{8}\right)^2 = 4 \times 8 = 32$$

12. **The difference between squares** can be stated as $x^2 - y^2 = (x+y)(x-y)$:

$$\underbrace{(\sqrt{7} + \sqrt{3})(\sqrt{7} - \sqrt{3})}_{(x+y)(x-y)} = \underbrace{(\sqrt{7})^2 - (\sqrt{3})^2}_{x^2 - y^2} = 7 - 3 = 4$$

13. To simplify a fraction with a radical in its denominator, multiply the top and bottom of the fraction **by whatever makes the radical disappear**. In most cases, you can rid a denominator of its square root by multiplying the fraction by the **same square root**:

$$\frac{12\sqrt{6}}{\sqrt{10}} = \frac{12\sqrt{6}}{\sqrt{10}} \times \boxed{\frac{\sqrt{10}}{\sqrt{10}}} = \frac{12\sqrt{6 \times 10}}{10} = \frac{6\sqrt{3 \times 2 \times 2 \times 5}}{5} = \frac{12\sqrt{15}}{5}$$

14. To simplify an irrational fraction with a "complex" denominator, **multiply the numerator and denominator by the conjugate** of the denominator:

$$\frac{1}{4 + \sqrt{15}} \rightarrow \frac{1}{4 + \sqrt{15}} \times \boxed{\frac{4 - \sqrt{15}}{4 - \sqrt{15}}} = \frac{1(4 - \sqrt{15})}{(4)^2 - (\sqrt{15})^2} = \frac{4 - \sqrt{15}}{16 - 15} = 4 - \sqrt{15}$$

15. The fastest way to simplify "complex" roots is to **factor them**. When doing so, always look for perfect squares:

$$\sqrt{9(18) + 27(6)} = \sqrt{\underbrace{9(9)(2)}_{18} + \underbrace{9(3)(6)}_{18}} = \sqrt{9\underbrace{(18 + 18)}_{\text{factor 9}}} = \sqrt{9(36)} = \sqrt{9} \times \sqrt{36} = 3 \times 6 = 18$$

(13) Cheat Sheet – In the table below, you will find a shorthand listing of every operation involving roots tested by the GRE.

Root Rule	Example With Variables	Example With Numbers
Simplification	$\sqrt{k^2 h} = \sqrt{k \times k \times h} = k\sqrt{h}$	$\sqrt{28} = \sqrt{2 \times 2 \times 7} = 2\sqrt{7}$
Addition/Subtraction	$5\sqrt{w} + 7\sqrt{w} = 12\sqrt{w}$	$6\sqrt{7} - 2\sqrt{7} = 4\sqrt{7}$
Multiplication	$3\sqrt{p} \times 4\sqrt{q} = 12\sqrt{pq}$	$\sqrt{33} \times \sqrt{11} = \sqrt{3 \times 11 \times 11} = 11\sqrt{3}$
Division	$\dfrac{8\sqrt{xy}}{4\sqrt{y}} = \dfrac{8}{4} \times \sqrt{\dfrac{xy}{y}} = 2\sqrt{x}$	$\dfrac{10\sqrt{15}}{2\sqrt{5}} = \dfrac{10}{2} \times \sqrt{\dfrac{15}{5}} = 5\sqrt{3}$
Simple vs. Complex	*Simple*: $\sqrt{36 \times 36} = 36$ *Complex*: $\sqrt{36 + 36} = \sqrt{72}$	*Simple*: $\sqrt{\dfrac{16}{9}} = \dfrac{\sqrt{16}}{\sqrt{9}} = \dfrac{4}{3}$ *Complex*: $\sqrt{100 - 36} = \sqrt{64}$
Irrational Fractions (rare)	$\dfrac{8}{\sqrt{n}} = \dfrac{8}{\sqrt{n}} \times \dfrac{\sqrt{n}}{\sqrt{n}} = \dfrac{8\sqrt{n}}{n}$	$\dfrac{4}{\sqrt{3}} = \dfrac{4}{\sqrt{3}} \times \dfrac{\sqrt{3}}{\sqrt{3}} = \dfrac{4\sqrt{3}}{3}$

Root Rule	Examples With Numbers Only
Values from $\sqrt{2}$ to $\sqrt{10}$	Benchmark: $\sqrt{4} = 2$. Larger roots increase by 0.2, smaller roots decrease by 0.3.
Approximation	$\sqrt{55} \approx 7.4$, since $\sqrt{55}$ is slightly closer to $\sqrt{49} = 7$ than to $\sqrt{64} = 8$
Factoring Complex Roots (rare)	$\sqrt{9(4) + 9(5)} = \sqrt{9(4 + 5)} = \sqrt{9(9)} = \sqrt{9} \times \sqrt{9} = 9$
Conjugation (rare)	$\dfrac{5}{2 + \sqrt{3}} = \dfrac{5}{2 + \sqrt{3}} \times \dfrac{2 - \sqrt{3}}{2 - \sqrt{3}} = \dfrac{5(2 - \sqrt{3})}{(2)^2 - (\sqrt{3})^2} = \dfrac{5(2 - \sqrt{3})}{4 - 3} = 5(2 - \sqrt{3})$
Roots as Exponents (rare)	$\sqrt{4} = 4^{\frac{1}{2}} \quad \sqrt[3]{8} = 8^{\frac{1}{3}} \quad \sqrt[4]{16} = 16^{\frac{1}{4}}$
Decimals in Roots (rare)	$\sqrt[3]{0.000064} = 0.04$, since $0.04 \times 0.04 \times 0.04 = 0.000064$

(14) Problem Sets – The following questions have been arranged into three groups: fundamental, intermediate, and rare or advanced.

• Whether you're aiming for a perfect score or a score closer to average, mastery of the concepts in the FUNDAMENTAL questions is absolutely essential.

➤ As you might expect, the INTERMEDIATE questions are more difficult but are essential for test-takers who need an above-average score or higher.

• Finally, the RARE or ADVANCED questions test concepts that are very sophisticated or seldom encountered on the GRE. Mastery of such questions is required only if you need a math score above the 90th percentile.

• As always, if you find yourself confused, bogged down with busy work, or stuck, don't be afraid to fall back on your "Plan B" strategies!

Fundamental

	Quantity A	Quantity B
1.	$\sqrt{4^2}$	$4\sqrt{4}$

	Quantity A	Quantity B
2.	$\sqrt{8} \times \sqrt{6}$	7

	Quantity A	Quantity B
3.	$\dfrac{\sqrt{12}}{\sqrt{4}}$	$\dfrac{\sqrt{18}}{\sqrt{6}}$

	Quantity A	Quantity B
4.	$\dfrac{10}{\sqrt{5}}$	$2\sqrt{5}$

	Quantity A	Quantity B

5. $\qquad\qquad$ $5+3\sqrt{3}$ $\qquad\qquad\qquad$ $3+5\sqrt{3}$

6. Which of the following is closest to $\sqrt[3]{59}$

$$(A)\ 6 \quad (B)\ 5 \quad (C)\ 4 \quad (D)\ 3 \quad (E)\ 2$$

	Quantity A	Quantity B

7. $\qquad\qquad$ $\sqrt{49+49}$ $\qquad\qquad\qquad$ 14

8. The value of $\sqrt[3]{8} \cdot \sqrt[4]{81} =$

$$(A)\ 2 \quad (B)\ 4 \quad (C)\ 6 \quad (D)\ 8 \quad (E)\ 10$$

	Quantity A	Quantity B

9. $\qquad\qquad$ $\sqrt{\dfrac{25}{36}}$ $\qquad\qquad\qquad$ $\dfrac{5}{6}$

10. The value of $\sqrt{12}+\sqrt{12}$ equals:

$$(A)\ 3\sqrt{2} \quad (B)\ 2\sqrt{6} \quad (C)\ 4\sqrt{3} \quad (D)\ 6\sqrt{2} \quad (E)\ 8\sqrt{2}$$

	Quantity A	Quantity B

11. $\qquad\qquad$ $\sqrt{125}-\sqrt{80}$ $\qquad\qquad\qquad$ $2\sqrt{5}$

Intermediate

Quantity A	Quantity B
12. $\left(\sqrt{12.5} + \sqrt{12.5}\right)^2$	100

13. What is the distance between two points on a number line if the coordinates of the points are $6+\sqrt{3}$ and $3-\sqrt{3}$?

(A) $3-2\sqrt{3}$ (B) 3 (C) $3+2\sqrt{3}$ (D) 9 (E) $9+2\sqrt{3}$

Quantity A	Quantity B
14. $\sqrt{\dfrac{3}{2}}$	$\dfrac{1}{2}\sqrt{6}$

15. If $n > 0$, then $\left(\sqrt{3n} + \sqrt{12n}\right)^2 =$

(A) $8n$ (B) $9n$ (C) $15n$ (D) $27n$ (E) $36n$

16. $\left(\sqrt{8} + \sqrt{3}\right)\left(\sqrt{8} - \sqrt{3}\right) =$

(A) 3 (B) 4 (C) 5 (D) 6 (E) 8

Quantity A	Quantity B
17. $\sqrt{8 + \sqrt{40}}$	4

Rare or Advanced

	Quantity A	Quantity B

18. $(6+\sqrt{3})(6-\sqrt{3})$ $(-\sqrt{3}-6)(\sqrt{3}-6)$

19. $\sqrt{\sqrt[3]{0.000064}} = ?$ Give your answer as a decimal.

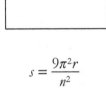

$$s = \frac{9\pi^2 r}{n^2}$$

n and r are positive.

	Quantity A	Quantity B

20. n $3\pi\sqrt{\dfrac{r}{s}}$

21. If $m > 0$ and $n > 0$, which of the following is equivalent to $\dfrac{m}{n}\sqrt{\dfrac{n}{m^2}}$?

(A) 1 (B) $\dfrac{\sqrt{m}}{\sqrt{n}}$ (C) $\sqrt{m}$ (D) $\dfrac{1}{\sqrt{m}}$ (E) $\dfrac{1}{\sqrt{n}}$

	Quantity A	Quantity B

22. $\dfrac{1+\sqrt{2}}{1-\sqrt{2}}$ -5

23. If $x = \dfrac{\frac{3}{4}}{\sqrt{\frac{3}{4}}}$, which of the following is equal to x?

(A) $\dfrac{3}{4}$ (B) $\dfrac{\sqrt{3}}{2}$ (C) $3\sqrt{\dfrac{1}{2}}$ (E) $3\sqrt{2}$ (E) $4\sqrt{3}$

	Quantity A	Quantity B

24. $\sqrt{3}+\sqrt[3]{3}+\sqrt[4]{3}$ 5.1

(15) Solutions – Video solutions for each of the previous questions can be found on our website at **www.sherpaprep.com/videos**.

- BOOKMARK this address for future visits!

  ➢ To view the videos, you'll need the LOGIN and PASSWORD that you created upon registering your copy of <u>Number Properties & Algebra</u>.

- If you have yet to register your book yet, please go to **www.sherpaprep.com/activate** and enter your email address, last name, and shipping address.

- Be sure to provide the SAME last name and shipping address that you used to purchase your copy of <u>Master Key to the GRE</u> or to enroll in your GRE course with Sherpa Prep!

  ➢ When checking your answers, we encourage you to watch the solution for any problem that you answered INCORRECTLY

- The same goes for any problem that took you MORE than TWO MINUTES to solve.

- After digesting the explanation, REVISIT your mistake a couple of days later to ensure that the problem no longer poses issues to you.

  ➢ If you struggle to solve the problem a SECOND time, add it to your "LOG of ERRORS" and redo it every few weeks.

- Solving tricky questions MORE THAN ONCE is the best way to learn from your mistakes and to avoid similar difficulties on your actual exam.

Fundamental	Intermediate	Rare or Advanced
1. B	12. B	18. C
2. B	13. C	19. 0.2
3. C	14. C	20. C
4. C	15. D	21. E
5. B	16. C	22. B
6. C	17. B	23. B
7. B		24. B
8. C		
9. C		
10. C		
11. B		

Chapter 5

Algebra

Algebra

To be discussed:

Fundamental Concepts

Whether you're aiming for a perfect score or a score closer to average, mastery of the following concepts is essential.

1 Introduction
2 Solving for X
3 Distribution & Factoring
4 Get Rid of Denominators!
5 One Variable "In Terms Of" Another
6 Inequalities
7 Absolute Value
8 Combining Equations
9 Working With Exponents or Roots
10 Quadratic Equations

11 "FOIL"
12 The "FOIL" Identities
13 "Plug-Ins"
14 Manipulating "Plug-Ins"

Rare or Advanced Concepts

The following concepts are either advanced or are tested only on rare occasions. If you don't need an elite math score, don't waste your time!

15 Combining Inequalities
16 Advanced Shortcuts
17 Maximization Problems

18 Integer Constraints
19 Absolute Value Graphs

Practice Questions

There's no substitute for elbow grease. Practice your new skills to ensure that you internalize what you've studied.

20 Drills
21 Problem Sets
22 Solutions

Fundamental Concepts
---

(1) Introduction – Of all the concepts tested by the revised GRE, few are more important than Algebra.

• Not only do 10-15% percent of GRE questions test Algebra directly, but a majority of the other questions also require its use in one way or another.

 ➢ Word Problems, Geometry problems, and problems involving Charts and Graphs all demand the ability to solve for x.

• In other words, Algebra — like Arithmetic — lies at the "heart" of GRE math: we can't solve the exotic concepts without it.

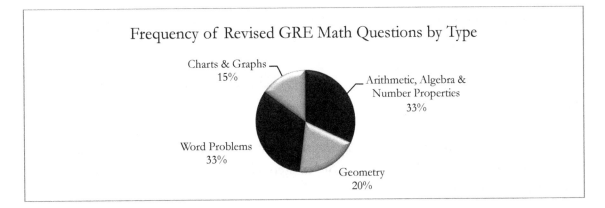

• To this point, we've covered a number of topics with you: PEMDAS, Arithmetic, Fractions, Decimals, "Plan B" Strategies, Integer Properties, Exponents, and Roots.

 ➢ You will encounter all of these topics within your Algebra problems.

• If you haven't done so already, be sure to reacquaint yourself with them before jumping into Algebra. It will make much of what's to follow easier for you.

• Finally, be sure to take your time with the easier stuff. In many ways, **the simpler something may seem, the more important it is**. Algebra is the foundation of many things to follow, so let's be sure that foundation is solid!

<u>**(2) Solving for X**</u> – The goal of most algebraic equations is to solve for a variable, such as x, which represents an unknown value.

• In all likelihood, you already have some familiarity with how to do so. It may have been years since you've had to, but you probably have a sense of how this works.

➢ Let's pretend, however, that you don't remember a thing. Let's start at the beginning.

• Imagine that you were given the statement $\boxed{?} - 3 = 1$. You'd probably have no problem determining that the "mystery box" equals 4, since you know that $4 - 3 = 1$.

• Likewise, if you were given the statement $2 + \odot = 5$, you'd probably have no trouble realizing that the "bulls-eye" equals 3, since $2 + 3 = 5$.

➢ In Algebra, we generally don't use "mystery boxes" or "bulls-eyes" to represent numbers we don't know.

• We use letters, such as x or y. Thus, we write statements such as $x - 3 = 1$ and $2 + y = 5$, instead of $\boxed{?} - 3 = 1$ and $2 + \odot = 5$.

• The letters simply mean "this value is unknown" and are commonly referred to as VARIABLES. We use variables instead of "mystery boxes" because it's a lot easier to say "$5x$" than to say "5 mystery boxes".

➢ Algebra, in many ways, is like solving a puzzle. If, for example, we are told that $5 + x = 8$ our mission is to identify the unknown value — i.e. to "solve for the variable".

• Now a statement such as $5 + x = 8$ is easy to solve. We know that $x = 3$, since we know that $5 + 3 = 8$.

• In most cases, however, "solving for x" isn't as easy. The sort of Algebra that you'll encounter on the GRE will be more complex. You'll need a proven approach that will allow you to determine unknown values that are harder to identify.

➢ As a general rule, we recommend the following process for solving for a variable, such as x.

• FIRST, identify what you want to REMOVE to get x alone. THEN, remove it by doing the OPPOSITE. In math, the opposite of addition is subtraction, while the opposite of multiplication is division.

• FINALLY, do the opposite operation to BOTH sides.

➢ Take the statement $x + 3 = 15$. To get x alone, we want to remove the $+ 3$, like so: $x \cancel{+3} = 15$.

• Therefore, we need to subtract $–3$ from x, since $–3$ is the opposite of $+3$. However, we need to subtract 3 from both sides of the equal sign:

$$x + 3 = 15$$
$$\underline{-3 \quad -3}$$

• Thus, we know that $x = 12$, since $15 – 3 = 12$.

➢ The reason we do the same thing to both sides of the equal sign is to preserve the BALANCE of the information.

• An EQUAL SIGN denotes that the information to left of the equal sign has the SAME value as the information to the right of the equal sign.

• For example, the statement $4x – 3 = 2x + 5$ indicates that $4x – 3$ has the same value as $2x + 5$.

➢ As long as we do the SAME thing to BOTH sides of the equal sign, we preserve the balance.

• Hence, if we double both sides of the statement $6 = 6$, we get $12 = 12$, which is true. Likewise, if we add 3 to both sides of the statement $4 = 4$, we get $7 = 7$, which is also true.

• However, if we only triple one side of the statement $5 = 5$, we get $15 = 5$, which is false. By doing something to just ONE side of the statement, we have failed to maintain its balance.

➢ We call a statement such as $4x - 3 = 2x + 5$ an EQUATION, because it has an equal sign.

• However, we call statements such as $4x - 3$ and $2x + 5$ EXPRESSIONS. We do so because expressions and equations are NOT the same thing. An equation has an equal sign. An expression does not.

EQUATION   EXPRESSION

$3x - 6 = 9$ $4x + 7$

➢ The distinction between an expression and an equation is an important one because ONLY EQUATIONS can be used to solve for x.

• An EXPRESSION is just a puzzle piece. On its own, its value is dependent on whatever we PLUG into it.

• Take the expression $7x - 1$. Notice how it has one value if we plug in $x = 3$ but has another value if we plug in $x = 7$. The same is true of the expression $2y + 5$: it's value changes as we insert different values for y.

➢ As equations become more complicated, you will need to remove several pieces of information to get x alone.

• Take the equation $3x + 4 = 16$. To isolate x, we need to remove two things: the $+ 4$ and the 3.

• However, we cannot remove these items in any order that we choose. We have to follow the order of operations. If you've read through the Arithmetic chapter of our book on Arithmetic & "Plan B" Strategies, you may recall this as PEMDAS.

➢ When isolating a variable, you generally need to do PEMDAS BACKWARDS. In other words, first remove anything you can by addition or subtraction.

• Then, remove what you can by multiplication or division. As a last step, remove any exponents or roots and resolve any parentheses, if your equation has them. Here, 4 is being added to $3x$, so our first step should be to subtract 4 from both sides, like so:

$$
\begin{array}{r}
3x + 4 = 16 \\
\underline{-4 \quad -4} \\
3x \quad\; = 12
\end{array}
$$

➤ Next, we need to simplify the statement $3x = 12$. The expression $3x$ is shorthand notation for 3 "times" x.

• Thus, since x is being multiplied by 3, we must divide both sides of the equation by 3, like this, to solve for x:

$$\frac{3x}{3} = \frac{12}{3}$$

• Doing so cancels the 3's on the left side of the equation and reduces the right side of the equation to 4. Hence, the value of x is 4, since:

$$\frac{3x}{3} = \frac{12}{3} \quad \rightarrow \quad \frac{\cancel{3}x}{\cancel{3}} = \frac{4(\cancel{3})}{\cancel{3}} \quad \rightarrow \quad x = 4$$

➤ If we've done our work correctly, we should be able to PLUG our result BACK into the original equation and obtain a true statement.

• The original equation stated $3x + 4 = 16$. If we replace x with 4, we get $3(4) + 4 = 16$. We can simplify this to $12 + 4 = 16$, which is a true statement.

• In other words, $x = 4$ is a solution to the equation since the information to the left of the equal sign equals the information to the right when $x = 4$. If our work had given us an incorrect value for x, such as 6, the two halves of the equation would not equal one another.

➤ To ensure that you've got it, let's work through a second example. Consider the equation $7 = 4x - 5$.

• To isolate x, we need to remove the -5 and the 4 from the right side of the equation. Since -5 indicates subtraction, we first need to add 5 to both sides of the equation to get rid of it:

$$\begin{array}{r} 7 = 4x - 5 \\ +5 = +5 \\ \hline 12 = 4x \end{array}$$

➤ Then, we need to simplify the statement $12 = 4x$, which indicates that x is being multiplied by 4.

• We can do so by dividing both sides of the equation by 4, to cancel out the multiplication. Thus, x equals 3, since:

$$\frac{12}{4} = \frac{4x}{4} \quad \rightarrow \quad \frac{3(\cancel{4})}{\cancel{4}} = \frac{\cancel{4}x}{\cancel{4}} \quad \rightarrow \quad 3 = x$$

(3) Distribution & Factoring – As equations become more complicated, you'll often need to group "like terms" in order to solve them.

- LIKE TERMS are terms that share the SAME variable and the SAME exponent.

- For example, $5x^2$ and $2x^2$ are like terms, since they share a common variable and a common exponent. The same goes for $4y$ and y. $5x$ and $2y$ are NOT like terms, nor are $4x^2$ and $3x$: $5x$ and $2y$ have different variables, while $4x^2$ and $3x$ have different exponents.

  ➢ Grouping like terms simplifies an equation, and is generally an important step in solving for a variable.

- To ensure that you are comfortable grouping like terms, let's work through a sample problem:

If $6x - 12 = 2x + 4$, what is the value of x?

(A) –4   (B) –2   (C) 4   (D) 6   (E) 8

Answer. C. Before we can solve for x, we first need to group our like terms: $6x$ and $2x$. To do so, we can either subtract $6x$ or $2x$ from both sides of the equation. Here, it is easier to subtract $2x$, since **subtracting $6x$ from $2x$ would result in a negative value.**

Once we subtract $2x$ from both sides of the equation, we can isolate x as follows:

$6x - 12 = 2x + 4$	The initial equation.
$4x - 12 = 4$	Subtract $2x$ from both sides.
$4x = 16$	Add 12 to both sides.
$x = 4$	Divide both sides by 4.

Thus, (C) is the correct answer.

  ➢ Before we can group like terms, however, it's often necessary to DISTRIBUTE something within an equation.

- In math, the term "distribute" generally means to multiply out (or to expand) the parts of an expression. For example, the distribution of $4(3n + 5)$ results in $12n + 20$, since:

$$4(3n + 5) = 4(3n) + 4(5) = 12n + 20$$

- In other words, to distribute an expression such as $4(3n + 5)$, we must multiply the term outside the parentheses (in this case 4) with **everything within the parentheses** ($3n$ and 5).

  ➤ When distributing, watch out for expressions involving the **distribution of negative signs.**

- Expressions such as $4 - (3x - 1)$ are often misunderstood as $4 - 3x - 1$. However, the notation indicates that **we are subtracting both $3x$ and -1** from 4. Thus, we have to subtract BOTH elements within the parentheses, like so:

$$4 - (3x - 1) \;\rightarrow\; 4 - (3x) - (-1) \;\rightarrow\; 4 - 3x + 1 \;\rightarrow\; 5 - 3x$$

  ➤ In other words, you can think of $- (3x - 1)$ as $-1(3x - 1)$, which equals $-3x + 1$ after distribution.

- Let's work through an equation involving distribution:

  If $3 - 6(x - 4) = x + 6$, what is the value of x?

  (A) -4 (B) 0 (C) 3 (D) 4 (E) 6

Answer. C. To solve for x, we need to group the x's on the left side of the equation with those on the right side. Before we can do so, however, we must first distribute $- 6(x - 4)$:

$$-6(x - 4) = -6(x) + -6(-4) = -6x + 24$$

Thus, our original equation equals $3 - 6x + 24 = x + 6$, which we can solve as follows:

$27 - 6x = x + 6$	Group $3 + 24$.
$27 = 7x + 6$	Add $6x$ to both sides.
$21 = 7x$	Subtract 6 from both sides.
$3 = x$	Divide both sides by 7.

Therefore, (C) is the correct answer.

  ➤ Distribution in REVERSE is known as FACTORING.

- As we saw in our discussion of Exponents, the term factoring refers to the "splitting" of an expression into simpler terms that multiply to the original. For example, each term in the expression $2x + 6y$ is a multiple of 2, so we can "factor" it as $2(x + 3y)$, since:

$$2(x + 3y) = 2x + 6y$$

➢ Sometimes, however, factoring can be TRICKY.

• When factoring an intimidating expression, there are two questions you should always ask yourself:

1. What is the **largest element** in COMMON to all of my terms?
2. What do I have to multiply with that common element to **recreate the original** expression?

• For example, imagine that you needed to factor $12n^3 + 4n^2 + 8n$. To start, you would need to identify the largest element in common to $12n^3$, $4n^2$, and $8n$.

➢ Since each of these terms is both a multiple of 4 (4, 8, 12) and contains at least one n (n, n^2, and n^3), that element must be $4n$.

• Next, you would need to multiply $4n$ by $3n^2 + n + 2$ to recreate $12n^3 + 4n^2 + 8n$:

$$12n^3 + 4n^2 + 8n$$

$$4n \times \boxed{3n^2} = 12n^3 \qquad 4n \times \boxed{n} = 4n^2 \qquad 4n \times \boxed{2} = 8n$$

• In other words, $12n^3 + 4n^2 + 8n$ can be factored as $4n(3n^2 + n + 2)$, since:

$$4n(3n^2 + n + 2) \;\rightarrow\; 4n(3n^2) + 4n(n) + 4n(2) \;\rightarrow\; 12n^3 + 4n^2 + 8n$$

➢ $\boxed{\text{Tip}}$: When solving equations, it is usually in your best interest to factor expressions that can be factored and to distribute expressions that can be distributed.

• So if you see an opportunity to factor or distribute an expression, go for it: you will likely find it helpful. Consider the following:

If $x = xz + yz$, then $z =$

(A) $\dfrac{xy}{x+y}$ (B) $\dfrac{y}{x+y}$ (C) $\dfrac{x+y}{x}$ (D) $\dfrac{x(x-y)}{y}$ (E) $\dfrac{x}{x+y}$

Answer: E. To solve for z, we first need to factor z from the right side of the equation. Once factored, z can then be isolated by dividing both sides of the equation by $x + y$:

$$x = z(x + y) \qquad \text{Factor out } z.$$
$$\frac{x}{x+y} = z \qquad \text{Divide both sides by } x + y.$$

Thus, (E) is the correct answer.

(4) Get Rid of Denominators! – For many people, solving for x starts to become difficult once equations contain denominators.

• If you skip ahead to our section on common Algebra mistakes, you'll notice that many of these mistakes occur in equations with denominators.

> ➤ Fortunately, most of these errors are easily avoided with one simple trick. We like to call it $\boxed{\textbf{The Denominator Trick}}$.

• If your equation contains a denominator, immediately **put parentheses around the ENTIRE equation** and **MULTIPLY it by the denominator** you wish to eliminate. Upon distribution, the denominator will cancel out, leaving you with a much simpler problem.

• To get a sense of how this works, consider the following:

$$\text{If } 4-\frac{x}{5}=2 \text{, what is the value of } x?$$

$$\text{(A) } -6 \quad \text{(B) } -5 \quad \text{(C) } 8 \quad \text{(D) } 10 \quad \text{(E) } 15$$

Answer. D. To solve for x, let's first get rid of its denominator. Since the denominator here is 5, we can do so by multiplying the entire equation by 5. When multiplying, be sure to put parentheses around the equation before you carry out the arithmetic:

$$5(4-\tfrac{x}{5}=2) \quad \rightarrow \quad 5(4)-\cancel{5}(\tfrac{x}{\cancel{5}})=5(2) \quad \rightarrow \quad 20-x=10$$

Now that we've eliminated our denominator, we can solve for x as follows:

$20 - x = 10$	Our equation after the "denominator trick".
$20 = x + 10$	Add x to both sides.
$10 = x$	Subtract 10 from both sides.

Thus, the correct answer is (D).

> ➤ Note that there are alternative ways to solve the equation above. For example, we could subtract 4 from both sides and then multiply the remaining equation by 5.

• These other approaches, however, **always** involve the same step: multiplying the entire equation by the denominator. In most instances, it will **save you time** to take care of this step early before performing other operations.

➤ If your equation contains **MULTIPLE denominators**, you can eliminate all of them by multiplying the equation by the **lowest common denominator (LCD)**.

• Multiplying by the lowest common denominator will eliminate all of your denominators at the same time. Let's take a look at an example:

$$\text{If } \frac{2}{3}x - 4 = \frac{1}{2}x + 1 \text{, what is the value of } x?$$

$$\text{(A) } -25 \quad \text{(B) } -10 \quad \text{(C) } 15 \quad \text{(D) } 25 \quad \text{(E) } 30$$

Answer. E. Since this equation contains denominators of 2 and 3, let's multiply the **ENTIRE** equation by 6, since 6 is the smallest number divisible by both 2 and 3:

$$6(\frac{2}{3}x - 4 = \frac{1}{2}x + 1) \;\rightarrow\; {}^2\!\cancel{6}(\frac{2}{\cancel{3}}x) - 6(4) = {}^3\!\cancel{6}(\frac{1}{\cancel{2}}x) + 6(1) \;\rightarrow\; 4x - 24 = 3x + 6$$

Now that we've eliminated our denominators, we can solve for x as follows:

$4x - 24 = 3x + 6$	Our equation after the "denominator trick".
$x - 24 = 6$	Subtract $3x$ from both sides.
$x = 30$	Add 24 to both sides.

Thus, the correct answer is (E).

➤ In an equation where a FRACTION EQUALS a FRACTION, you may find it easier to CROSS-MULTIPLY than to use the denominator trick.

• Although both strategies will result in the same answer, cross-multiplying is usually a simpler approach.

• To cross-multiply two fractions, just multiply each denominator with the opposing numerator, like this:

$$\frac{4}{12} \bowtie \frac{1}{3} \;\rightarrow\; 3 \times 4 = 12 \times 1$$

➤ Of course, the cross-multiplication that you'll encounter on the GRE will be a bit more involved than this.

• To ensure that you've got the hang of it, let's work through a sample problem together. Consider the following:

If $\dfrac{3x-1}{4} = \dfrac{5x+9}{12}$, then $x =$

(A) −3   (B) −2   (C) 2   (D) 3   (E) 6

Answer. D. When one fraction equals another, we can always cross-multiply to solve for x:

$$\dfrac{3x-1}{4} \diagup\!\!\!\!\diagdown \dfrac{5x+9}{12}$$

Doing so gives us $12(3x-1) = 4(5x+9)$, which equals $36x - 12 = 20x + 36$ after we carry out the distribution. The correct answer is therefore (D), since we can solve for x as follows:

$16x - 12 = 36$	Subtract $20x$ from both sides.
$16x = 48$	Add 12 to both sides.
$x = 3$	Divide both sides by 3.

➢ Note, however, that there is an even FASTER shortcut we can use to solve this equation.

• The denominators in this equations have a very specific relationship: 12 is <u>3 times</u> as great as 4.

• Therefore, we can CONVERT the fraction on the left to a value over 12 by multiplying its top and its bottom by 3. Doing so DOESN'T change the value of the fraction, since 3/3 = 1 and **anything times 1 equals itself**:

$$\dfrac{3}{3} \cdot \dfrac{3x-1}{4} = \dfrac{3(3x-1)}{3(4)} = \dfrac{9x-3}{12}$$

➢ Once we realize that the equation can be understood as $\dfrac{9x-3}{12} = \dfrac{5x+9}{12}$, we simply need to set the numerators equal to one another to solve for x.

• After all, if the two fractions are equal, and their denominators are equal, then their numerators must be equal as well.

• Thus, we can prove that $x = 3$, since:

$9x - 3 = 5x + 9$	Set the numerators equal.
$4x = 12$	Subtract $5x$ from both sides. Then add 3 to both sides.
$x = 3$	Divide both sides by 4.

➤ Before cross-multiplying, remember that cross-multiplication can ONLY be performed when one fraction equals another.

• If either side of an equation is NOT a fraction, the equation should be solved with the "denominator trick". Consider the following:

If $\dfrac{3}{4} - 2 = -\dfrac{5}{n}$, what is the value of n?

(A) –3 (B) –2 (C) 2 (D) 3 (E) 4

Answer. E. Because the left side of this equation is not a fraction, we cannot use cross-multiplication to solve for n. We can, however, use the "denominator trick". Since this equation contains denominators of 4 and n, let's multiply the entire equation by $4n$:

$$4n\left(\frac{3}{4} - 2 = -\frac{5}{n}\right) \;\rightarrow\; \cancel{4}n\left(\frac{3}{\cancel{4}}\right) + 4n(-2) = 4\cancel{n}\left(-\frac{5}{\cancel{n}}\right) \;\rightarrow\; 3n - 8n = -20$$

Doing so proves that (E) is the correct answer, since we can solve for n as follows:

$3n - 8n = -20$	Our equation after the "denominator trick".
$-5n = -20$	Group like terms.
$n = 4$	Divide both sides by –5.

➤ On a final note, if a variable has a fraction for a coefficient, you may find it easier to MULTIPLY by its RECIPROCAL than to use the denominator trick.

• For example, if $\dfrac{2}{3}n = 4$, we can multiply both sides of the equation by $\dfrac{3}{2}$ to solve for n, like so:

$$\frac{2}{3}n = 4 \;\rightarrow\; \left(\frac{\cancel{3}}{\cancel{2}}\right)\frac{\cancel{2}}{\cancel{3}}n = 4\left(\frac{3}{2}\right) \;\rightarrow\; n = \frac{12}{2} = 6$$

• Multiplying by the reciprocal works in situations like this because we need to divide $\dfrac{2}{3}n$ by $\dfrac{2}{3}$, and (as we saw in our book on <u>Arithmetic and "Plan B" Strategies</u>) dividing something by a fraction is the same thing as multiplying it by the reciprocal of that fraction.

➤ Before multiplying by the reciprocal, just be sure that your variable **stands alone**.

• If there's anything beside your variable (other than its coefficient), you'll need to use the denominator trick or to isolate the variable before multiplying by the reciprocal.

MULTIPLY by the RECIPROCAL	Use the DENOMINATOR trick
$\dfrac{2}{3}n = 4$	$\dfrac{2}{3}n - 2 = 4$

(5) One Variable "In Terms Of" Another – Some Algebra problems will ask you to express one variable "in terms of" another.

• The goal of such problems is to solve for a given variable. Knowing which variable to solve for, however, can seem tricky.

> ➤ The key lies in the phrasing of the question. If a question asks you to "solve for x in terms of y and z", then solve for x.

• If a question asks you "in terms of x and y, what is z?", then solve for z. In other words, always **SOLVE for the variable QUESTION**.

• The phrase "in terms of" means that the answer choices will contain that variable (or variables). NEVER solve for the "in terms of" variable.

> ➤ When solving for "one variable in terms of another", be sure to solve for that variable in the same manner that you would solve for any variable.

• Get rid of denominators, factor, or distribute whenever possible. Group like terms together. And expect the Algebra to be a little bit tricky.

• In some cases, it may be necessary to use the $\boxed{\textbf{Complex Numerator Shortcut}}$ in order to solve "one variable in terms of another" problems. Consider the following:

$$\text{If } \frac{n}{p+1} = \frac{2}{5}, \text{ what is } p \text{ in terms of } n?$$

$$\textbf{(A) } \tfrac{2}{5}n \quad \textbf{(B) } \tfrac{2}{5}n + \tfrac{2}{5} \quad \textbf{(C) } \tfrac{2}{5}n + 1 \quad \textbf{(D) } \tfrac{5}{2}n - \tfrac{2}{5} \quad \textbf{(E) } \tfrac{5}{2}n - 1$$

Answer. E. The question asks us "what is p", so the goal of the problem is to isolate p. The phrase "in terms of n" tells us the answer choices contain n's, so we know not to solve for n.

> ➤ To solve for p, let's first get rid of our denominators. This equation has one fraction equal to another, so we can cross-multiply like this:

$$\frac{n}{p+1} \diagdown\!\!\!\!\diagup \frac{2}{5} \quad \rightarrow \quad 5n = 2(p+1)$$

• Once distributed, our equation becomes $5n = 2p + 2$, so we can isolate p as follows:

$$5n - 2 = 2p \qquad \text{Subtract 2 from both sides.}$$
$$\frac{5n - 2}{2} = p \qquad \text{Divide both sides by 2.}$$

➤ Although we've solved for p, you'll notice that our answer is not located among the answer choices. We haven't made a mistake: we simply need to reduce our fraction.

• As you may recall, if the NUMERATOR of a fraction contains addition or subtraction, that fraction can be split using the "Complex Numerator Shortcut":

$$p = \frac{5n-2}{2} \quad \rightarrow \quad p = \frac{5n}{2} - \frac{2}{2} \quad \rightarrow \quad p = \frac{5n}{2} - 1$$

• Since, $\frac{5n}{2} - 1$ is equal to $\frac{5}{2}n - 1$, the correct answer is (E).

➤ To be sure you've got the hang of it, let's work through one more example together. Consider the following:

If $D = (A - B)C$ and $D \neq 0$, then A in terms of B, C, and D =

(A) $B - \dfrac{C}{D}$ **(B)** $\dfrac{D}{C} + B$ **(C)** $CD - B$ **(D)** $CD + B$ **(E)** $D + BC$

Answer: B. To solve for A, let's first distribute $(A - B)C$ as follows:

$$D = (A - B)C = AC - BC$$

Next, we'll need to isolate A. We can start by adding BC to both sides of the equation, and then dividing by C:

$D = AC - BC$	The distributed equation.
$D + BC = AC$	Add BC to both sides of the equation.
$\dfrac{D + BC}{C} = A$	Divide both sides of the equation by C.

Finally, we'll need to use the "Complex Numerator Shortcut" to split our fractions as follows, in order to simplify it:

$$A = \frac{D+BC}{C} \quad \rightarrow \quad A = \frac{D}{C} + \frac{B\cancel{C}}{\cancel{C}} \quad \rightarrow \quad A = \frac{D}{C} + B$$

Thus, the correct answer is (B). ALTERNATIVELY, we can divide both sides by C and then add B to both sides like this:

$$\frac{D}{C} = A - B \quad \rightarrow \quad \frac{D}{C} + B = A$$

(6) Inequalities – In math, we use the following symbols to indicate that one expression is larger than another:

$x < 3$	"x is less than 3".
$x > 5$	"x is greater than 5".
$x \leq 4$	"x is less than or equal to 4".
$x \geq 8$	"x is greater than or equal to 8".

• Such statements are known as inequalities. And as with equations, the goal of most inequalities is to solve for a variable.

➤ By and large, inequalities can be solved in precisely the same manner as equations.

• For example, given the statement $2x - 3 \geq 5$, we can determine that x can equal any value equal to or greater than 4 by adding 3 to both sides and isolating x:

$2x \geq 8$	Add 3 to both sides.
$x \geq 4$	Divide both sides by 2.

• There is, however, one <u>critical</u> difference between equations and inequalities.

➤ **When inequalities are MULTIPLIED or DIVIDED by a NEGATIVE value, the direction of their inequality sign must always be FLIPPED.**

• Take the statement $-2x + 3 > 11$. To isolate x, we first need to subtract 3 from both sides of the inequality. We then have to divide both sides by –2. Dividing both sides by –2, however, forces us to flip the direction of the inequality sign. In other words:

$-2x > 8$	Subtract 3 from both sides.
$x < -4$	Divide both sides by –2. Flip the sign!

• Be sure to note that adding or subtracting negative values does NOT flip the inequality sign. The same goes for multiplying and dividing by positive values. If you are multiplying or dividing by a positive value, LEAVE the sign ALONE.

FLIP the sign	DON'T FLIP the sign
$-4x < 16$	$3x > 18$
$x > -4$	$x > 6$

➢ To understand why we flip the inequality sign when multiplying or dividing by a negative value, consider the statement $10 > 5$.

• This statement indicates that 10 is greater than 5, which is true. If we were to multiply both sides by -1, but leave the sign unchanged, we would get $-10 > -5$. However, this is false: -10 is not greater than -5. Flipping the sign gives us the true relationship: $-10 < -5$.

• In other words, when multiplying or dividing inequalities by negative numbers, we need to flip their signs in order to maintain the validity of their relationships. If we don't flip their signs, we get false statements such as $-10 > -5$.

➢ When working with inequalities, **BEWARE of multiplying or dividing by a variable**.

• Unless you know whether that variable represents a positive or negative value, you DON'T know whether to flip the sign.

• If you need to multiply or divide an inequality by a variable, you must consider TWO scenarios: (I) what happens if the variable is positive, and (II) what happens if the variable is negative. Consider the following:

$$d \neq 0 \text{ and } ad > bd$$

Quantity A	**Quantity B**
a	b

Answer: D. According to question, $ad > bd$. Dividing both sides of this inequality by d gives us $a > b$, which seems to indicate that (A) is the correct answer. However, this is false.

➢ Because we do not know whether d represents a positive value or a negative value, there are two scenarios that we have to consider:

I. $\boxed{d > 0}$. **If d is positive**, $ad > bd$ will yield $a > b$ when divided by d, since dividing an inequality by a positive value does not change the direction of the inequality sign.

II. $\boxed{d < 0}$. **If d is negative**, $ad > bd$ will yield $a < b$ when divided by d, since dividing an inequality by a negative value forces us to flip the direction of the inequality sign.

• Thus, the correct answer is (D): it is uncertain whether $a > b$, since we do not know whether $ad > bd$ will yield $a > b$ or $a < b$ when divided by d.

➤ To graph an inequality on a number line, simply **shade** every point on the number line that is a **valid solution** to the inequality.

• For example, to graph $x \geq 4$, we have to shade every point on the number line that is 4 or greater. To graph $x < 3$, we have to shade every point less than 3:

• Note that we **shade the number 4** in the diagram to the left, since 4 is included in the statement $x \geq 4$. Conversely, we leave the number 3 **open** (unshaded) in the diagram to the right, since 3 is not included in the statement $x < 3$.

➤ Finally, some inequalities contain more than one statement. Such inequalities are commonly known as **COMPOUND inequalities.**

• The examples below would be considered compound inequalities:

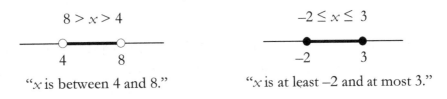

• Problems involving compound inequalities are rare. Should you find one on your exam, don't panic! They may look daunting, but they're easy to solve. Simply **isolate the variable in the middle** of the compound by doing the same thing to **all three sides** of the inequality.

• Take the statement $3 \leq -2n + 7 < 15$. To simplify it, we only need to isolate n. We can do so by subtracting 7 from all three sides, and then by dividing all three sides by -2:

$$3 \leq -2n + 7 < 15 \qquad \text{The given inequality.}$$
$$-4 \leq -2n < 8 \qquad \text{Subtract 7 from all three sides.}$$
$$2 \geq n > -4 \qquad \text{Divide all three sides by } -2. \text{ Flip both signs!}$$

• We can even graph $3 \leq -2n + 7 < 15$ by depicting its solution as follows:

"n is greater than -4 but no greater than 2."

(7) Absolute Value – Earlier, in our discussion of Integer Properties, we introduced the concept of absolute value.

• As you may recall from that discussion, the absolute value of a number is indicated by **two vertical bars**, commonly known as "absolute value brackets".

  ➢ These brackets measure **the distance** on the number line **between the number inside them and zero**.

• For example, $|-4| = 4$, since -4 is four "steps" from zero on the number line. Likewise, $|4| = 4$, since 4 is also four "steps" from zero on the number line.

• With **variables**, absolute value brackets work the same way. For example, if $|x| = 5$, we know that there are two values on the number line that are "five steps" from zero: 5 or -5. Thus, we can say that $x = \pm 5$, or that $\pm x = 5$, since the two equations are equal.

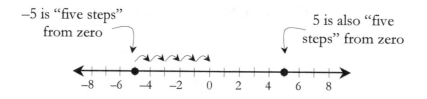

  ➢ On the GRE, absolute value questions often involve equations with variables AND numbers inside their absolute value brackets.

• Should you find one on your exam, don't panic! Such equations may look daunting, but they're easier than most test-takers realize.

• To solve them, first **isolate the absolute value brackets** (if necessary). Then DROP the brackets and place $\pm$, the "plus/minus" symbol, in front of the Algebra, like so:

$$\boxed{\;|\text{Algebra}| = \text{Answer} \quad \rightarrow \quad \pm\,(\textbf{Algebra}) = \textbf{Answer}\;}$$

  ➢ The resulting statement will give you TWO equations. Be sure to SOLVE BOTH of them.

• With absolute value, you should expect to find two solutions. You'll need to know both to answer certain GRE questions. If you only identify one solution, exam-makers may find a way to take advantage of your mistake.

• Consider the following:

$$\text{If } \frac{2|x+5|}{3} = 4 \text{, then } x + 4 \text{ could equal which of the following?}$$

Indicate all such values.

$\boxed{\text{A}}\ -15 \quad \boxed{\text{B}}\ -7 \quad \boxed{\text{C}}\ -3 \quad \boxed{\text{D}}\ 1 \quad \boxed{\text{E}}\ 5 \quad \boxed{\text{F}}\ 9$

Answer: B and E. To solve the equation, we first need to isolate the absolute value brackets, which we can do as follows:

$$2|x + 5| = 12 \qquad \text{Multiply the equation by 3.}$$
$$|x + 5| = 6 \qquad \text{Divide both sides by 2.}$$

Next, we need to drop the brackets and to place the $\pm$ symbol in front of $(x + 5)$:

$$|x+5| = 6 \quad \rightarrow \quad \pm(x+5) = 6$$

Finally, we have to solve BOTH equations:

EQUATION #1	EQUATION #2
$(x + 5) = 6$	$-(x + 5) = 6$
$x + 5 = 6$	$x + 5 = -6$
$x = 1$	$x = -11$

Since $x = 1$ or -11, there are two possible solutions for $x + 4$: $1 + 4 = 5$ and $-11 + 4 = -7$. Thus, $\boxed{\text{B}}$ and $\boxed{\text{E}}$ are both possible solutions.

➢ But **BEWARE: both solutions are not always valid.** PLUG both solutions back into the question to ensure that each works.

• In the problem above, both solutions are valid, since $|1 + 5| = 6$ and $|(-11) + 5| = 6$. This is not always the case. In a statement such as $|x + 8| = 3x$, note how only one of the solutions is valid:

$$|x+8| = 3x \quad \rightarrow \quad \pm(x+8) = 3x$$

EQUATION #1	EQUATION #2
$(x + 8) = 3x$	$-(x + 8) = 3x$
$x + 8 = 3x$	$x + 8 = -3x$
$8 = 2x \ \rightarrow \ 4 = x$	$8 = -4x \ \rightarrow \ -2 = x$

• Although the Algebra predicts that $x = 4$ or -2, **the second solution isn't valid.** Plugging $x = -2$ into the original statement gives us $|-2 + 8| = 3(-2)$, which is false: $|6| \neq -6$.

Sherpa
  Prep

➤ Inequalities that involve absolute value can be solved in exactly the same manner as equations that involve absolute value.

• As with equations, first **isolate the absolute value brackets**, if necessary. Then drop the brackets and place ±, the "plus/minus" symbol, in front of the Algebra:

$$\boxed{\;\left|\text{Algebra}\right| < \text{Answer} \quad \rightarrow \quad \pm(\textbf{Algebra}) < \textbf{Answer}\;}$$

• The resulting statement will give you TWO inequalities. Once you solve BOTH of them, be sure to COMBINE their results into a single statement.

If $\left|x-3\right| \leq 5$, then which of the following is true?

(A) $-8 < x < 2$ (B) $-2 < x < 8$ (C) $-1 < x < 1$ (D) $2 < x < 8$ (E) $5 < x < 8$

Answer: B. To solve this inequality, we first need to drop its absolute value brackets and to place the ± symbol in front of $(x-3)$:

$$\left|x-3\right| \leq 5 \quad \rightarrow \quad \pm(x-3) \leq 5$$

➤ Then we have to solve BOTH equations. Be sure to flip the sign when you multiply the second inequality by -1:

INEQUALITY #1	INEQUALITY #2
$(x-3) \leq 5$	$-(x-3) \leq 5$
$x-3 \leq 5$	$-x+3 \leq 5$
$x \leq 8$	$-x \leq 2$
	$x \geq -2$ (multiply by -1)

• Since **inequality #1** proves that x can be no greater than 8, and **inequality #2** proves that x must be at least -2, x must be at least -2 but no greater than 8. Algebraically, we can state this as $-2 \leq x \leq 8$. Thus, (B) is the correct answer.

➤ As with equations, it can be helpful to plug your solutions back into the question to ensure that each solution works.

• Although GRE inequalities almost NEVER require such careful proofing, **testing the edges of each range** can expose unexpected wrinkles. In this case, the edges of our ranges are 8 and -2. Plugging each into the inequality proves that there are no such wrinkles here, since both of our values yield true statements: $\left|8-3\right| \leq 5$ and $\left|(-2)-3\right| \leq 5$.

(8) Combining Equations – Given two equations, there are two ways to solve for the variables within those equations.

- The first way is known as a substitution.

  ➢ SUBSTITUTION involves the "substitution" of one equation into another in order to solve for a given variable.

- To substitute one equation into another, first **isolate a variable** that they have in common. Then **plug that variable into the other equation**. The aftermath will leave you with something easy to solve: a single equation with only one variable. Let's work through an example together:

$$\text{If } 4x + y = 9 \text{ and } 3x - 6y = 0, \text{ then } x + y =$$

$$\text{(A) } 3 \quad \text{(B) } 4 \quad \text{(C) } 6 \quad \text{(D) } 7 \quad \text{(E) } 9$$

Answer. A. To solve for x and y, we must first isolate a variable that they have in common. In general, it is preferable to **isolate a variable with no coefficient**, since this will help us avoid fractions. In the problem above, the first equation contains a y with no coefficient, so:

$$4x + y = 9$$
$$y = 9 - 4x$$

- Now that y has been isolated, we can substitute $(9 - 4x)$ for y **wherever y appears** in the "other equation".

  ➢ In this case, the other equation is $3x - 6y = 0$, since **we already used $4x + y = 9$** to isolate y:

$$\text{Substitute}$$
$$3x - 6y = 0 \qquad (9 - 4x) \text{ for } y$$
$$3x - 6(\mathbf{9 - 4x}) = 0$$
$$3x - 54 + 24x = 0$$
$$27x = 54 \;\rightarrow\; x = 2$$

- Since $x = 2$, this value can be plugged into either of the original equations to determine the value of y:

$$
\begin{array}{ccc}
4x + y = 9 & \text{OR} & 3x - 6y = 0 \\
4(2) + y = 9 & & 3(2) - 6y = 0 \\
8 + y = 9 & & 6 = 6y \\
y = 1 & & 1 = y
\end{array}
$$

- Thus, the correct answer is (A), since $x + y = 2 + 1 = 3$.

: If asked to solve for a specific variable, always SUBSTITUTE the OTHER variable.

• This tip isn't particularly important, but it will save you time. If you look back at our last example, notice that **we substituted *y*, but ended up solving for *x*.** If we had substituted *x*, we would have ended up solving for *y*.

• If time weren't an issue, this point wouldn't matter. Unfortunately, time is always a hidden enemy on the GRE, so it's always a good thing to be as efficient as possible.

➢ Equations can also be combined through a technique commonly known as elimination.

• ELIMINATION involves the addition or subtraction of two equations in order to "eliminate" one of their variables. To combine equations through elimination:

(1) **Stack** the two equations atop one another.
(2) **Arrange the variables** in the same order.
(3) **Add or subtract** the equations to ELIMINATE one of the variables.

• As with substitution, the aftermath will leave you with something easy to solve: a single equation with only one variable. Consider the following:

If $-2x + y = 8$ and $5y + 2x = 4$, what is the value of $y - x$?

(A) 3   (B) 4   (C) 5   (D) 7   (E) 9

Answer: C. To solve for *x* and *y*, first stack the equations and arrange their variables in the same order. Then add the two equations as follows:

$$
\begin{array}{r}
-2x + y = 8 \\
+\ \ 2x + 5y = 4 \\
\hline
6y = 12
\end{array}
$$

➢ Adding the equations eliminates the *x*'s, leaving us with $6y = 12$. Since $y = 2$, we can plug this information into either of the original equations to solve for *x*, like so:

$$
\begin{array}{ccc}
5y + 2x = 4 & \text{OR} & -2x + y = 8 \\
10 + 2x = 4 & & -2x + 2 = 8 \\
2x = -6 & & -2x = 6 \\
x = -3 & & x = -3
\end{array}
$$

• Thus, the correct answer must be (C), since $y - x = 2 - (-3) = 5$.

➢ It is important to understand that <u>elimination ONLY works</u> when combining the equations CANCELS OUT one of the variables.

• For a variable to cancel out, it must have **opposite coefficients**.

• For example, the equations $-2x + 3y = 7$ and $2x + 5y = 9$ are easily solved through elimination, since their "x-terms" have opposite coefficients: -2 and 2. **Thus, $-2x$ and $2x$** will cancel out when the equations are added.

➢ If adding or subtracting the equations does not eliminate one of the variables, the strategy will NOT work.

• UNLESS, that is, you **MULTIPLY one (or both) of the equations by some value** to give either variable opposite coefficients.

• For example, given the equations $-x + 2y = 3$ and $3x + 4y = 1$, you could multiply the first equation by 3, making it $-3x + 6y = 9$, so that the "x-terms" ($3x$ and $-3x$) cancel when the equations are added. To get a better sense of how this works, consider the following:

$$7a - 3b = 4$$
$$3a + 5b = 8$$

Quantity A	**Quantity B**
$5a + b$	6

Answer: C. To solve this problem with the elimination strategy, we need one of the variables to have opposite coefficients. As it stands, neither variable does.

➢ If we were to multiply the top equations by 5 and the bottom equation by 3, however, the b's would cancel, like so:

$$
\begin{array}{l}
7a - 3b = 4 \\
\underline{3a + 5b = 8} \\
\text{nothing cancels}
\end{array}
\quad
\begin{array}{l}
\xrightarrow{\text{Multiply} \times 5} \\
\xrightarrow{\text{Multiply} \times 3}
\end{array}
\quad
\begin{array}{l}
35a - 15b = 20 \\
\underline{9a + 15b = 24} \\
44a \qquad\; = 44
\end{array}
$$

• Thus, we know that $a = 1$, since $44a = 44$. If $a = 1$, then the correct answer is (C), since plugging $a = 1$ into either of the original equations shows us that $b = 1$, proving that Quantity A equals $5(1) + 1 = 6$:

$$
\begin{array}{ccc}
7(1) - 3b = 4 & \text{OR} & 3(1) + 5b = 8 \\
-3b = -3 & & 5b = 5 \\
b = 1 & & b = 1
\end{array}
$$

➤ In general, **elimination is a much faster technique than substitution**. This is particularly true when equations are already stacked atop one another.

• That said, make sure that you are comfortable using both techniques. There are plenty of situations where you'll need to use substitution.

• As a general approach, we think it's always worthwhile to ask yourself "can I combine these equations easily through elimination?" Elimination is often the difference between "**spotting the shortcut**" and a minute or two of tedious calculations. If you can't see a way to use elimination easily, you can always fall back on substitution.

➤ Be aware, however, that questions involving multiple equations often test your ability to "**Solve for Chunks**".

• When combining equations, it's easy to assume that you have to solve for each variable separately. The truth of the matter is that you can often bypass this step with GRE questions.

• Think back to the previous problem. We did quite a bit of work to determine the value of $5a + b$. Did we really need to do all that work? The question wanted to know whether Quantity A was bigger than 8. Was there a way to solve for $5a + b$ "as a chunk"?

$$7a - 3b = 4$$
$$3a + 5b = 8$$

Quantity A	**Quantity B**
$5a + b$	6

Answer: C. Before combining the equations to solve for the variables separately, be sure to ask yourself whether you can add or subtract the equations to get $5a + b$ directly. Here, if we add the equations, we get:

$$7a - 3b = 4$$
$$\underline{3a + 5b = 8}$$
$$10a + 2b = 12$$

• Thus, the busy work on the previous page wasn't needed to prove that the two quantities are equals, since dividing this equation by 2 gives us

$$\frac{10a+2b}{2} = \frac{12}{2} \quad \rightarrow \quad \frac{2(5a+b)}{2} = 6 \quad \rightarrow \quad 5a + 6$$

(9) Working with Exponents or Roots – As you may recall from our discussion of Integer Properties, exponents and roots are opposite operations.

• Opposite operations are operations that "undo" or negate one another. For example, a square cancels out a square root, and a square root cancels out a square.

> ➤ To solve for a variable underneath a root or an exponent, first ISOLATE the root or the exponent. Then, perform the OPPOSITE operation.

• Use a root to get rid of an exponent, and an exponent to get rid of a root. The one will always cancel out the other. Let's look at a pair of examples, side by side. On the left, you will find an equation with a root. On the right, you will find an equation with an exponent:

$4\sqrt{x+6} - 5 = 11$ ROOT equation. $3(x-5)^3 + 6 = 30$ EXPONENT equation.

$4\sqrt{x+6} = 16$ Add 5. $3(x-5)^3 = 24$ Subtract 6.

$\sqrt{x+6} = 4$ Divide by 4. $(x-5)^3 = 8$ Divide by 3.

$x+6 = 16$ SQUARE both sides. $x-5 = 2$ CUBE ROOT both sides.

$x = 10$ Subtract 6. $x = 7$ Add 5.

• In each case, **notice how the root and the exponent negate one another**. In the root equation, squaring the square root eliminated the root. In the exponent equation, taking the cube root of the cube eliminated the exponent.

> ➤ BEWARE of equations containing **EVEN exponents**. An equation with an even exponent typically has TWO solutions: one positive and one negative.

• For example, if $x^2 = 25$, then $x = 5$ or -5, since 5^2 and $(-5)^2$ both equal 25. The same goes for more complex equations. If $(x-3)^2 = 25$, then:

$$x - 3 = 5 \qquad\qquad x - 3 = -5$$

• Exam-makers LOVE to design questions involving even exponents, since it's easy to forget that an equation with an even exponent generally has two solutions.

> ➤ Thankfully, equations with **ODD exponents** are easy: they always have ONE solution.

• For example, if $x^3 = 27$, then $x = 3$ only, since $3^3 = 27$ but $(-3)^3 = -27$. Likewise, if $(x+6)^3 = -8$, then $x + 6 = -2$ only, since $(-2)^3 = -8$ but $2^3 = 8$.

➤ To illustrate the difference between EVEN and ODD exponents, let's compare two problems side by side.

• On the left, you will find an equation with an even exponent. On the right, you will find an equation with an odd exponent:

$$(x+4)^2 = 9 \qquad \text{EVEN exponent.} \qquad\qquad (x-7)^3 = 64 \qquad \text{ODD exponent.}$$
$$x+4 = \pm 3 \qquad \text{SQUARE root.} \qquad\qquad x-7 = 4 \qquad \text{CUBE root.}$$

$$x+4 = 3 \qquad x+4 = -3 \qquad\qquad\qquad x = 11$$
$$x = -1 \qquad\;\; x = -7$$

• The equation with the EVEN exponent ends up with TWO solutions, as $9 = 3^2$ and $(-3)^2$. The equation with the ODD exponent ends up with ONE solution, as $64 = 4^3$ but not $(-4)^3$.

➤ It's worth pointing out that taking the root of an expression with an EVEN exponent technically results in its ABSOLUTE VALUE.

• This is something that the GRE almost NEVER tests. However, if you need to score a 170 and want to make sure that you've covered all your bases, it may be worth your time to note that:

$$(x-5)^2 = 9 \;\rightarrow\; \sqrt{(x-5)^2} = \sqrt{9} \;\rightarrow\; |x-5| = 3$$

• To understand how this might help you solve an actual GRE problem, consider the following:

If $n \neq 0$, then $\dfrac{\sqrt{n^2}}{n}$ is equal to which of the following?

(A) 1 (B) –1 (C) $\dfrac{|n|}{n}$ (D) n^3 (E) n^4

Answer: C. If we attack this problem by testing out numbers, we end up with either 1 or –1:

$$\frac{\sqrt{4^2}}{4} = \frac{\sqrt{16}}{4} = \frac{4}{4} = 1 \qquad\qquad \frac{\sqrt{(-4)^2}}{-4} = \frac{\sqrt{16}}{-4} = \frac{4}{-4} = -1$$

• The correct answer, however, is (C), since taking the root of an even exponent results in its absolute value:

$$\frac{\sqrt{n^2}}{n} = \frac{|n|}{n}$$

> Understanding that an expression such as $\sqrt{(x+3)^2}$ equals $|x+3|$ can come in handy when working with INEQUALITIES that involve EVEN EXPONENTS.

- Consider the following:

If $(2x-1)^2 \leq 9$, then x equals

(A) $-3 \leq x \leq 2$ **(B)** $-2 \leq x \leq 1$ **(C)** $-1 \leq x \leq 2$ **(D)** $1 \leq x \leq 3$ **(E)** $2 \leq x \leq 3$

- To determine the range of solutions for x, we can take the square root of both sides of the inequality and convert the expression $\sqrt{(2x-1)^2}$ into its absolute value, like so:

$$(2x-1)^2 \leq 9 \ \rightarrow \ \sqrt{(2x-1)^2} \leq \sqrt{9} \ \rightarrow \ |2x-1| \leq 3$$

> From here, we can drop the absolute value brackets and place $\pm$, the "plus/minus" symbol, in front of the Algebra:

$$\pm(2x-1) \leq 3$$

- If we solve both inequalities, we get:

INEQUALITY #1	INEQUALITY #2
$2x - 1 \leq 3$	$-(2x-1) \leq 3$
$2x \leq 4$	$-2x + 1 \leq 3$
$x \leq 2$	$-2x \leq 2$
	$x \geq -1$

- Since inequality #1 proves that x can be no greater than 2, and inequality #2 proves that x must be at least -1, we know that x must be at least -1 but no greater than 2. Algebraically, we can state this as $-1 \leq x \leq 2$. Thus, (C) is the correct answer.

> Alternatively, if you prefer to avoid working with absolute value, you can think about the question logically.

- According to the problem, $(2x-1)^2 \leq 9$. We know that there are TWO values, when SQUARED, that equal 9: 3 and -3.

- However, any value GREATER than 3 or LESS than -3, when squared, will result in a value that EXCEEDS than 9. Thus, we know that **$2x -1$ cannot be greater than 3 or less than -3**. Algebraically, we can state this as: $2x - 1 \leq 3$ and $2x - 1 \geq -3$. If we solve these inequalities and combine their results, we get $-1 \leq x \leq 2$, again proving that (C) is the answer.

(10) Quadratic Equations – Any equation that contains a variable raised to both the first and second powers is commonly known as a quadratic equation.

• Such equations differ from the other sorts of equations we've seen so far in that **quadratics can have an "x^2 term" AND an "x term"**, whereas the other equations we've seen ONLY have a single variable term to some power.

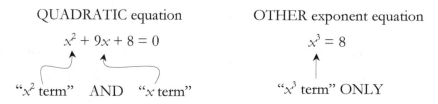

QUADRATIC equation   OTHER exponent equation

$$x^2 + 9x + 8 = 0$$ $$x^3 = 8$$

"x^2 term"   AND   "x term"   "x^3 term" ONLY

• Although quadratic equations are often written in the form $ax^2 \pm bx \pm c = 0$, any equation that contains BOTH an x^2 term and an x term is a quadratic. Thus, the first equation below would be considered a quadratic, as would the two equations to its right:

$$x^2 + 7x + 10 = 0 \qquad x^2 + 5x = -6 \qquad -x^2 = 8x + 7$$

➢ The reason that we distinguish quadratic equations from other equations is that quadratic equations CANNOT be solved by traditional means.

• To solve a quadratic equation, you either have to factor it, "complete the square", or use the quadratic formula.

• Fortunately, for the GRE, you only need to know how to FACTOR. The other techniques, though useful in various ways, are too slow to help you on the GRE.

➢ To factor a quadratic, first set the equation EQUAL to ZERO. Then make sure the x^2 term is POSITIVE.

• Once your quadratic is in the form $ax^2 \pm bx \pm c = 0$, set up two sets of parentheses, like this: $(x \quad)(x \quad) = 0$. Then complete the parentheses by choosing two numbers:

The numbers should MULTIPLY to the LAST value in your quadratic, but ADD to the MIDDLE value.

• For example, to factor $x^2 + 7x + 10 = 0$, we would need to choose two numbers that:

$$x^2 + 7x + 10 = 0$$

Add to 7 ⟶   ⟵ Multiply to 10

- The numbers that multiply to 10 are 1×10, 2×5, -1×-10, and -2×-5. Of these, only $2 + 5$ add to 7. Thus, we can factor $x^2 + 7x + 10 = 0$ as $(x + 2)(x + 5) = 0$:

$$\overbrace{(x + 2)}^{\text{add to 7}}\underbrace{(x + 5)}_{} = 0$$
$$\underbrace{}_{\text{multiply to 10}}$$

> ➢ Once a quadratic has been factored, its solutions, also known as "ROOTS", can be determined by setting EACH FACTOR equal to ZERO.

- For example, the equation $(x + 2)(x + 5) = 0$ has the solutions $x = -2$ or -5, since setting both factors equal to zero gives us:

$$x + 2 = 0 \qquad \text{OR} \qquad x + 5 = 0$$
$$x = -2 \qquad\qquad\qquad x = -5$$

- Note, by the way, that the solutions of a quadratic equation are so-called because they produce a **true statement** when plugged into the factored equation. For example, $x = -2$ is a solution to $x^2 + 7x + 10 = 0$, since plugging -2 into $(x + 2)(x + 5) = 0$ produces the true statement $(-2 + 2)(-2 + 5) = (0)(3) = 0$.

> ➢ Make sure that you learn the terms SOLUTIONS, ROOTS, and FACTORS.

- Exam-makers will use this terminology in their questions, so if you don't understand the terms, you may not be able to solve their problems. Consider the following:

$$x^2 - 15 = 2x$$

Quantity A	**Quantity B**
Twice the sum of the roots of the equation	4

Answer: C. Since $x^2 - 15 = 2x$ has both an "x^2 term" AND an "x term" it is a quadratic. To solve it, we'll need to **set the equation equal to zero**, but keep the x^2 term positive. To do this, let's subtract $2x$ to both sides.

$$x^2 - 2x - 15 = 0$$

- Next, we'll need to set up two parentheses, $(x \quad)(x \quad) = 0$, and identify two numbers that **multiply to -15** (the last number) but **add to -2** (the middle number).

Chapter 5: Algebra

➤ The numbers that multiply to –15 are –1 × 15, 1 × –15, –5 × 3, and 5 × –3. Of these, only –5 + 3 add to –2. Therefore, we can factor our quadratic as:

$$(x - \underbrace{\overbrace{5)(x + 3}^{\text{add to –2}}}_{\text{multiply to –15}}) = 0$$

• Now that our quadratic has been factored, we can **set each factor equal to zero** to determine its solutions:

$$x - 5 = 0 \qquad \text{OR} \qquad x + 3 = 0$$
$$x = 5 \qquad\qquad\qquad x = -3$$

• Since the solutions of a quadratics can also be referred to as the roots, the sum of the roots equals 5 + (–3) = 2. Thus, the correct answer is (C), since twice the sum would be 4.

➤ On a last note, keep your eye out for HIDDEN quadratics. To make quadratic equations more difficult, exam-makers sometimes disguise them in unexpected ways.

• Remember, no matter how odd an equation may look, if it has an x^2 term and an x term, you MUST factor it to solve it. Consider the following:

$$6x^2 = x$$

Quantity A	**Quantity B**
x	$\dfrac{1}{6}$

Answer. D. Although it may be tempting to divide both sides of this equation by x to solve it, doing so would be a mistake.

➤ For starters, dividing both sides of an equation by x when you don't know whether $x = 0$ is always a **dangerous** game: you may miss out on a possible solution.

• Moreover, this equation has both an x^2 term and an x term, so it is a quadratic. To solve it properly, we MUST set it equal to zero and factor it:

$$6x^2 - x = 0 \quad \rightarrow \quad (x)(6x - 1) = 0$$

• The correct answer here is (D), since setting each factor equal to zero proves that x **can equal 1/6 or 0**, making Quantity A equal to or less than Quantity B:

$$x = 0 \qquad \text{OR} \qquad 6x - 1 = 0$$
$$6x = 1 \ \rightarrow \ x = 1/6$$

<u>**(11) "FOIL": First, Outer, Inner, Last**</u> – The distribution of factors is generally known by the term "FOIL".

• "FOIL" stands for First, Outer, Inner, Last. It is a mnemonic device designed to help us remember how to multiply expressions such as $(n + 5)(n - 2)$.

> ➤ As you may recall, to multiply such expressions, every term in the first parentheses must be multiplied by every term in the second parentheses.

• "FOIL" reminds us which terms we need to multiply so that we do so correctly. Thus, to multiply the expression $(n + 5)(n - 2)$, we would "FOIL" it as follows:

FIRST	OUTER	INNER	LAST
$(n + 5)(n - 2)$	$(n + 5)(n - 2)$	$(n + 5)(n - 2)$	$(n + 5)(n - 2)$
$n \times n = n^2$	$n \times (-2) = -2n$	$5 \times n = 5n$	$5 \times (-2) = -10$

• In other words, the multiplication of $(n + 5)(n - 2) = n^2 - 2n + 5n - 10$. **Combining like terms** simplifies the result to $n^2 + 3n - 10$.

> ➤ As you may have noticed from the example above, the "FOILING" of two factors can create a QUADRATIC expression.

• In general, if a problem contains the product of two factors, it may be necessary to "FOIL" the factors into a quadratic to solve the equation.

• Consider the following:

If $(y + 2)(y + 3) = 6$, then y could equal which of the following?

Indicate <u>all</u> such values.

$\boxed{\text{A}}$ –6 $\boxed{\text{B}}$ –5 $\boxed{\text{C}}$ –2 $\boxed{\text{D}}$ –1 $\boxed{\text{E}}$ 0

Answer: B and E. To solve for y, first combine the factors by using "FOIL".

FIRST	OUTER	INNER	LAST
$(y + 2)(y + 3)$	$(y + 2)(y + 3)$	$(y + 2)(y + 3)$	$(y + 2)(y + 3)$
$y \times y = y^2$	$y \times 3 = 3y$	$2 \times y = 2y$	$2 \times 3 = 6$

➢ Next, combine the like terms and factor the quadratic:

$y^2 + 3y + 2y + 6 = 6$	The "FOILed" equation.
$y^2 + 5y + 6 = 6$	Combine like terms.
$y^2 + 5y = 0$	Set the quadratic equal to zero.
$y(y + 5) = 0$	Factor out y.

• Finally, to solve for y, set each factor equal to zero. As we can see, y can equal 0 or −5, so the correct answer is $\boxed{B}$ and $\boxed{E}$.

$$y = 0 \qquad \text{OR} \qquad \begin{aligned} y + 5 &= 0 \\ y &= -5 \end{aligned}$$

➢ But beware: if the factors of an equation are ALREADY set equal to ZERO, it is a MISTAKE to "FOIL" it.

• Take the equation $(x + 2)(x + 3) = 0$. "FOILing" it creates the quadratic $x^2 + 5x + 6 = 0$. To solve this quadratic, we would have to factor it as $(x + 2)(x + 3) = 0$, leaving us back where we started!

• To solve $(x + 2)(x + 3) = 0$, we only need to set each factor equal to zero. Such an equation is simply a quadratic that had already been factored.

➢ Consider the following:

If $\left(\dfrac{2}{3}n - 4\right)\left(\dfrac{1}{2}n + 3\right) = 0$, then the least possible value of n equals

(A) −8 **(B)** −6 **(C)** −4 **(D)** −3 **(E)** −2

Answer: B. Although we might be tempted to "FOIL" this equation, doing so would be a mistake. Not only would we **waste our time** creating a monstrous quadratic, but that quadratic would also be extremely difficult to factor.

➢ Further, **the factors of this equation are already set equal to zero**. To solve for n, we only need to set each factor equal to zero:

$$\begin{aligned} \tfrac{2}{3}n - 4 &= 0 \\ \tfrac{2}{3}n &= 4 \\ n &= 4 \times \tfrac{3}{2} = 6 \end{aligned} \qquad\qquad \begin{aligned} \tfrac{1}{2}n + 3 &= 0 \\ \tfrac{1}{2}n &= -3 \\ n &= -3 \times \tfrac{2}{1} = -6 \end{aligned}$$

• If n can equal 6 or −6, the least possible value of n is −6. Thus, (B) is the correct answer.

(12) The "FOIL" Identities – There are three special equations that will henceforth be referred to as the "FOIL" identities.

• These identities are extremely IMPORTANT. Not only are they frequently tested by the GRE, but exam-makers also design problems that cannot be solved without them.

SIMPLE	"FOILED"
$(x + y)^2$	$x^2 + 2xy + y^2$
$(x - y)^2$	$x^2 - 2xy + y^2$
$(x + y)(x - y)$	$x^2 - y^2$

• You may recognize the last equation from our chapter on Exponents and Roots: it's the **difference between squares**.

➢ To solve problems that involve the "FOIL" identities, you will first need to MEMORIZE the equations in BOTH their forms.

• Simply put, there are problems that cannot be solved if you do not know that $(x + y)^2 = x^2 + 2xy + y^2$ or that $x^2 + 2xy + y^2 = (x + y)^2$.

You will also need to REWRITE each equation in its OPPOSITE form.

• For example, the opposite form of $(x + y)^2$ is $x^2 + 2xy + y^2$. Conversely, the opposite form of $x^2 - 2xy + y^2$ is of $(x - y)^2$. Putting these equations in their opposite form is the KEY to solving almost ANY problem that involves them. Consider the following:

If $r^2 - 2rs + s^2 = 4$, then $(r - s)^4 = ?$

(A) 2 (B) 8 (C) 16 (D) 32 (E) 64

Answer. C. Since $r^2 - 2rs + s^2$ is one of the "FOIL" identities, we'll need to rewrite it in its opposite form to solve the question.

➢ The OPPOSITE form of $r^2 - 2rs + s^2$ is $(r - s)^2$, so we can rewrite the initial equation, like so:

$$r^2 - 2rs + s^2 = 4 \quad \rightarrow \quad (r - s)^2 = 4$$

• We can simplify $(r - s)^2 = 4$ by taking the square root of both sides of the equation. An even exponent typically has two solutions, so doing so proves that $r - s = 2$ **and** -2. If we plug this information into $(r - s)^4$, we get 16, since $(2)^4$ and $(-2)^4$ both equal 16.

➢ To solve more DIFFICULT examples, you may need to recognize these identities in a variety of "hidden" or "scrambled" forms.

• While it would be impossible to compile an exhaustive list, you should be prepared to recognize examples such as:

HIDDEN	FACTORED
$x^2 - 1$	$(x+1)(x-1)$
$x^4 - y^4$	$(x^2 + y^2)(x^2 - y^2)$
$x^2 - 4x + 4$	$(x-2)^2$
$x^2 + y^2 = -2xy + 16$	$x^2 + 2xy + y^2 = 16 \rightarrow (x+y)^2 = 16$

• Consider the following:

$$x^4 - y^4 = 10$$
$$x^2 + y^2 = 2$$

Quantity A	**Quantity B**
$x^2 - y^2$	5

Answer. C. The opposite form of $x^4 - y^4$ is $(x^2 + y^2)(x^2 - y^2)$. Therefore, we can rewrite the statement $x^4 - y^4 = 10$ as $(x^2 + y^2)(x^2 - y^2) = 10$.

➢ If $x^2 + y^2 = 2$, then $x^2 - y^2$ must equal 5, since we can substitute this information into the factored equation as follows:

$(x^2 + y^2)(x^2 - y^2) = 10$ The factored equation.

$2(x^2 - y^2) = 10$ Since $x^2 + y^2 = 2$, plug in 2 for $x^2 + y^2$.

$(x^2 - y^2) = 5$ Divide both sides by 2.

• Thus, the two quantities are equal, so the correct answer is (C).

(13) "Plug-Ins" – You now know the concepts of Algebra tested by the GRE. To excel at GRE Algebra, however, there's still something more that you need to know.

• Quite frequently, Quantitative Comparison questions ask test-takers to COMPARE algebraic EXPRESSIONS.

> ➢ In fact, of all the Algebra concepts tested by the GRE, none is tested more FREQUENTLY than the comparison of expressions.

• We call such questions "Plug-Ins". As you may recall, an expression differs from an equation in that an equation has an equal sign, whereas an expression does not:

EQUATION   EXPRESSION   No equal sign

$2x - 3 = 5$ $4x + 2$ ◄

• Unlike equations, in which we can solve for a particular variable, **expressions are dependent on the values that we PLUG into them**. For example, the expression $4x + 2$ has a different value when we plug in $x = 3$ than it does when we plug in $x = 7$.

> ➢ There are two ways to solve "Plug-Ins": you can either PLUG IN numbers or MANIPULATE the Algebra.

• In general, plugging in numbers is the **easier** approach. This is especially true if you don't like math. Manipulating the Algebra is **more difficult but can be faster**. If you like math, you'll probably prefer this strategy.

• Whichever approach you prefer, bear in mind that some problems work better with one strategy, and some with the other.

> ➢ In some cases, a combination of the two strategies may prove the fastest of all. **So, do your best to learn both**.

• Before examining either approach, however, let's first address the most important question of all: **how do you know that you have a "Plug-In" problem?**

• In essence, a "Plug-In" problem compares EXPRESSIONS that can have LIMITLESS, or nearly limitless, values. For example, the question at the top of the next page would be considered a "Plug-In", since x and y can equal ANY VALUES whose difference is greater than zero.

- This is a "Plug-In" question:

$$x - y > 0$$

Quantity A	**Quantity B**
$2x + 3y$	$x + 4y$

> ➢ However, if an expression can only have ONE or two SPECIFIC values, the problem is not a "Plug-In".

- Thus, the question below is not a "Plug-In", since we can combine the initial equations to SOLVE for $x + 2y$:

$$2x + 3y = 8$$
$$x - y = 4$$

Quantity A	**Quantity B**
$3x + 2y$	4

> ➢ As mentioned, in many instances, the easiest way to solve "Plug-Ins" is to plug in numbers.

- When plugging, your goal is ALWAYS as follows:

To PROVE an INCONSISTENT relationship between the two quantities.

- If one set of numbers makes A larger, and another set makes B larger, your answer will always be (D): the relationship cannot be determined from the given information.

> ➢ To plug PROPERLY, you should ALWAYS test at least <u>THREE</u> numbers, unless you are able to determine (D) with fewer tries.

- If you plug at least 3 different numbers and the same expression is larger each time, you can generally assume that particular expression is always larger.

- The numbers you plug, however, MUST be as DIFFERENT as possible to assure that you are not missing something. If you plug 3 similar numbers you may not discover less obvious relationships than only EXTREME numbers can identify.

> ➤ To start, it's usually best to look for a number that might MAKE the two quantities EQUAL. In many cases, 1 or 0 is a great first choice.

• Your next choices should then try to make the quantities dissimilar or to REVERSE the relationship established with your first plug.

• In general, we recommend that you $\boxed{\textbf{always test 1, 0, and –1}}$. Not only are these numbers easy to work with, but they often reveal special or unexpected results. To get a sense of what we mean by all this, let's work through a sample problem together:

Quantity A	**Quantity B**
$\lvert r + s \rvert$	$\lvert r \rvert + \lvert s \rvert$

Answer. D. Depending on the values of r and s, these expressions can have a nearly unlimited number of values, so this is a "Plug-In" problem.

> ➤ To solve it, let's **first let $r = 1$ and $s = 1$**. Doing so proves the two quantities can be equal, since:

Quantity A	Quantity B
$\lvert 1 + 1 \rvert = \lvert 2 \rvert = 2$	$\lvert 1 \rvert + \lvert 1 \rvert = 1 + 1 = 2$

• Next, let's **try to disprove this relationship** by testing 0 and –1.

• Remember, 1, 0, and –1 always great numbers to test, since they're easy to work with and often reveal unexpected results!

> ➤ Choosing DIFFERENT COMBINATIONS of 1, 0, –1 is a smart tactic when choosing TWO variables, since these numbers often combine in unexpected ways.

• If we choose 1 and 0, the two quantities remain equal. But if we choose 1 and –1, we get:

Quantity A	Quantity B
$\lvert 1 + (-1) \rvert = \lvert 0 \rvert = 0$	$\lvert 1 \rvert + \lvert -1 \rvert = 1 + 1 = 2$

• Thus, **the answer is (D) since the quantities have an inconsistent relationship**: depending on the values we choose, they can either be equal or one can be larger than the other.

➤ If your problem restricts the use of 1, 0, or –1, consider EXTREME values such as values BETWEEN –1 and 1 or very LARGE or SMALL numbers.

• Like 1, 0, and –1, values between –1 and 1 have special properties that often reveal unexpected results. Consider the following:

$x > 0$ and cannot equal 1

Quantity A	**Quantity B**
$\sqrt{x}$	x^2

Answer. D. According to the restriction at the top of the problem, x can't equal 1, 0, or –1, so let's **first let $x = 4$, since 4 is easy to test here**. If $x = 4$, B is greater than A, since:

Quantity A	Quantity B
$\sqrt{4} = 2$	$4^2 = 16$

➤ Next, let's try to disprove this relationship. Since we can't use 0 or negative numbers, let's next try a value between 0 and 1.

• As you may recall, **values between 0 and 1 do the opposite of normal numbers**: they get BIGGER when you take their square root and get SMALLER when you square them.

• Thus, if x is a value between 0 and 1 (e.g. 0.5), Quantity A will increase in value and Quantity B will decrease in value, proving that the correct answer is (D), since A can be greater than B and B can be greater than A:

Quantity A	Quantity B
$\sqrt{0.5} \approx 0.7$	$(0.5)^2 = 0.25$

➤ If you can't choose 1, 0, and –1, or fractions between 1 and –1, be sure to test numbers that are EASY to work with but that DIFFER in some fashion.

• For example, you might consider choosing a positive number and a negative number (–2 vs. 2), a small number and a large number (2 vs. 10), or an odd number and an even number (2 vs. 3).

• If your problem restricts a variable to a range of values, such as $3 \leq x \leq 8$, you should test numbers at the ENDS of that range (3 vs. 8). In DIFFICULT problems, you may need to test numbers that are microscopically different (1.01 vs. 0.99).

➢ Finally, BEFORE you plug, remember to REMOVE any terms SHARED by the two expressions. Doing so will make plugging much easier and faster.

• Consider the following:

$$xy \neq 0$$

Quantity A	**Quantity B**
$x^2 + 2xy + y^2$	$x^2 + y^2$

• To solve this "Plug-In", let's first remove x^2 and y^2 from both expressions, as these terms are common to both quantities. Doing so leaves us with:

Quantity A	Quantity B
$2xy$	0

➢ Since we always want to try the special numbers 1, 0, and –1 whenever possible, let's next plug $x = 1$ and $y = 1$ into both expressions.

• As you can see, doing so gives Quantity A a value of 2. There are no variables in Quantity B, so Quantity B remains 0. Thus, A can be greater than B:

Quantity A	Quantity B
$2(1)(1) = 2$	0

• Now let's **try to disprove this relationship**. Remember, choosing DIFFERENT combinations of 1, 0, –1 is a smart tactic when choosing TWO variables, since these numbers often combine in odd and surprising ways.

➢ According to the problem, we can't choose 0 for either x or y because $xy \neq 0$. We can, however, let $x = 1$ and $y = -1$.

• Doing so proves that B can be greater than A, since:

Quantity A	Quantity B
$2(1)(-1) = -2$	0

• Since A can be greater than B and B can be greater than A, the quantities have an inconsistent relationship. Therefore, the correct answer is (D).

(14) Manipulating "Plug-Ins" – As mentioned in the preceding section, many "Plug–In" problems can also be solved by manipulating their Algebra.

• On the whole, this approach is more DIFFICULT than plugging in numbers, but can often be FASTER. So if you don't like math, you're probably better off plugging in numbers. If you like math, however, you may prefer this strategy.

➢ Whichever approach you prefer, bear in mind that some problems work better with one strategy and some with the other.

• And in some cases, a combination of the two strategies is the fastest of all. **So, do your best to learn both**. And remember: if one approach is giving you problems, be prepared to try the other.

• As a general rule, the manipulation approach becomes more effective as the Algebra becomes MORE COMPLEX. There are two reasons for this:

1. Plugging in numbers is usually **time-consuming** when expressions have multiple parts.

2. Exam-makers often **disguise simple relationships** by putting them in arrangements that appear complicated or confusing.

• Imagine a question like the following:

$$x > 1$$

Quantity A

$$\frac{x(x+1)+x+1}{(x+1)^2}$$

Quantity B

$$1$$

➢ Although you could attack this problem by plugging in values for x, doing so would be time consuming, since testing a number would require multiple substitutions.

• Worse still, you might need to test 3 or 4 numbers to determine a relationship between the quantities.

• As you may recall from our book on Arithmetic & "Plan B" Strategies, **exam-makers are never interested in your ability to perform a series of slow, tedious calculations**. They're interested in your ability to find smart, effective ways to solve questions that appear time consuming or difficult. This is particularly true of Quantitative Comparison questions and "Plug-Ins".

➢ As a rule of thumb, it's generally worthwhile to ask yourself whether it's possible to SIMPLIFY the Algebra in your "Plug-In" questions.

• **Quantitative Comparison questions are nothing more than UNSTATED inequalities**. "Is Quantity A greater than Quantity B?" That's just a wordy way of asking "is A > B?" And like any inequality, such questions can be simplified by doing the SAME thing to BOTH sides of the inequality. Or in this case, both QUANTITIES.

• When simplifying "Plug-In" questions, there are several things you can do to manipulate the Algebra. You can:

    1. ADD or SUBTRACT anything you want from both quantities.
    2. MULTIPLY or DIVIDE both quantities by a POSITIVE value.
    3. SQUARE or SQUARE ROOT both quantities, if they are POSITIVE.

➢ You CANNOT multiply or divide the quantities by NEGATIVE values, or square or take the square root negative quantities.

• Doing so would cause your "unstated inequality sign" to flip directions. To give you a sense of how this works, let's go back to the previous question:

$$x > 1$$

Quantity A	**Quantity B**
$\dfrac{x(x+1)+x+1}{(x+1)^2}$	1

Answer: C. According to the problem $x > 1$. Thus, we know that $(x + 1)^2$ is positive. Since $1 = \frac{1}{1}$, each quantity has a positive denominator, so cross-multiplication yields the following:

Quantity A	Quantity B
$x(x+1)+x+1$	$(x+1)^2$

➢ Quantity A can then be distributed, like so: $x(x + 1) + x + 1 \rightarrow x^2 + x + x + 1$. And if we add the $x + x$, we get:

Quantity A	Quantity B
$x^2 + 2x + 1$	$(x+1)^2$

• As you can see, Quantities A and B are opposite forms of the same "FOIL" identity: $(x + 1)^2 = x^2 + 2x + 1$. Thus, they are equal and the correct answer is (C).

➤ In other words, manipulating "Plug-Ins" is just like simplifying inequalities: do the same thing to both quantities and avoid multiplying or dividing by negative values.

• To give you some additional practice, here are two more examples for you:

$$s > r$$

Quantity A	**Quantity B**
$\dfrac{r + 3s}{2}$	$\dfrac{3r + 7s}{5}$

Answer. A. As with any inequality, you always want to **get rid of the denominators**. Since 2 and 5 are both positive numbers, we are free to cross-multiply the fractions, giving us:

Quantity A	Quantity B
$5(r + 3s) \rightarrow 5r + 15s$	$2(3r + 7s) \rightarrow 6r + 14s$

➤ Both quantities now contain at least 5r's and 14s's, so we can subtract 5r and 14s from each, leaving Quantity A with a single s and Quantity B with a single r:

Quantity A	Quantity B
$5r + 15s$	$6r + 14s$
$-5r - 14s$	$-5r - 14s$
s	r

• According to the problem, $s > r$. Since A = s and B = r, the correct answer has to be (A).

$$n > 1$$

Quantity A	**Quantity B**
$\dfrac{n^3}{3}$	$\dfrac{n^2}{2}$

Answer. D. To start, let's **cross-multiply** the fractions to get rid of their denominators. Doing so makes Quantity A = $2n^3$ and Quantity B = $3n^2$. Next, let's **divide** both sides by n^2. According to the problem $n > 1$, so we are free to do so, since n^2 must be positive:

Quantity A	Quantity B
$2n^3 \rightarrow \dfrac{2n^3}{n^2} \rightarrow 2n$	$3n^2 \rightarrow \dfrac{3n^2}{n^2} \rightarrow 3$

• Finally, we can **isolate n** by dividing both quantities by 2, making A = n and B = 3/2. According to the problem, $n > 1$. If $n = 2$, then A > B. However, if $n = 1.1$, then A < B. Thus, the correct answer is (D), since A can be greater than B and B can be greater than A.

Rare or Advanced Concepts

(15) Combining Inequalities – Like equations, inequalities can be combined.

• To do so, simply stack the inequalities atop one another. As long as their inequality signs point in the SAME direction, you can then ADD them.

➢ When combining inequalities, you do NOT need to eliminate variables, as you do when you combine equations.

• To combine inequalities, you only need to add them. In other words, if a problem gives you two (or more) inequalities:

(1) Stack them atop one another.
(2) Make sure their inequality signs point in the same direction.
(3) Add them.

• Consider the following:

$$x + y + z > 0 \ \text{ and } \ x + y + 1 < 0.$$

Quantity A	**Quantity B**
z	1

Answer. A. To solve this problem, we need to ADD the inequalities. Before we can do so, however, we need to STACK them atop one another and make sure their inequality signs point in the SAME direction.

➢ To start, let's flip the sign of the bottom inequality by multiplying it by –1:

$x + y + 1 < 0$	The given inequality.
$-x - y - 1 > 0$	Multiply by –1. Flip sign.

• Next, let's stack the inequalities and add them together, like this:

$$\begin{array}{c} \cancel{x} + \cancel{y} + z > 0 \\ \underline{-\cancel{x} - \cancel{y} - 1 > 0} \\ z - 1 > 0 \end{array}$$

• Finally, since $z - 1 > 0$, let's add 1 to both sides of the inequality to define z. Doing so gives us $z > 1$, proving that (A) is the correct answer.

➤ An INEQUALITY can also be combined with an EQUATION. It's rarely necessary to do so on the GRE, but there are problems in which it can prove helpful.

• Should you need to combine an equation and an inequality:

    (1) ISOLATE a variable that they share in common.
    (2) SUBSTITUTE the equation into the inequality.

• To get a sense of how this works, consider the following:

$$x < 4 \text{ and } 4y - 2x = 0$$

Quantity A	**Quantity B**
y	2

Answer: B. To solve this problem, we need to combine the equation and the inequality. To do so, we first need to **isolate** a variable that they share, which in this case is x:

The INEQUALITY	The EQUATION
$x < 4$	$4y - 2x = 0$
	$-2x = -4y$
	$x = 2y$

➤ Next, we need to plug the equation into the inequality:

$x < 4$	The given inequality.
$2y < 4$	**Substitute** $2y$ for x.
$y < 2$	Divide both sides by 2.

• Doing so reveals that Quantity B must be larger than Quantity A, since the statement $y < 2$ proves that y is less than 2.

(16) Advanced Shortcuts – There are four shortcuts that can save you a lot of time (and aggravation) with more difficult Algebra problems.

• None are particularly difficult to use. So if you are determined to attain an elite math score, we strongly encourage you to add them to your "bag of tricks".

➤ Shortcut #1: $\boxed{x-1 \text{ vs. } 1-x}$

• As is apparent, the expressions $x-1$ and $1-x$ are mirror images of one another. What may be less apparent, however, is that $1-x$ is simply $x-1$ "times -1":

$$-1(x-1) \;\rightarrow\; -x+1 \;\rightarrow\; 1-x$$

• In other words, expressions of the form $1-x$ can be factored as follows:

SIMPLE	FACTORED
$1-x$	$-(x-1)$
$3-n$	$-(n-3)$
$2-5y$	$-(5y-2)$

➤ Recognizing that expressions such as $2-4x$ can be factored as $-(4x-2)$ can mean the difference between a lot of time-consuming busy work and none at all.

• Consider the following:

Multiplying which of the following by the nonzero number $\dfrac{4-5n}{9}$ will give a product of -1?

(A) $\dfrac{9}{4-5n}$ (B) $\dfrac{-9}{5n-4}$ (C) $\dfrac{9}{5n-4}$ (D) $\dfrac{5n-4}{9}$ (E) $9(5n-4)$

Answer: C. Although there are many ways to solve this question, the fastest is to recognize that $5n-4$ can be factored as $-(4-5n)$. Thus, (C) is the correct answer, since:

$$\frac{4-5n}{\cancel{9}}\cdot\frac{\cancel{9}}{5n-4} \;\rightarrow\; \frac{\cancel{4-5n}}{-(\cancel{4-5n})} \;\rightarrow\; \frac{1}{-1}=-1$$

➤ Shortcut #2: **Multiplying Equations**

• Earlier, we saw that equations can be combined through substitution and elimination. They can also be combined through MULTIPLICATION.

• Although the opportunity to do so is not particularly common, multiplying equations can save you a lot of time when the chance does arise. Consider the following:

If $abc \neq 0$ and if $r = \dfrac{ac}{b}$ and $s = \dfrac{ab}{c}$, then $\dfrac{1}{rs} =$

(A) $\dfrac{a}{c}$ **(B)** $\dfrac{a}{b}$ **(C)** abc **(D)** a^2 **(E)** $\dfrac{1}{a^2}$

Answer. E. If $r = \dfrac{ac}{b}$ and $s = \dfrac{ab}{c}$, then $rs = a^2$, since:

$$r \times s = \dfrac{ac}{b} \times \dfrac{ab}{c} = \dfrac{a^2 \, \cancel{bc}}{\cancel{bc}} = a^2$$

• And if $rs = a^2$, then $\dfrac{1}{rs} = \dfrac{1}{a^2}$, since we can flip both terms. Thus, the correct answer is (E).

➤ Shortcut #3: **The "Something" Shortcut**

• There are several ways to solve the equation $6 - \dfrac{x}{5} = 4$.

• One way that rarely occurs to most test-takers is to realize that the statement $6 - \boxed{\dfrac{x}{5}} = 4$ indicates that "6 minus SOMETHING equals 4".

➤ Since that "something" must equal 2, we therefore know that $\dfrac{x}{5} = 2$ and, thus, that $x = 10$.

• The "Something" Shortcut is particularly effective for solving complicated equations that seem to require a lot of busy work. Consider the following:

If $\dfrac{8a}{6 - \dfrac{2b}{3c}} = 2a,$ then which of the following is true?

(A) $3b = 2c$ **(B)** $2b = c$ **(C)** $b = 3c$ **(D)** $6b = c$ **(E)** $b = 6c$

Answer. C. According to the equation above, "8a divided by SOMETHING equals 2a." Since that "something" must be 4, we therefore know that $6 - \dfrac{2b}{3c} = 4$.

• From the statement $6 - \boxed{\dfrac{2b}{3c}} = 4$, we know that "6 minus SOMETHING equals 4". Since that something must be 2, we also know that $\dfrac{2b}{3c} = 2$. Thus, the correct answer is (C), as:

$$\dfrac{2b}{3c} = 2 \;\rightarrow\; 2b = 6c \;\rightarrow\; b = 3c$$

> Shortcut #4: **Avoiding Quadratics**

• Plugging an equation containing ADDITION or SUBTRACTION into an equation containing MULTIPLICATION will produce a quadratic equation — if those equations have the SAME two variables.

• To solve problems with two such equations, it is considerably faster to "avoid the quadratic".

> Avoiding the quadratic is easy: FIND two numbers that MULTIPLY to your product but ADD to your sum.

• Those numbers will be your solutions. Consider the following:

$$x + y = 6 \text{ and } xy = -7$$

Quantity A	**Quantity B**
$(x-y)^2$	64

Answer: C. To solve this question, we need to find two numbers that multiply to –7 but add to 6.

• Since the numbers that multiply to –7 are $7 \times (-1)$ and $1 \times (-7)$, x and y must equal 7 and –1, because only 7 and –1 add to 6.

> Although we don't know whether $x = 7$ and $y = -1$ or $x = -1$ and $y = 7$, the same would be true if we combined the equations and factored the resulting quadratic.

• The correct answer here must be (C), since either combination of x and y results in a product of 64:

$$(x-y)^2 = (7-(-1))^2 = 8^2 = 64 \qquad (x-y)^2 = (-1-7)^2 = (-8)^2 = 64$$

> To ensure that you've got the hang of it, let's take a look at one more practice problem.

• As with the first question, note that you cannot identify which solution belongs to which variable but that the same is true if you combine the equations and factor the resulting quadratic.

• Consider the following:

If $v + w = 8$ and $vw = 12$, which of the following are possible values of w?

Indicate <u>all</u> such values.

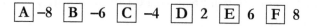

Answer: $\boxed{\text{D}}$ and $\boxed{\text{E}}$. There are two ways to solve this problem. **The slow way** is to combine the equations and to solve the resulting quadratic.

- To do so, first isolate v. Then plug $v = 8 - w$ into $vw = 12$ as follows:

$(8 - w)w = 12$	Substitute $8 - w$ for v.
$8w - w^2 = 12$	Distribute.
$0 = w^2 - 8w + 12$	Set the quadratic equal to zero.
$0 = (w - 6)(w - 2)$	Factor.

➤ Thus, the correct answer is $\boxed{\text{D}}$ and $\boxed{\text{E}}$, since setting each factor equal to zero proves that w can equal 6 or 2:

$$w - 6 = 0 \qquad\qquad w - 2 = 0$$
$$w = 6 \qquad\qquad\qquad w = 2$$

- The **fast way** is to avoid the quadratic. To sidestep the work above, we simply need to identify two numbers that multiply to 12 but add to 8.

- Although there are several sets of numbers that multiply to 12, the only set that adds to 8 is 6 and 2. Thus, w can equal 6 or 2.

(17) Maximization Problems – Every now and then, exam-makers design problems asking test-takers to identify the **greatest or smallest value** for a particular variable or expression.

- We call such problems "maximization" problems.

  ➢ To solve them, first identify the GREATEST and SMALLEST values that are possible for each input.

- Then test out EVERY combination of those inputs. Consider the following:

If −4 ≤ x ≤ 8 and −6 ≤ y ≤ 2, what is the greatest possible value for x − y?

(A) −2 (B) 6 (C) 8 (D) 14 (E) 16

Answer. D. To determine the greatest possible value of x − y, first identify the greatest and smallest possible values of x and y:

$$x = 8 \text{ and } -4 \qquad\qquad y = 2 \text{ and } -6$$

Then determine all the possible combinations of x − y:

(i) 8 − 2 = 6   (ii) 8 − (−6) = 14   (iii) (−4) − 2 = −6   (iv) (−4) − (−6) = 2

Since scenario (ii) produces the largest output, the greatest possible value of x − y is therefore 14.

  ➢ To ensure that you've got the hang of it, let's work through one more example together. Consider the following:

$$-5 \le p \le 4 \text{ and } -9 \le q \le 11$$

Quantity A	**Quantity B**
The greatest possible value of *pq*	44

Answer. A. To determine the greatest possible value of *pq*, first identify the greatest and smallest possible values of p and q:

$$p = 4 \text{ and } -5 \qquad\qquad q = 11 \text{ and } -9$$

Then determine all the possible combinations of *pq*:

(i) 4(11) = 44   (ii) 4(−9) = −36   (iii) −5(11) = −55   (iv) −5(−9) = 45

Since 45 is greater than −55, −36, and 44, the greatest possible value of *pq* is 45. Thus, Quantity A is greater than Quantity B.

(18) Integer Constraints – Given one equation with two or more variables, it is usually impossible to solve for those variables.

• Take the equation $2a + 3b = 5$. It is impossible to determine the values of a and b, since a and b can equal any two fractions or decimals that satisfy $2a + 3b = 5$.

> ➢ If, however, those variables MUST be INTEGERS, it MAY be possible to solve for them.

• To do so, you'll need to know the ⎡**Addition or Subtraction Multiple Rule**⎤. In short, this rule states:

> **If two terms in an equation are multiples of M, then the remaining term in that equation must also be a multiple of M.**

• Take the equation $49 - x = 14$. Since 49 and 14 are both multiples of 7, x must also be a multiple of 7. Likewise, if $x + 18 = 42$, x must be a multiple of 2, 3, and 6, since 18 and 42 are also multiples of 2, 3, and 6.

• To understand how this might help you solve an equation with an integer constraint, consider the following:

> **If a and b are positive integers, and $5a + 7b = 63$, then $a + b =$**
>
> **(A) 10   (B) 11   (C) 12   (D) 13   (E) 14**

Answer: B. Since a and b must be positive integers, this equation has an integer constraint: its variables must be integers. To solve it, notice that $7b$ and 63 are both multiples of 7. This means that $5a$ must also be a multiple of 7.

Positive multiples of 7 include 7, 14, 21, 28, etc. If a were to equal 7, b would equal 4, since:

$$5(7) + 7b = 63 \ \rightarrow \ 7b = 28 \ \rightarrow \ b = 4$$

However, if a were to equal a larger multiple of 7, such as 14, b would be negative:

$$5(14) + 7b = 63 \ \rightarrow \ 7b = -7 \ \rightarrow \ b = -1$$

According to the problem, a and b must be positive integers. When $a = 7$, $b = 4$, but when $a = 14$ or larger, b is negative. Thus, a can only be 7, meaning that b must equal 4. As such, the correct answer is (B), since $7 + 4 = 11$.

(19) Absolute Value Graphs – On extremely rare occasions, GRE questions will require test-takers to translate a number line into an equation or inequality involving absolute value.

• Such questions can be easily solved with the following FORMULA, in which the midpoint represents the average of the two endpoints:

$$|x - \text{Midpoint}| \leq \text{Distance From Endpoints to Midpoint}$$

• To get a sense of how this works, consider the following:

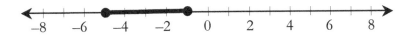

Which of the following inequalities represents the number line above?

(A) $|x| \leq -1$ (B) $|x| \geq -5$ (C) $|x - 3| \geq 2$ (D) $|x + 3| \leq 2$ (E) $|x - 1| \leq 4$

Answer. D. According to the graph, the shaded line ends at –5 and –1 and has a midpoint of –3, since the average of –5 and –1 is –3. The distance from the endpoints to the midpoint is less than or equal to 2, since every point on the shaded line is **no more than 2 spaces from the midpoint**.

Thus, the algebraic expression for the shaded portion of the number line is $|x - (-3)| \leq 2$, or $|x + 3| \leq 2$, since the graph has a midpoint of –3 and the distance from the midpoint to every point on the shaded line is 2 spaces or less.

A certain board game has been designed for children between the ages of 8 and 16. Which of the following inequalities can be used to determine whether a child's age is suitable for this game?

(A) $|a| < 16$ (B) $|a - 4| < 12$ (C) $|a - 8| < 8$ (D) $|a - 12| < 4$ (E) $|a - 16| < 0$

Answer. D. According to the question, the game has been designed for children between the ages of 8 and 16. On a number line, this information would be graphed as follows:

Since the **midpoint of this graph is 12**, and every point on the graph is **less than 4 spaces** from the midpoint, the algebraic expression for the shaded portion of the number line is $|x - 12| < 4$.

Chapter 5: Algebra

Drills

(20) Drills – The following drills have been broken down into three levels: fundamental, intermediate, and tricky.

• For each equation or inequality, solve for the variables involved (if possible). For each expression, simplify as much as possible. Solutions can be found on the following pages.

Fundamental

1. $4(x+1) = 5x - 1$

2. $\dfrac{x+3}{2} + x = 9$

3. $-5x + \dfrac{1}{3} > 2$

4. $-9 \le -4x + 3 \le 7$

5. $\dfrac{5}{4-x} = \dfrac{3}{4+x}$

6. $\sqrt[3]{x+3} - 4 = -2$

7. $6(x-5)^2 + 7 = 31$

8. $x^2 - 7x + 12 = 0$

Intermediate

9. $3x + 4y = 12$
    $2x - 4y = 8$

10. $\dfrac{2x - (4 - 4x)}{x + 3} = -5$

11. $-x^2 + 18 = -3x$

12. $x + 4y = 10$ and $x + 2y = 4$

13. $|2x - 3| = 11$

14. $(x+3)(x-8) = 0$

15. $|x + 5| > 11$

16. $x^2 - 2xy + y^2 = 9$, so $x - y =$

Tricky

17. $4x - [y - (2x - 8y)] =$

18. $2x^2 = x$

19. $\dfrac{x-3}{2} - \dfrac{x-2}{3} = x$

20. $\dfrac{x^2 + 8x + 16}{x^2 - 16} =$

21. $\dfrac{5-x}{x-5} =$

22. $3x + y > 10$ and $5 > 2x + y$

Solutions

---

1. When solving equations, it is usually in your best interest to factor expressions that can be factored, and to distribute expressions that can be distributed:

$4(x+1) = 5x - 1$	The given equation.
$4x + 4 = 5x - 1$	Distribute $4(x + 1)$.
$5 = x$	Subtract $4x$ from both sides. Add 1 to both sides.

2. To solve an equation with a denominator, use the "denominator trick". **Immediately** put parentheses around the equation and multiply each term in the equation by the denominator you wish to remove. Thus:

$$2\left(\frac{x+3}{2} + x = 9\right) \;\rightarrow\; \cancel{2}\left(\frac{x+3}{\cancel{2}}\right) + 2(x) = 2(9) \;\rightarrow\; x + 3 + 2x = 18$$

$3x = 15$	Add $x + 2x$. Subtract 3 from both sides.
$x = 5$	Divide both sides by 3.

3. The "denominator trick" also works for inequalities. Remember to **flip the direction of the inequality sign** if you multiply or divide the inequality by a **negative** value:

$$3\left(-5x + \frac{1}{3} > 2\right) \;\rightarrow\; 3(-5x) + \cancel{3}\left(\frac{1}{\cancel{3}}\right) > 3(2) \;\rightarrow\; -15x + 1 > 6$$

$-15x > 5$	Subtract 1 from both sides.
$x < -\frac{5}{15} \;\rightarrow\; x < -\frac{1}{3}$	Divide both sides by -15. FLIP the sign. Reduce.

4. To solve a compound inequality ("three-part inequality"), isolate the variable in the middle by doing **the same thing to every side** of the inequality:

$-9 \le -4x + 3 \le 7$	The given inequality.
$-12 \le -4x \le 4$	Subtract 3 from every side.
$3 \ge x \ge -1$	Divide every side by -4. Flip BOTH signs.

5. When **a fraction equals a fraction**, you can cross-multiply to solve:

$$\frac{5}{4-x} = \frac{3}{4+x} \;\rightarrow\; 5(4+x) = 3(4-x) \;\rightarrow\; 20 + 5x = 12 - 3x$$

$8x = -8$	Add $3x$ to both sides. Subtract 20 from both sides.
$x = -1$	Divide both sides by 8.

6. To solve an equation with a cube root, first **isolate the root.** Then **cube both sides.** The exponent will cancel out the root:

$$\sqrt[3]{x+3}-4=-2 \qquad \text{The given equation.}$$
$$\sqrt[3]{x+3}=2 \qquad \text{Add 4 to both sides.}$$
$$x+3=8 \qquad \text{CUBE both sides.}$$
$$x=5 \qquad \text{Subtract 3 from both sides.}$$

7. To solve an equation with an exponent, first isolate the exponent then "root" both sides. The root will cancel out the exponent. But remember, **an even exponent typically has two solutions:** one positive, one negative.

$$6(x-5)^2+7=31 \qquad \text{The given equation.}$$
$$6(x-5)^2=24 \qquad \text{Subtract 7 from both sides.}$$
$$(x-5)^2=4 \qquad \text{Divide both sides by 6.}$$
$$x-5=2,-2 \qquad \text{SQUARE ROOT both sides.}$$

If $x-5=2$ and $x-5=-2$, then $x=7$ or 3.

8. An equation with **a variable to the second power (e.g. x^2) and the first power (e.g. x)** is a quadratic equation. To solve quadratics, set them equal to zero and factor:

$$x^2-7x+12=0 \;\rightarrow\; (x-4)(x-3)=0$$

Be sure to **set each factor equal to zero** to determine the solutions ("roots") of the equation. Here, the solutions are $x=4$ and 3, since the factors are $x-4$ and $x-3$.

9. Equations can be combined through substitution or elimination. In general, **elimination is the faster strategy**, especially if one variable cancels upon addition or subtraction. Adding these equations gives us:

$$3x+4y=12$$
$$2x-4y=8$$
$$5x=20 \;\rightarrow\; x=4$$

To solve for y, plug $x=4$ into either of the original equations. Thus, $y=0$, since:

$$3x+4y=12 \;\rightarrow\; 3(4)+4y=12 \;\rightarrow\; 4y=0 \;\rightarrow\; y=0$$

10. The "denominator trick" gives us:

$$(x+3)\left(\frac{2x-(4-4x)}{x+3}=-5\right) \rightarrow \cancel{(x+3)}\left(\frac{2x-(4-4x)}{\cancel{x+3}}\right)=(x+3)(-5)$$

When distributing, be sure to **distribute to every term** within your parentheses:

$$2x-(4-4x)=(x+3)(-5) \rightarrow 2x-4+4x=x(-5)+3(-5)$$

$2x-4+4x=-5x-15$	Multiply $x(-5)$ and $3(-5)$.
$6x-4=-5x-15$	Add $2x + 4x$.
$11x-4=-15$	Add $5x$ to both sides.
$11x=-11$	Add 4 to both sides.
$x=-1$	Divide both sides by 11.

11. When solving quadratics, **make sure the "x^2 term" is positive** before factoring:

$$-x^2+18=-3x \rightarrow 0=x^2-3x-18 \rightarrow \overbrace{(x-6)(x+3)}^{\text{add to }-3}=0$$
$$\underbrace{}_{\text{multiply to }-18}$$

The solutions are $x = 6$ and -3, since the factors are $x - 6$ and $x + 3$.

12. If we **subtract** the equations, we get:

$$\begin{array}{r} x+4y=10 \\ \underline{x+2y=4} \\ 2y=6 \rightarrow y=3 \end{array}$$

Plugging $y = 3$ into either of the original equations proves that $x = -2$:

$$x + 2y = 4 \rightarrow x + 2(3) = 4 \rightarrow x = -2$$

13. To solve an equation with absolute value brackets, first isolate the brackets. Then drop the brackets and place $\pm$, the "plus/minus" symbol, in front of the Algebra, as follows:

$$\left|\text{Algebra}\right| = \text{Answer} \rightarrow \pm(\text{Algebra}) = \text{Answer}$$

Doing so here gives us: $\left|2x-3\right|=11 \rightarrow \pm(2x-3)=11$. Then solve both equations:

$2x-3=11$	$-(2x-3)=11$
$2x=14$	$2x-3=-11$
$x=7$	$2x=-8 \rightarrow x=-4$

14. If the factors of an equation **are already set equal to zero**, it is a mistake to "FOIL" the equation. To solve $(x + 3)(x - 8) = 0$, we only need to set each factor equal to zero:

$$x + 3 = 0 \qquad\qquad x - 8 = 0$$
$$x = -3 \qquad\qquad x = 8$$

15. Solving an inequality with absolute value brackets is just like solving an equation with absolute value brackets:

$$|x + 5| > 11 \quad \rightarrow \quad \pm(x + 5) > 11$$

Here, x can be any value greater than 6 or less than −16, since:

$$x + 5 > 11 \qquad\qquad -(x + 5) > 11$$
$$x > 6 \qquad\qquad x + 5 < -11 \text{ (multiply by } -1)$$
$$\qquad\qquad\qquad x < -16$$

16. Be sure to memorize the "FOIL" identities. And when you see one, **always put it in its opposite form**. Since $x^2 - 2xy + y^2 = (x - y)^2$, doing so here gives us:

$$x^2 - 2xy + y^2 = 9 \quad \rightarrow \quad (x - y)^2 = 9 \quad \rightarrow \quad x - y = 3, -3$$

17. When working with parentheses within brackets, be sure to **solve the parentheses first**. And be careful with the distribution. Make sure you distribute the negative signs to everything within the parentheses or brackets:

$4x - [y - (2x - 8y)]$	The given expression.
$4x - [y - 2x + 8y]$	Distribute the negative sign to $2x$ and $-8y$.
$4x - [9y - 2x]$	Add $y + 8y$.
$4x - 9y + 2x$	Distribute the negative sign to $9y$ and $-2x$.
$6x - 9y$	Add $4x + 2x$.

18. An equation with **a variable to the second power and the first power** is a quadratic equation. To solve quadratics, set them equal to zero and factor:

$$2x^2 = x \quad \rightarrow \quad 2x^2 - x = 0 \quad \rightarrow \quad x(2x - 1) = 0$$

Be sure to set each factor equal to zero to determine the solutions ("roots") of the equation. Here, the solutions are $x = 0$ and $1/2$, since the factors are 0 and $2x - 1$.

19. To solve an equation with two denominators, **multiply the equation by the lowest common denominator:**

$$6\left(\frac{x-3}{2} - \frac{x-2}{3} = x\right) \rightarrow {}^3\cancel{6}\left(\frac{x-3}{\cancel{2}}\right) - {}^2\cancel{6}\left(\frac{x-2}{\cancel{3}}\right) = 6(x)$$

Here, the initial distribution leads to a second round of distribution:

$$3(x-3) - 2(x-2) = 6(x) \rightarrow 3x - 9 - 2x + 4 = 6x$$

Finally, we can solve for x like so:

$x - 5 = 6x$	Subtract $3x - 2x$. Add $-9 + 4$.
$-5 = 5x$	Subtract x from both sides.
$-1 = x$	Divide both sides by 5.

20. Both of these expressions are "FOIL" identities. Since $x^2 + 8x + 16 = (x+4)^2$ and $x^2 - 16 = (x+4)(x-4)$, we can simplify this expression as follows:

$$\frac{x^2 + 8x + 16}{x^2 - 16} = \frac{(x+4)^2}{(x+4)(x-4)} = \frac{\cancel{(x+4)}(x+4)}{\cancel{(x+4)}(x-4)} = \frac{(x+4)}{(x-4)}$$

21. $5 - x$ can be factored as $-(x-5)$, so this expression equals -1:

$$\frac{5-x}{x-5} = \frac{-\cancel{(x-5)}}{\cancel{x-5}} = \frac{-1}{1} = -1$$

22. Like equations, inequalities can be combined. To do so, stack the inequalities atop one another. As long as their **inequality signs point in the same direction**, you can then **add** them. Doing so here gives us:

$$\begin{array}{c} 3x + y > 10 \\ 5 > 2x + y \\ \hline 3x + y + 5 > 10 + 2x + y \end{array}$$

Be sure to simplify the result:

$3x + y + 5 > 10 + 2x + y$	The sum of the inequalities.
$3x + 5 > 10 + 2x$	Subtract y from both sides.
$x + 5 > 10$	Subtract $2x$ from both sides.
$x > 5$	Subtract 5 from both sides.

Chapter 5: Algebra

Practice Questions

(21) Problem Sets – The following questions have been arranged into three groups: fundamental, intermediate, and rare or advanced.

• Whether you're aiming for a perfect score or a score closer to average, mastery of the concepts in the FUNDAMENTAL questions is absolutely essential.

➢ As you might expect, the INTERMEDIATE questions are more difficult but are essential for test-takers who need an above-average score or higher.

• Finally, the RARE or ADVANCED questions test concepts that are very sophisticated or seldom encountered on the GRE. Mastery of such questions is required only if you need a math score above the 90th percentile.

• As always, if you find yourself confused, bogged down with busy work, or stuck, don't be afraid to fall back on your "Plan B" strategies!

Fundamental

$$p \times 24 \times 26 \times 28 = 12 \times 13 \times 14$$

Quantity A	Quantity B

1. $\quad\quad\quad p \quad\quad\quad\quad\quad\quad\quad\quad 0.125$

$$xy + xz = 44 \text{ and } y + z = 11$$

Quantity A	Quantity B

2. $\quad\quad\quad x \quad\quad\quad\quad\quad\quad\quad\quad 3$

3. $3[4x - (2x - 5x)] - (2x + 5x) =$

   (A) $-16x$ (B) $-6x$ (C) 0 (D) $14x$ (E) $16x$

Quantity A	Quantity B

4. $\quad\quad\quad \dfrac{r}{2} \quad\quad\quad\quad\quad\quad\quad\quad \dfrac{r + s}{2}$

5. If $\frac{3}{n} + \frac{5}{4n} = \frac{1}{4}$, then $n =$

(A) 11   (B) 13   (C) 15   (D) 17   (E) 19

6. If $\frac{3x - 2}{4} = \frac{15}{12}$, then x equals

(A) $\frac{5}{3}$ (B) $\frac{7}{3}$ (C) 6   (D) $\frac{15}{4}$ (E) 9

7. If $0 < ab < 1$, then which of the following can be true?

(A) $a < -1$ and $b > 0$ (B) $a < -1$ and $b < -1$ (C) $a > -1$ and $b < -1$
(D) $a > 1$ and $b < -1$ (E) $a > 1$ and $b > 1$

8. If $(d - 1)^2 = 225$, which of the following could be the value of the $d - 4$?

(A) 14   (B) 16   (C) 18   (D) –16   (E) –18

$$a < b < c$$

Quantity A	Quantity B

9. $\dfrac{a + b + c}{3}$ b

10. If $4x - 3y = 3x - 2y$, what is y in terms of x?

(A) $\frac{x}{4}$ (B) $\frac{x}{3}$ (C) x (D) $3x$ (E) $4x$

Quantity A	Quantity B

11. $(x - 2)(x + 2)$ x^2

12. If $\dfrac{3}{2 + \frac{2}{z}} = 1$, then $z = ?$

(A) $\frac{1}{2}$ (B) $\frac{2}{3}$ (C) $\frac{3}{4}$ (D) $\frac{4}{3}$ (E) 2

13. If $p^2 - 4p + 3 < p^2 - 5p - 12$, which of the following are a possible value of p?

Indicate <u>all</u> such values.

$\boxed{A}$ 8 $\boxed{B}$ 4 $\boxed{C}$ −4 $\boxed{D}$ −8 $\boxed{E}$ −16

$$2 < m < 3$$
$$n = 8$$

Quantity A	Quantity B

14. $\dfrac{m}{n}$ — 0.35

$$x + y = 10$$
$$x - y = 6$$

Quantity A	Quantity B

15. x — y

16. If $3(p + q) = 7$, then, in terms of p, $q =$

(A) $\dfrac{7}{3} - p$ (B) $\dfrac{7}{3} + p$ (C) $7 - 3p$ (D) $7 - \dfrac{p}{3}$ (E) $\dfrac{7}{3} + \dfrac{p}{3}$

$$w^2 + 5w - 24 = 0$$

Quantity A	Quantity B

17. w^2 — 3

$$p \neq 0$$

Quantity A	Quantity B

18. $|p| + |-3|$ — $|p - 3|$

$$(x + 3)^3 < -27$$

Quantity A	Quantity B

19. x — -3

20. If $a - b = x$, then $a^2 - 2ab + b^2 =$

   (A) $2x$ (B) x^2 (C) $x(a - b)$ (D) $x^2 + 2b(x - a)$ (E) $x^2 + ax - a^2$

$$|-4| = -k$$

Quantity A	Quantity B
k	4

21.

$$0 < a < b < 1$$

Quantity A	Quantity B
ab	$a + b$

22.

23. If $x^2 - 2xy + y^2 = 4$, then $(x - y)^4 =$

   (A) 4   (B) 6   (C) 8   (D) 12   (E) 16

$$y = \frac{4x}{5}, \quad x = \frac{3z}{4}, \text{ and } z = 30$$

Quantity A	Quantity B
y	18

24.

$$(p + 4)(p - 4) = 0$$
$$(q + 4)(q - 4) = 0$$

Quantity A	Quantity B
$p + 4$	$q + 4$

25.

26.   Of the following, which could be the graph of $4 - 7x \geq \dfrac{3x + 5}{-2}$?

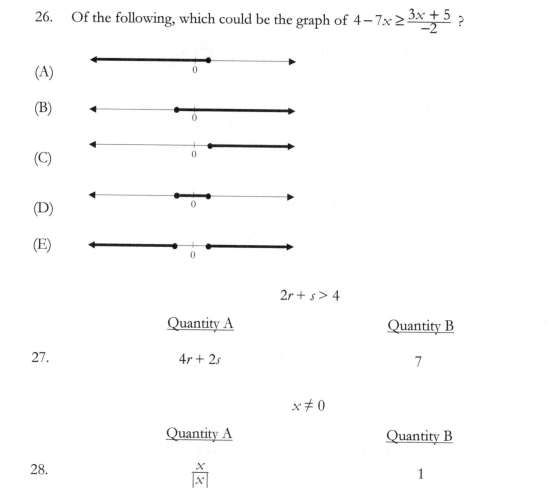

(A)

(B)

(C)

(D)

(E)

$$2r + s > 4$$

Quantity A	Quantity B
$4r + 2s$	7

27.

$$x \neq 0$$

Quantity A	Quantity B
$\dfrac{x}{|x|}$	1

28.

29.   If $|n - 5| > 8$, which of the following could be the value of n?

Indicate all such values.

A   –9   B   –6   C   –3   D   9   E   15

Intermediate

30.　$103^2 - 97^2 =$

(A) 36　(B) 120　(C) 360　(D) 1,200　(E) 3,600

31.　If $b = 4a$ and $c = 3b$, then in terms of a, $a + b + c =$

(A) $17a$　(B) $13a$　(C) $12a$　(D) $8a$　(E) $7a$

$$x^2 - 11x + 30 = 0$$

Quantity A	Quantity B
32.　Thrice the sum of the roots of the equation	11

$$pq \neq 0$$

Quantity A	Quantity B
33.　$(p + q)^2$	$p^2 + q^2$

34.　$\left(2 + \dfrac{1}{5}\right)^2 - \left(2 - \dfrac{4}{5}\right)^2 =$

(A) $1\dfrac{1}{5}$　(B) $2\dfrac{2}{5}$　(C) $2\dfrac{3}{5}$　(D) $3\dfrac{2}{5}$　(E) $4\dfrac{4}{5}$

35.　If $y - z = 7$, and $x + z = 18$, then $x + y =$

(A) 20　(B) 25　(C) 30　(D) 33　(E) 40

-8 is a solution for x in the equation $x^2 - px + 8 = 0$.

Quantity A	Quantity B
36.　p	10

$$x^2 + 2xy = 4 - y^2$$

Quantity A	Quantity B
$x + y$	2

37.

$$mn > 0$$

Quantity A	Quantity B
$\dfrac{2}{m} + \dfrac{5}{n}$	$\dfrac{2n}{m} + \dfrac{5m}{n}$

38.

39. If $t > 0$ and $t = \sqrt{\dfrac{x}{t}}$, what is t in terms of x?

(A) $\sqrt[3]{x}$ (B) $\sqrt{x}$ (C) x (D) x^2 (E) x^3

40. If $z\left(\dfrac{4w - 5}{7}\right) = z$ and $z \neq 0$, then w equals

(A) $\dfrac{1}{2}$ (B) $\dfrac{2}{3}$ (C) $\dfrac{3}{2}$ (D) 2   (E) 3

$$(x + 2)(x + 3) = 6$$

Quantity A	Quantity B
-2	x

41.

42. If $x + y = 20$, then $\left(x + \dfrac{y}{4}\right) + \left(y + \dfrac{x}{4}\right)$ equals

(A) 10   (B) 20   (C) 25   (D) 35   (E) 40

$$(x - 1)^3 = 8$$
$$(y - 1)^4 = 16$$

Quantity A	Quantity B
x	y

43.

$$\frac{k^2 + 2k + 1}{k + 1} = 5$$

Quantity A	Quantity B
44. k	4

45. If $\left(\frac{1}{5}x - 2\right)\left(\frac{2}{3}x + 4\right) = 0$, then x could equal

(A) –8   (B) –6   (C) 0   (D) 6   (E) 8

$$x > 1$$

Quantity A	Quantity B
46. $7x - 4$	$2x + 5$

47. If $w^3 + 8w^2 + 7w = 0$ and $w \geq 0$, what is the value of w?

(A) 0   (B) 1   (C) 7   (D) 8   (E) 10

$$6x = -x^2 - 9$$

Quantity A	Quantity B
48. The number of roots in the equation above	2

49. If p can have only the values –4, $\frac{1}{2}$, and 3, and q can have only the values –4, $\frac{2}{3}$, and 3, what is the greatest possible value for $p^2 + 3q$?

(A) 12   (B) 15   (C) 18   (D) 25   (E) 28

$$3x + 4y = 10$$
$$2x + 5y = 8$$

Quantity A	Quantity B
50. $x - y$	2

51. If z is an integer, what is the least possible value of $|14 - 3z|$?

(A) 1   (B) 2   (C) 3   (D) 4   (E) 5

$$xy = \sqrt{12}$$

Quantity A	Quantity B
52. $\quad x^2$	$\dfrac{20}{y^2}$

$$\sqrt{k + 12} - \sqrt{18 - 2k} = 0$$

Quantity A	Quantity B
53. $\quad k$	2

$$xz > yz$$

Quantity A	Quantity B
54. $\quad x$	y

$$|x + 4| = 3x$$

Quantity A	Quantity B
55. $\quad x$	2

$$x > 0$$

Quantity A	Quantity B
56. $\quad \dfrac{x^2 + 2}{x}$	$x + \dfrac{1}{x}$

$$6x^2 = x$$

Quantity A	Quantity B
57. $\quad x$	$\dfrac{1}{6}$

$$m < 0$$

Quantity A	Quantity B
58. $\quad (m - 1)(m)(m + 1)$	$(m)(m)(m)$

$$9a + 4b = 20$$
$$4a + 9b = 10$$

59.   If a and b satisfy the system of equations above, what is the value of $a - b$?

(A) $\frac{1}{2}$ (B) $\frac{2}{5}$ (C) 2   (D) $\frac{5}{2}$ (E) 20

60.   If $\sqrt{\sqrt{3z} + 7} = 4$, what is the value of z?

(A) 3   (B) 9   (C) 18   (D) 27   (E) 81

Quantity A	Quantity B
$\sqrt{x^4 + 8x^2 + 16}$	$x^2 + 4$

61.

$$x^2 + y^2 = 49 \text{ and } xy = 24$$

Quantity A	Quantity B
$(x - y)^2$	1

62.

63.   If $0 > -xy - 2 > -2$, which of the following must be true?

Select all possible statements.

$\boxed{A}$ $xy > -2$ $\boxed{B}$ $xy < 0$ $\boxed{C}$ $\frac{x}{y} < 0$

Quantity A	Quantity B
$\dfrac{x + 2y}{3}$	$\dfrac{2x + 4y}{6}$

64.

65.   If $r \geq 7$ and $s \leq 2$, then it must be true that

(A) $r + s \geq 5$ (B) $r + s \leq 9$ (C) $r - s \geq 5$ (D) $r - s \leq 5$ (E) $r - s \leq 9$

$$x^2 + kx + 5 = (x - 1)(x - 5) \text{ for all } x.$$

Quantity A	Quantity B
k	-5

66.

$$(n + 1)(n - 2)(2n + 3)(3n + 6)(n - 1) = 0$$

	Quantity A	Quantity B
67.	The number of possible values of n that are integers	5

$$n > 5$$

	Quantity A	Quantity B
68.	$\dfrac{1}{n + 5}$	$\dfrac{1}{n - 4}$

69. The expression $(n + 5)(3n - 2)$ is equivalent to which of the following?

Select <u>all</u> such values.

$\boxed{\text{A}}$ $3n(n + 5) - 2(n + 5)$ $\boxed{\text{B}}$ $(n - 5)(3n + 2)$ $\boxed{\text{C}}$ $3n^2 - 10$ $\boxed{\text{D}}$ $n(3n - 2) + 5(3n - 2)$

$$n > 1$$

	Quantity A	Quantity B
70.	$(n + 7)(2n + 5)$	$(n + 5)(2n + 7)$

$$\frac{2n + 1}{4} - \frac{n - 1}{8} = \frac{n - 1}{4} - \frac{2n + 1}{8}$$

	Quantity A	Quantity B
71.	$2n + 1$	$n - 1$

72. If $\dfrac{a}{b + 1} = \dfrac{3}{7}$, what is b in terms of a?

(A) $\dfrac{3}{7}a$ (B) $\dfrac{3}{7}a + \dfrac{3}{7}$ (C) $\dfrac{3}{7}a + 1$ (D) $\dfrac{7}{3}a - \dfrac{3}{7}$ (E) $\dfrac{7}{3}a - 1$

Rare or Advanced

$$nk = 24 \text{ and } n + k = -10$$

Quantity A	Quantity B

73. n k

74.   At an ice cream company, machine A fills a container with ice cream and machine B accepts the container only if the number of ounces is between $15\frac{3}{4}$ and $16\frac{1}{4}$. If machine B accepts a container containing n ounces, which of the following describes all possible values of n?

     (A) $|n - 16| = \frac{1}{4}$ (B) $|n + 16| = \frac{1}{4}$ (C) $|n - 16| < \frac{1}{4}$

           (D) $|n + 16| < \frac{1}{4}$ (E) $|n - 16| > \frac{1}{4}$

75. $(1 - n)(n - 1) =$

     (A) $-(n - 1)^2$ (B) $(n - 1)^2$ (C) 0 (D) $n^2 - 1$ (E) $1 - n^2$

76. If $3a = 4b = 5c = 12$, then $15abc =$

77.   If $x^2 \geq 1$, then x equals

     (A) $x \leq -1$ (B) $x \geq -1$ (C) $-1 \leq x \leq 1$ (D) $x \leq -1$ or $x \geq 1$ (E) $x \geq 1$

78. $\left(1 - \frac{x}{x+1}\right) - \frac{1-x}{x+1} =$

     (A) 0 (B) 1 (C) $\frac{1}{x+1}$ (D) $\frac{x}{x+1}$ (E) $\frac{-2x}{x+1}$

79.　Which of the following equals $x + xy + (x + xy)y$?

　　(A) $x(1 + y)^2$　(B) $x(2 + y + y^2)$　(C) $2x(1 + y) + y$　(D) $2xy(1 + y)$　(E) $x^2(1 + y^2)y$

80.　If $pq = p^2$, which of the following cannot be true?

Select all possible statements.

$\boxed{A}$ $q = p$　$\boxed{B}$ $p = 0$　$\boxed{C}$ $pq < 0$

81.　If $n > 0$ and $2n - 1 = \dfrac{1}{2n + 1}$, then $n =$

　　(A) $\dfrac{1}{2}$　(B) $\dfrac{\sqrt{2}}{2}$　(C) 1　(D) $\sqrt{2}$　(E) $\sqrt{2} + 1$

82.　If $|r + 2| \le 6$ and $|s - 2| \le 4$, what is the least possible value of the product rs ?

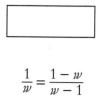

$$\frac{1}{w} = \frac{1 - w}{w - 1}$$

Quantity A	Quantity B

83.　w　　　　　　　　　　　　　　　$\dfrac{1}{2}$

84.　Which of the following indicates all n such that $n^2 < n$?

　　(A) $-1 < n < 0$　(B) $-1 < n < 1$　(C) $0 < n < 1$　(D) $n < 0$　(E) $n > 1$

85.　$(2rs)^2 + (r^2 - s^2)^2 =$

　　(A) $2rs$　(B) $r^2 - s^2$　(C) $r^2 + s^2$　(D) $(2rs)^2 + (r^2 + s^2)^2$　(E) $(r^2 + s^2)^2$

86. If $n = \dfrac{r}{r+s}$ and $k = \dfrac{r}{s}$, then n in terms of $k =$

   (A) $-\dfrac{1}{k}$ (B) $1 + k$ (C) $1 + \dfrac{1}{k}$ (D) $\dfrac{1}{1+k}$ (E) $\dfrac{k}{1+k}$

$$x > 1$$

	Quantity A	Quantity B
87.	$\dfrac{x}{x+1}$	$\dfrac{-x}{1-x}$

88. If $\dfrac{6q}{7 - \dfrac{2r}{3s}} = 2q,$ then which of the following is true?

   (A) $3r = 2s$ (B) $2r = 3s$ (C) $r = 6s$ (D) $6r = s$ (E) $3r = s$

89. If r and s are positive integers, and $4r + 9s = 72$, then $r + s =$

   (A) 8   (B) 9   (C) 11   (D) 12   (E) 13

(22) Solutions – Video solutions for each of the previous questions can be found on our website at **www.sherpaprep.com/videos**.

• BOOKMARK this address for future visits!

> ➤ To view the videos, you'll need the LOGIN and PASSWORD that you created upon registering your copy of <u>Number Properties & Algebra</u>.

• If you have yet to register your book yet, please go to **www.sherpaprep.com/activate** and enter your email address, last name, and shipping address.

• Be sure to provide the SAME last name and shipping address that you used to purchase your copy of <u>Master Key to the GRE</u> or to enroll in your GRE course with Sherpa Prep!

> ➤ When checking your answers, we encourage you to watch the solution for any problem that you answered INCORRECTLY

• The same goes for any problem that took you MORE than TWO MINUTES to solve.

• After digesting the explanation, REVISIT your mistake a couple of days later to ensure that the problem no longer poses issues to you.

> ➤ If you struggle to solve the problem a SECOND time, add it to your "LOG of ERRORS" and redo it every few weeks.

• Solving tricky questions MORE THAN ONCE is the best way to learn from your mistakes and to avoid similar difficulties on your actual exam.

Fundamental	Intermediate		Rare or Advanced
1. C	30. D	62. C	73. D
2. A	31. A	63. A, B, C	74. C
3. D	32. A	64. C	75. A
4. D	33. D	65. C	76. 432
5. D	34. D	66. B	77. D
6. B	35. B	67. B	78. D
7. C	36. B	68. B	79. A
8. E	37. D	69. A, D	80. C
9. D	38. D	70. A	81. B
10. C	39. A	71. C	82. –48
11. B	40. E	72. E	83. B
12. E	41. D		84. C
13. E	42. C		85. E
14. D	43. D		86. E
15. A	44. C		87. B
16. A	45. B		88. C
17. A	46. D		89. E
18. D	47. A		
19. B	48. B		
20. B	49. D		
21. B	50. C		
22. B	51. A		
23. E	52. B		
24. C	53. C		
25. D	54. D		
26. A	55. C		
27. A	56. A		
28. D	57. D		
29. A, B, E	58. A		
	59. C		
	60. D		
	61. C		

Functions & Sequences

Functions & Sequences

To be discussed:

Fundamental Concepts

Whether you're aiming for a perfect score or a score closer to average, mastery of the following concepts is essential.

1   Introduction
2   Monster Formulas
3   Symbolism
4   Functions
5   Sequences
6   Drills
7   Picking Numbers

Rare or Advanced Concepts

The following concepts are either advanced or are tested only on rare occasions. If you don't need an elite math score, don't waste your time!

8   Finding Patterns
9   Embedded Functions

Practice Questions

There's no substitute for elbow grease. Practice your new skills to ensure that you internalize what you've studied.

10   Problem Sets
11   Solutions

Fundamental Concepts

(1) Introduction – If you hated math in high school, the term "Function" may bring back memories you'd rather not relive.

• We understand your fear. Functions are ugly. The notation is confusing, and if you don't understand it, even the most basic questions can seem like witchcraft.

> ➤ However, we think that the fear is misplaced. For starters, Function questions are relatively RARE.

• Most exams contain no more than 1 or 2 examples, if they have any at all.

• Thus, even if you know nothing about Functions, it's unlikely to affect your score by more than a point or two.

> ➤ More importantly, questions that involve Functions are generally easier than you might think.

• A Function is simply a FORMULA for which any INPUT (or set of inputs) has exactly one OUTPUT.

• Take the statement $2x = y$. Believe it or not, this is a Function. The proof? If we plug in the input $x = 5$, we get exactly one output: $y = 10$.

> ➤ The chief difference between $2x = y$ and the sort of Functions that you find on the GRE is the NOTATION.

• GRE Functions simply look strange. The trick is DISTINGUISHING the inputs from the formula.

• However, once you understand "what goes where", you'll see that most Functions are little more than a fancy game of "Plug In".

(2) Monster Formulas – The simplest Function questions are easy to spot.

- They always contain a MONSTER FORMULA such as $Q = \dfrac{2P}{R+S}$ or $C = \dfrac{2\pi x^2}{d}$ atop the question or within it.

> ➤ To solve such problems, you simply need to solve for a VARIABLE within the formula.

- In most cases, you can do so by plugging values supplied by the question into the OTHER variables. Here's a typical example:

$$E = \frac{I}{D^2}$$

The illumination, E, in footcandles, provided by a light source of intensity I, in candles, at a distance D, in feet, is given by the formula above.

Quantity A	Quantity B
The intensity of a source for an illumination of 8 footcandles at a distance of 5 feet from the source	**200 candles**

- Because of the formula $E = I/D^2$ atop the problem, this is a "Monster Formula" problem. To solve it, let's plug in the supplied information.

> ➤ According to the problem, the illumination is 8 footcandles at a distance of 5 feet from the source.

- Since E = illumination and D = distance, we therefore know that $E = 8$ and $D = 5$. If we insert this information into the formula, we get:

$$E = \frac{I}{D^2} \;\rightarrow\; 8 = \frac{I}{5^2} \;\rightarrow\; 8 \cdot 5^2 = I$$

- The intensity, I, of the illumination therefore equals 200 candles, since $8 \times 25 = 200$. Thus, the correct answer is (C).

> In more difficult examples, you may need to plug in TWICE in order to solve for a
> CONSTANT.

- Consider the following:

**For a sound that has an intensity of 80 decibels at its source, the intensity in decibels,
S, of the sound at a point d feet from the source is given by the formula $S = 40E/d^2$,
where E is a constant. The intensity of the sound is 20 decibels at a distance of 4 feet
from the source.**

<u>Quantity A</u>	<u>Quantity B</u>
The intensity of the sound, in decibels, at a distance of 40 feet from the source	2

- Because of the formula $S = 40E/d^2$ within the problem, this is a "Monster Formula"
problem. To solve it, let's plug in the supplied information.

> According to the problem, the intensity of the sound is 20 decibels at a distance of 4
> feet from the source.

- Since S = intensity and d = distance, we therefore know that $S = 20$ and $d = 4$. If we
insert this information into the formula, we get:

$$S = \frac{40E}{d^2} \quad \rightarrow \quad 20 = \frac{40E}{4^2} \quad \rightarrow \quad 20 = \frac{40E}{16}$$

- The constant E must therefore equal 8, since:

$$20 = \frac{40E}{16} \quad \rightarrow \quad 320 = 40E \quad \rightarrow \quad E = 8$$

> If $E = 8$, then Quantity A must equal 1/5 of a decibel, since plugging $E = 8$ and
> $d = 40$ gives us:

$$S = \frac{40E}{d^2} \quad \rightarrow \quad S = \frac{40 \cdot 8}{40^2} \quad \rightarrow \quad S = \frac{40 \cdot 8}{40 \cdot 40} = \frac{8}{40} = \frac{1}{5}$$

- Thus, the correct answer is (B).

➢ Finally, every now and then problems involving Monster Formulas may IMPLY information rather than state it directly.

• This is particularly true of examples involving GEOMETRY. Consider the following:

$$A = \frac{16\pi d^2}{x^2}$$

The formula given above gives the area A of a circle in terms of its diameter d. If x is greater than zero, what is the value of x?

(A) $\frac{1}{4}$ (B) $\frac{1}{2}$ (C) 4 (D) 8 (E) 16

• Because of the formula $A = \frac{16\pi d^2}{x^2}$ atop the problem, this is a "Monster Formula" problem.

➢ Before solving it, let's first recall two basic Geometry formulas, both of which will be introduced properly in our book on <u>Geometry</u>.

• In each case, r = the radius of the circle:

The AREA of a Circle = πr^2 The DIAMETER of a Circle = $2r$

• According to the problem, A = the area of a circle and d = the diameter. The area of a circle ALSO equals πr^2 and the diameter of a circle ALSO equals $2r$, so we know that:

$$A = \pi r^2 \qquad\qquad d = 2r$$

➢ If we insert this information into $A = \frac{16\pi d^2}{x^2}$, we get:

Replace A
with πr^2

$$\pi r^2 = \frac{16\pi (2r)^2}{x^2}$$

Replace d
with $2r$

• Therefore x^2 equals 64, since:

$x^2 \pi r^2 = 16\pi \cdot 4r^2$ Multiply both sides by x^2. $(2r)^2 = 2r \times 2r = 4r^2$.

$x^2 = \frac{64\pi r^2}{\pi r^2}$ Divide both sides by πr^2. Multiply $16\pi \times 4r^2$.

$x^2 = \frac{64\,\cancel{\pi r^2}}{\cancel{\pi r^2}} = 64$ Cancel πr^2.

• If $x^2 = 64$, then $x = 8$ or -8. However, the problem states that x is greater than zero, so the correct answer must be (D).

<u>**(3) Symbolism**</u> – Some Functions contain funny symbols such as $\odot$, *, or $\boxed{x}$.

- Here's an example:

$$\text{If } x \odot y = \frac{x+y}{x-y} \text{ for all } x \text{ and } y \text{ such that } x \neq y, \text{ then } 5 \odot 3 = ?$$

$$\textbf{(A) } 1 \quad \textbf{(B) } 4 \quad \textbf{(C) } 5 \quad \textbf{(D) } 8 \quad \textbf{(E) } 15$$

- If you're like many people who take the GRE, you may find such problems intimidating because the symbols look strange and unfamiliar.

  ➢ Fortunately, you're in luck. These problems are total frauds. Their difficulty is only skin deep.

- Let's demystify them.

- For starters, the exam does NOT expect you to know the symbols in advance. The symbols are ALWAYS defined within the problem.

  ➢ In some cases, the definition will be obvious because the exam will tell you something like "$a * b$ is defined as $a^2 - b^2$".

- In other cases, you will just find an EQUAL sign. For example, in the problem above, you were told that $x \odot y = \frac{x+y}{x-y}$.

- This is a bit trickier, since an equal sign technically means the two expressions are equal. In Symbolism problems, however, the equal sign ALSO means "IS DEFINED AS".

  ➢ Once you find the DEFINITION, simply TREAT it as a FORMULA. For example, in the problem above, you were given a definition and a question:

<u>The DEFINITION</u>   <u>The QUESTION</u>

$x \odot y$ is defined as $\frac{x+y}{x-y}$ $5 \odot 3 = ?$

- If you compare the phrases $x \odot y$ and $5 \odot 3$, notice that the x has been REPLACED with a 5 and that the y has been REPLACED with a 3:

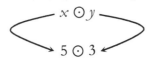

➤ Thus, to solve this problem, we only need to PLUG $x = 5$ and $y = 3$ into the FORMULA (aka the definition) as follows:

$$\frac{x+y}{x-y} \quad \rightarrow \quad \frac{5+3}{5-3}$$

• Since $\frac{5+3}{5-3} = \frac{8}{2} = 4$, the answer to the question on the previous page is therefore (B).

• And that's all there is to it. So if that didn't seem so bad, there's some good news for you: most Symbolism problems are just as easy.

➤ If that didn't quite click for you, let's work through a SECOND example together.

• Consider the following:

$a * b = a^2 - b^2$ **for all values a and b, what is the value of $6 * (-3)$?**

(A) 3   (B) 18   (C) 27   (D) 36   (E) 45

• According to the problem, $a * b = a^2 - b^2$. Remember, in symbolism problems the equal sign also means "is defined as". Thus, our problem has one definition and one question:

The DEFINITION	The QUESTION
$a * b$ is defined as $a^2 - b^2$	$6 * (-3) = ?$

➤ If we compare the definition to the question, notice how the a has been REPLACED with a 6 and the b has been REPLACED with a -3:

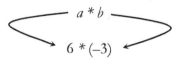

• Thus, to solve this problem, we only need to PLUG $a = 6$ and $b = -3$ into the FORMULA (i.e. the definition) as follows:

$$a^2 - b^2 \quad \rightarrow \quad 6^2 - (-3)^2$$

• Since $6^2 - (-3)^2 = 36 - 9 = 27$, the answer to the question is therefore (C).

Sherpa
Prep

➢ More difficult Symbolism problems often use their symbol TWICE. To solve such problems, simply perform the operation INSIDE the parentheses FIRST.

• Consider the following:

If $x \otimes y$ is defined as $x^y - y^x$, what is the value of $(4 \otimes 2) \otimes 3$?

(A) −1 (B) 0 (C) 1 (D) 2 (E) 3

• Unlike previous problems, this problem uses its symbol twice:

The DEFINITION   The QUESTION

$x \otimes y$ is defined as $x^y - y^x$ $(4 \otimes 2) \otimes 3 = ?$

➢ Therefore, let's start by performing the operation INSIDE the parentheses. If we compare $x \otimes y$ to $4 \otimes 2$, notice that the x is replaced with a 4 and the y with a 2:

• Thus, to resolve the parentheses, we simply need to plug $x = 4$ and $y = 2$ into the formula (i.e. the definition) as follows:

$$x^y - y^x \rightarrow 4^2 - 2^4$$

• Since $4^2 - 2^4 = 16 - 16 = 0$, **the information INSIDE the parenthesis has a value of zero.** The original question can therefore be rewritten like this:

$$(4 \otimes 2) \otimes 3 = ? \rightarrow 0 \otimes 3 = ?$$

Replace $(4 \otimes 2)$ with 0.

➢ If we next compare $x \otimes y$ to $0 \otimes 3$, we see that x now equals 0 and that y now equals 3. Thus, we can plug $x = 0$ and $y = 3$ into the formula as follows:

$$x^y - y^x \rightarrow 0^3 - 3^0$$

• Because any value to the zero power equals 1 (save for 0^0, which is undefined), the correct answer must be (A), since:

$$0^3 - 3^0 = 0 - 1 = -1$$

➢ Finally, every now and then problems involving Symbolism ALSO include OUTPUTS.

- Here's an example:

For all numbers r and s, the operation Θ is defined as $r \, \Theta \, s = (r - 2)(s + 1)$. If $7 \, \Theta \, t = -35$, then $t =$

(A) −15   (B) −8   (C) 6   (D) 7   (E) 20

- At first glance, a question like this may look significantly harder than the questions you've seen so far. The truth of the matter, however, is that it's really not much different.

➢ Let's compare the definition to the statement $7 \, \Theta \, t = -35$:

The DEFINITION	The STATEMENT
$r \, \Theta \, s = (r - 2)(s + 1)$	$7 \, \Theta \, t = -35$

- In essence, the statement tells us that if we replace r with 7 and s with t, the operation will equal −35:

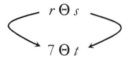

➢ To solve the problem, therefore, we simply need to plug $r = 7$ and $s = t$ into $(r - 2)(s + 1)$, and set the result equal to −35.

- We can do this as follows:

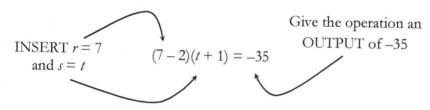

INSERT $r = 7$ and $s = t$

$(7 - 2)(t + 1) = -35$

Give the operation an OUTPUT of −35

- Thus, the correct answer is (B), since $t = -8$:

$5(t + 1) = -35$	Subtract 7 − 2.
$t + 1 = -7$	Divide both sides by 5.
$t = -8$	Subtract 1 from both sides.

(4) Functions – When most people think of Functions, they think of something like this:

> **If function f is defined for all numbers x as $f(x) = 4x^2 + 3$, what is the value of $f(-2)$?**
>
> **(A) –61   (B) –17   (C) –13   (D) 19   (E) 67**

- And understandably so. If you're like most people who take the GRE, your high-school years were filled with problems like this.

  ➢ Since it's probably been a while since you last saw this sort of Function, let's take some time to review the notation and the terminology.

- For starters, all Functions consist of a HEADER, a FORMULA, and an INPUT:

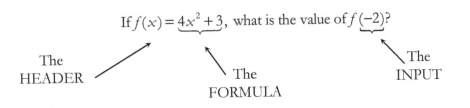

$$\text{If } f(x) = \underline{4x^2 + 3}, \text{ what is the value of } f\,(\underline{-2})?$$

  The
  HEADER

  The
  FORMULA

  The
  INPUT

  ➢ The HEADER indicates that the variable OUTSIDE the parentheses is dependent on the variable INSIDE them.

- For example, in the Function above, the header (pronounced "f of x") indicates that the value of f is dependent on the value of x. **It does NOT represent f times x.**

- If the function were $g(y) = 4y^2$, the header would be $g(y)$, indicating that the value of g is dependent on the value of y.

  ➢ The INPUT and FORMULA tell you "WHAT to plug in" and "WHERE to plug it".

- In the example above, the input is –2 and the formula $4x^2 + 3$. Thus, to determine the value of $f(-2)$, we simply need to plug "–2" into "$4x^2 + 3$" as follows:

$$4x^2 + 3 \;\rightarrow\; 4(-2)^2 + 3 \;\rightarrow\; 4(4) + 3 \qquad \text{Plug in (–2)}\atop \text{for } x$$

- Since $4(4) + 3 = 19$, the value of $f(-2)$ is 19, making (D) the correct answer.

➤ Like Functions involving funny symbols, Functions such as the one above sometimes contain OUTPUTS.

- Here's an example:

For all values y, function h is defined by $h(y) = 14 + y^2$. If p is a number such that $h(2p) = 30$, which two of the following could be the number p?

Indicate <u>two</u> such values.

$\boxed{A}$ –4 $\boxed{B}$ –2 $\boxed{C}$ 0 $\boxed{D}$ 2 $\boxed{E}$ 4 $\boxed{F}$ 8

- At first glance, the statement $h(2p) = 30$ may look confusing, but it simply states that an INPUT of $2p$ produces an OUTPUT of 30.

➤ Thus, to determine the value of p we simply have to PLUG $2p$ into the FORMULA $14 + y^2$, and set the result equal to 30.

- We can do this as follows:

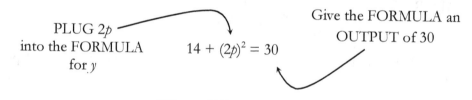

PLUG $2p$ into the FORMULA for y $14 + (2p)^2 = 30$ Give the FORMULA an OUTPUT of 30

- The correct answer is therefore $\boxed{B}$ and $\boxed{D}$, since p can equal 2 or –2:

$(2p)^2 = 16$	Subtract 14 from both sides.
$4p^2 = 16$	$2p \times 2p = 4p^2$.
$p^2 = 4$	Divide both sides by 4.
$p = 2, -2$	An even exponent has two solutions.

➢ Finally, every now and then you may need to determine the value of a CONSTANT to solve a Function.

• To do so, simply PLUG an input AND an output into the Function. Once you have the constant, insert its value into the Function before answering the question.

For all values x, function f is defined by $f(x) = mx^2 - 24$, where m is a constant. If $3f(4) = 24$, which is the value of $f(-4)$?

(A) –12   (B) –4   (C) 8   (D) 20   (E) 24

• According to the problem, $3f(4) = 24$. By dividing both sides of the equation by 3, we can simplify this statement to $f(4) = 8$. Thus, an INPUT of 4 has an OUTPUT of 8.

➢ To determine the value of m, let's plug 4 into $mx^2 - 24$, and set the result equal to 8. We can do this as follows:

Give it an
OUTPUT of 8

PLUG in 4
for x

$$m(4)^2 - 24 = 8$$

• Solving this equation proves that $m = 2$, since:

$$m(4)^2 - 24 = 8$$
$$16m = 32 \qquad \text{Add 24 to both sides.}$$
$$m = 2 \qquad \text{Divide both sides by 16.}$$

➢ If $m = 2$, then the original function can be rewritten as follows:

$$f(x) = mx^2 - 24 \;\rightarrow\; f(x) = 2x^2 - 24$$

• The value of $f(-4)$ is therefore 8, since inserting –4 into the formula $2x^2 - 24$ gives us:

$$2(-4)^2 - 24 \;\rightarrow\; 2(16) - 24 \;\rightarrow\; 32 - 24 = 8$$

PLUG in
–4 for x

• The correct answer must therefore be (C).

(5) Sequences – A Sequence is a set of numbers whose order is governed by a RULE or a FORMULA. On the GRE, Sequence problems usually look something like this:

For all positive integers n, the sequence $S_1, S_2, S_3, \ldots, S_n$, is such that $S_n = 2n - 7$. What is the value of S_6?

(A) 3   (B) 4   (C) 5   (D) 6   (E) 7

- If you're like most people taking the GRE, it's been a long time since you've seen a problem of this sort.

> In fact, if you never studied Algebra II, you may have never seen one at all. So let's take some time to breakdown the notation and terminology.

- Sequences are a lot like Functions. In most cases, they have a HEADER, a FORMULA, and an INPUT:

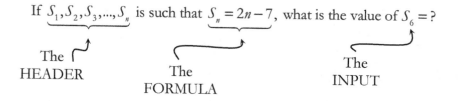

If $\underbrace{S_1, S_2, S_3, \ldots, S_n}$ is such that $\underbrace{S_n = 2n - 7}$, what is the value of $\underbrace{S_6} = ?$

The   The   The
HEADER   FORMULA   INPUT

> The HEADER indicates that EACH term in the Sequence is dependent on a particular variable.

- For example, in the sequence above, the header indicates that each term in Sequence S is dependent on the value of n.

- If the problem had been written "$x_1, x_2, x_3, \ldots, x_a$ such that $x_a = 4a - 3$", the header would indicate that each term in sequence x is dependent on the value of a.

> The INPUT and FORMULA tell you "WHAT to plug in" and "WHERE to plug it".

- In the example above, the input is 6 and the formula is $S_n = 2n - 7$. Thus, to determine the value of S_6 (which refers to the <u>sixth</u> term in the sequence), we simply need to plug "6" into "$S_n = 2n - 7$" as follows:

$$S_n = 2n - 7 \quad \rightarrow \quad S_6 = 2(6) - 7$$

- Thus, the correct answer to the question above would be (C), since $2(6) - 7 = 5$.

➢ In many cases, Sequences come with one or more CONSTRAINTS. Here's an example:

The sequence $a_1, a_2, a_3, \ldots, a_n$, is such that $a_n = 3n^2$ for all $n > 2$.

Quantity A	**Quantity B**
$a_4 - a_3$	$a_2 - a_1$

• The statement "for all $n > 2$" simply means that the FORMULA is only VALID for INPUTS with values greater than 2.

➢ The constraint does not affect Quantity A, since a_4 and a_3 have inputs of 4 and 3, respectively.

• However, the constraint does affect Quantity B. Because a_2 and a_1 have inputs of 2 and 1, we cannot use the formula to determine their values.

• The answer to the question is therefore (D), since it is impossible to establish the relationship between the two quantities if the value of Quantity B CANNOT be determined.

➢ In most cases, however, exam-makers use constraints to CLOSE technical LOOPHOLES within problems.

• Consider the following:

The sequence $S_1, S_2, S_3, \ldots, S_n$, is such that $S_n = \left(\dfrac{1}{n-2}\right)^{n-1}$ for all $n > 2$.

Quantity A	**Quantity B**
S_4	$\dfrac{1}{8}$

• Quantity A has an input of 4. If we plug this into the formula, we get:

$$S_n = \left(\frac{1}{n-2}\right)^{n-1} \rightarrow S_4 = \left(\frac{1}{4-2}\right)^{4-1} = \left(\frac{1}{2}\right)^3 = \frac{1}{8}$$

• The correct answer is therefore (C), since the two quantities are equal. The constraint $n > 2$ just serves to remind us that the Sequence is UNDEFINED for an input of 2:

$$S_n = \left(\frac{1}{n-2}\right)^{n-1} \rightarrow S_2 = \left(\frac{1}{2-2}\right)^{2-1} = \left(\frac{1}{0}\right)^1 = undefined$$

> In more difficult problems, the terms in a Sequence may be DEFINED by the terms that PRECEDE or SUCCEED them.

- Here's an example:

The sequence P_1, P_2, P_3,...P_n, is defined as $P_n = P_{n-1} + P_{n-2}$ for all $n > 2$.
If $P_1 = P_2 = 1$, which of the following equals P_5?

(A) 2 (B) 3 (C) 4 (D) 5 (E) 7

- The trick to solving questions like this is to TRANSLATE the FORMULA into a simple statement. For example, the formula "$P_n = P_{n-1} + P_{n-2}$ for all $n > 2$" just means:

> "EACH term (P_n) after the second ($n > 2$) equals the SUM of the PREVIOUS term (P_{n-1}) and the term BEFORE THAT (P_{n-2})."

- In other words, if we need to determine the value of P_5, we know that $P_5 = P_4 + P_3$. Similarly, we know that $P_4 = P_3 + P_2$ and that $P_3 = P_2 + P_1$

- Thus, if P_2 and P_1 both equal 1, then $P_3 = 1 + 1$. Likewise, if $P_3 = 2$ and $P_2 = 1$, then $P_4 = 2 + 1$. And finally if $P_4 = 3$ and $P_3 = 2$, then $P_5 = 3 + 2$. The correct answer is therefore (D).

> Here's a second example for you. This one is a bit TRICKIER than the first:

The sequence T_1, T_2, T_3,...T_n, is such that $T_n = \dfrac{T_{n-1} + T_{n-2}}{2}$ for all $n > 2$.
If $T_5 = 8$ and $T_7 = 10$, what is the value of T_8?

(A) 11 (B) 13 (C) 14 (D) 15 (E) 17

- According to the formula, "EACH term (T_n) after the SECOND ($n > 2$) is equal to the AVERAGE of the two PREVIOUS terms (T_{n-1} and T_{n-2})."

> Hence, T_8 should equal the average of T_7 and T_6, just as T_7 should equal the average of T_6 and T_5. If $T_7 = 10$ and $T_5 = 8$, then $T_6 = 12$, since:

$$T_7 = \frac{T_6 + T_5}{2} \rightarrow 10 = \frac{T_6 + 8}{2} \rightarrow 20 = T_6 + 8$$

- If $T_6 = 12$, $T_7 = 10$, and $T_8 = $ the average of T_7 and T_6, the correct answer must be (A), as:

$$T_8 = \frac{T_7 + T_6}{2} \rightarrow T_8 = \frac{10 + 12}{2} = 11$$

➤ Finally, it's worth pointing out that some sequence problems have NO EXPLICIT FORMULAS.

• Here's an example:

In the sequence of numbers A_1, A_2, A_3, A_4, A_5, each number after the first is three times the preceding number. If $A_4 - A_2 = 72$, what is the value of A_3?

(A) 27 (B) 36 (C) 45 (D) 54 (E) 63

• To solve sequence problems without explicit formulas, first LABEL the lowest (or highest) term in the sequence x. For example, here let's set $A_1 = x$.

➤ Then FLESH OUT the sequence until you have labeled ALL the terms specified in the problem.

• Thus, if each term in sequence A is "three times the preceding term", the remaining terms would be:

$$A_2 = 3x$$
$$A_3 = 9x$$
$$A_4 = 27x$$
$$A_5 = 81x$$

➤ LABELING the terms will allow you to SET UP an EQUATION to solve for x. Here, the problem states that "$A_4 - A_2 = 72$".

• If $A_4 = 27x$ and $A_2 = 3x$, then x must equal 3, since:

$$A_4 - A_2 = 72 \quad \rightarrow \quad 27x - 3x = 72 \quad \rightarrow \quad 24x = 72$$

• Once you know the value of x, be sure to SUBSTITUTE it back into the sequence to identify what you need. If $x = 3$, the answer to the question must therefore be (A), since:

$$A_3 = 9x = 9(3) = 27$$

Chapter 6: Functions & Sequences

(6) Drills – For each of the sections below, the exercises have been arranged in difficulty from least to greatest.

- Solutions can be found on the following pages.

Symbolism

1. If $g \neq 0$, and $k \triangle g$ is defined as $\dfrac{-k^2}{\sqrt{g}}$, what is the value of $3 \triangle 9$?

2. For all numbers a, b and c, if $a[b]c = ab - bc$, what is the value of $3[4]5$?

3. If $x \uparrow y$ is defined as $y^2 - x^2$, then what is the value of $(2 \uparrow 3) \uparrow 3$?

4. $x * y$ is defined as $(x + y)(x - y)$. If $5 * y = -11$, what does y equal?

Functions

5. If function f is defined as $f(x) = x^2 + 9$, what is the value of $f(4) + f(3)$?

6. Function h is defined as $h(m) = 2(m^3 - 3)$. When $h(m) = -60$, what is the value of $2 - 3m$?

7. $h(x) = x^2 + 4x$. If $h(2c) = 16c$, what are the possible values of c?

8. Function f is defined as $f(x) = x^3y + xy$. If $f(3) = 60$, then what is the value of $f(-1)$?

Sequences

9. If $S_n = 2n + 3$, what is the value of $S_{48} - (S_4)(S_3)$?

10. $Q_p = Q_{p-1} + 4$. If $Q_2 = 3$ and $Q_p = 15$, what does p equal?

11. $S_n = S_{n-1} + S_{n-2}$ for all $n > 2$. If $S_5 = 8$ and $S_6 = 10$, what is the value of S_8?

12. $T_n = 3(T_{n-1})$. If $T_4 - T_1 = 52$, then what does T_2 equal?

Solutions

1. If we compare $k \, \Delta \, g$ to $3 \, \Delta \, 9$, we see that $k = 3$ and $g = 9$. Plugging this into the formula gives us:

$$\frac{-k^2}{\sqrt{g}} \quad \rightarrow \quad \frac{-(3)^2}{\sqrt{9}} \quad \rightarrow \quad \frac{-9}{3} = -3$$

2. In Symbolism problems, the equal sign also means "is defined as". If we compare $a[b]c$ to $3[4]5$, we see that $a = 3$, $b = 4$, and $c = 5$. If we plug this into the formula, we get:

$$ab - bc \quad \rightarrow \quad 3(4) - 4(5) \quad \rightarrow \quad 12 - 20 = -8$$

3. To solve problems that use their symbol twice, FIRST perform the operation INSIDE the parentheses. Thus, $(2 \uparrow 3) = 5$, since:

$$y^2 - x^2 \quad \rightarrow \quad 3^2 - 2^2 \quad \rightarrow \quad 9 - 4 = 5$$

Then REWRITE the question. Since $(2 \uparrow 3) = 5$, the original question can be rewritten as:

$$(2 \uparrow 3) \uparrow 3 = ? \quad \rightarrow \quad 5 \uparrow 3 = ?$$

The answer is therefore –16, since:

$$y^2 - x^2 \quad \rightarrow \quad 3^2 - 5^2 \quad \rightarrow \quad 9 - 25 = -16$$

4. According to the problem, we get an OUTPUT of –11 when the INPUT is $5 * y$. Thus, if we insert $x = 5$ into the FORMULA, we get:

$$(x + y)(x - y) \quad \rightarrow \quad (5 + y)(5 - y) = -11$$

We can use this to solve for y as follows:

$25 - 5y + 5y - y^2 = -11$	FOIL.
$25 - y^2 = -11$	Add $-5y + 5y$.
$36 = y^2$	Add 11 and y^2 to both sides.
$y = 6$ or -6	An EVEN exponent has TWO solutions.

5. According to the problem, the formula is $f(x) = x^2 + 9$ and the inputs are 4 and 3:

$$f(4) = 4^2 + 9 = 25 \qquad\qquad f(3) = 3^2 + 9 = 18$$

Thus, $f(4) + f(3) = 43$, since $25 + 18 = 43$.

6. If $h(m) = 2(m^3 - 3)$ and $h(m) = -60$, then $2(m^3 - 3)$ and -60 BOTH equal $h(m)$. Therefore, $2(m^3 - 3) = -60$. We can use this equation to prove that $m = -3$, since:

$m^3 - 3 = -30$	Divide both sides by 2.
$m^3 = -27$	Add 3 to both sides.
$m = -3$	Take the cube root of both sides.

Thus, $2 - 3m = 11$, since:

$$2 - 3m \rightarrow 2 - 3(-3) \rightarrow 2 - (-9) = 11$$

7. According to the problem, we get an OUTPUT of $16c$ when the INPUT is $2c$. Thus, if we insert this information into the FORMULA, we get:

$$x^2 + 4x \rightarrow (2c)^2 + 4(2c) = 16c$$

We can use this equation to solve for c as follows:

$4c^2 + 8c = 16c$	$2c \times 2c = 4c^2$.
$4c^2 = 8c$	Subtract $8c$ from both sides.
$c^2 = 2c$	Divide both sides by 4.

Since $c^2 = 4c$ has a power of c to both the FIRST and SECOND powers, it is a quadratic equation. Therefore, we must set it equal to zero to solve it:

$c^2 - 2c = 0$	Subtract $2c$ from both sides.
$(c)(c - 2) = 0$	Factor out c.
$c = 0, 2$	Set both factors equal to zero.

8. According to the problem, we get an OUTPUT of 60 when the INPUT is 3. If we insert this into the formula, we get $y = 2$, since:

$$x^3 y + xy \rightarrow 27y + 3y = 60 \rightarrow 30y = 60$$

If $y = 2$, then the original function can be rewritten as:

$$f(x) = x^3 y + xy \rightarrow f(x) = 2x^3 + 2x$$

Thus, the value of $f(-1) = -4$, since:

$$2x^3 + 2x \rightarrow 2(-1)^3 + 2(-1) \rightarrow -2 + (-2) = -4$$

9. If the formula is $S_n = 2n + 3$, then $S_{48} = 99$, $S_4 = 11$, and $S_3 = 9$, since:

$$S_{48} = 2(48) + 3 = 99 \qquad S_4 = 2(4) + 3 = 11 \qquad S_3 = 2(3) + 3 = 9$$

Thus, $S_{48} - (S_4)(S_3) = 0$, since $99 - 11(9) = 0$.

10. According to the formula $Q_p = Q_{p-1} + 4$, each term in sequence Q is 4 greater than the term before it. Thus, if $Q_2 = 3$, then the next 3 terms in the sequence are:

$Q_3 = 7$
$Q_4 = 11$
$Q_5 = 15$

Since Q_p and Q_5 both equal 15, the value of p must therefore be 5.

11. If $S_n = S_{n-1} + S_{n-2}$ for all $n > 2$, then each term in sequence S equals the sum of the previous two (so long as that term isn't the first or second term in the sequence). Thus:

$$S_7 = S_6 + S_5$$
$$S_8 = S_7 + S_6$$

If $S_6 = 10$ and $S_5 = 8$, then $S_7 = 10 + 8 = 18$. Likewise, if $S_7 = 18$ and $S_6 = 10$, then $S_8 = 18 + 10 = 28$.

12. If $T_n = 3(T_{n-1})$, then each term in sequence T is 3 times as large as the term before it. Since we don't know the value of any specific term in the sequence, let's LABEL the first 4 terms in the sequence as follows:

$T_1 = x$
$T_2 = 3x$
$T_3 = 9x$
$T_4 = 27x$

According to the problem, $T_4 - T_1 = 52$. Since $T_4 = 27x$ and $T_1 = x$, we can rewrite this as follows:

$$27x - x = 52$$
$$26x = 52$$
$$x = 2$$

Thus, $T_2 = 6$, since $3x = 3(2) = 6$.

Chapter 6: Functions & Sequences

Rare or Advanced Concepts

(7) Picking Numbers – Some of the most challenging questions involving Functions & Sequences have NO CONCRETE VALUES.

- Here's an example:

For which of the following functions f is $f(x - 1) = f(1 - x)$ for all x?

Select all possible functions.

$\boxed{A}$ $f(x) = 1 - x$ $\quad \boxed{B}$ $f(x) = x + 1$ $\quad \boxed{C}$ $f(x) = (1 - x)^2$ $\quad \boxed{D}$ $f(x) = x^2 - 1$

- As discussed in section $\boxed{8}$ of the "Plan B" chapter of our book on <u>Arithmetic & "Plan B"</u> <u>Strategies</u>, the KEY to solving problems without concrete values is to PICK NUMBERS.

  ➤ When picking, be sure to keep your numbers SMALL and EASY to work with, and respect any constraints, should your problem have them.

- In the problem above, there are no concrete values and no constraints, so we are free to pick any value for x that we like. Let's choose 5.

- If $x = 5$, then $f(x - 1) = f(4)$, and $f(1 - x) = f(-4)$, since:

$$\text{Let } x = 5$$

$$f(x-1) = f(5-1) = f(4) \qquad f(1-x) = f(1-5) = f(-4)$$

  ➤ To find the functions for which $f(x - 1) = f(1 - x)$, therefore, we simply need to plug $f(4)$ and $f(-4)$ into the answers to see which give us the SAME response for BOTH.

- Doing so proves that $\boxed{D}$ is the only correct answer, since $\boxed{D}$ alone provides IDENTICAL outputs for both $f(4)$ and $f(-4)$:

		$f(4)$	$f(-4)$	
$\boxed{A}$	$f(x) = 1 - x$	$1 - 4 = -3$	$1 - (-4) = 5$	dissimilar
$\boxed{B}$	$f(x) = x + 1$	$4 + 1 = 5$	$(-4) + 1 = -3$	dissimilar
$\boxed{C}$	$f(x) = (1 - x)^2$	$(1 - 4)^2 = 9$	$(1 - (-4))^2 = 25$	dissimilar
$\boxed{D}$	$f(x) = x^2 - 1$	$4^2 - 1 = 15$	$(-4)^2 - 1 = 15$	identical

Sherpa
Prep

➢ "Monster Formula" problems, in particular, OFTEN lack concrete values.

• In many cases, one variable within the formula increases (or decreases) in value, while another remains constant. The following is a CLASSIC example:

The quantities A and B are positive and are related by the equation $A = \frac{x}{B}$, where x is a constant. If the value of B increases by 25 percent, then the value of A decreases by what percent?

(A) 20%   (B) 25%   (C) 40%   (D) 50%   (E) $66\frac{2}{3}$%

• To solve problems like this, first pick a value for the variable that changes, then pick another for the constant.

➢ Here, the value of B is said to increase by 25%. A good choice for B would therefore be 4, since 25% of 4 is 1.

• Likewise, if B equals 4, a good choice for x would be 40, since 4 and 40 work well together. Thus, if $B = 4$ and $x = 40$, then A initially equals 10, since:

$$A = \frac{x}{B} \quad \rightarrow \quad A = \frac{40}{4} = 10$$

➢ Next, let's see what happens to A when B changes. If B increases by 25%, then B must now equal 5, since 25% of 4 = 1.

• Because x is a constant, i.e. something that doesn't change, the value of x is still 40. Thus, if $B = 5$ and $x = 40$, the value of A decreases to 8, since:

$$A = \frac{x}{B} \quad \rightarrow \quad A = \frac{40}{5} = 8$$

• As you will learn in the Percents chapter of our book on <u>Word Problems</u>, the **percent change** of a value can be calculated by placing the **difference** between the old and new values over the **original value**.

➢ Therefore, if the value of A changes from 10 to 8, then the value of A decreases by 20%, since:

$$\frac{\text{Difference}}{\text{Original}} = \frac{10-8}{10} = \frac{2}{10} = 20\%$$

• Hence, the correct answer is (A).

(8) Finding Patterns – To solve some of the most difficult Sequence problems, you may need to recognize a pattern within a sequence.

- Consider the following problem:

For every integer n from 1 to 20 inclusive, the nth term of a certain sequence is defined as $(-1)^{n+1}\left(\dfrac{1}{4^n}\right)$. If z is the sum of the first 10 terms in the sequence, then z should have which of the following values?

(A) $z > 1$ (B) $\dfrac{1}{2} < z < 1$ (C) $\dfrac{1}{4} < z < \dfrac{1}{2}$ (D) $0 < z < \dfrac{1}{4}$ (E) $z < 0$

- Although there is no easy way to know when you'll have to recognize a pattern, it can be helpful to remember the following:

  ➤ You should NEVER need to perform a LOT of TEDIOUS computations to solve a problem on the GRE.

- Remember, the GRE is testing your ability to find a simple solution to something that seems complicated, not your ability to be a human calculator.

- Thus, in a question like the one above, it's highly unlikely that you'll need to calculate AND add all 10 terms to determine the value of z: it's too much work.

  ➤ If a Sequence problem seems to require difficult calculations or a lot of busy work, WRITE OUT the first 4 or 5 terms of the sequence and look for a pattern.

- In most cases, you should see a simple path to the solution. Here, if $n =$ every integer from 1 to 20, the first 4 terms of the sequence are:

$n = 1$: $\qquad$ $n = 2$: $\qquad$ $n = 3$: $\qquad$ $n = 4$:

$$(-1)^{1+1}\left(\frac{1}{4^1}\right) = \frac{1}{4} \qquad (-1)^{2+1}\left(\frac{1}{4^2}\right) = -\frac{1}{16} \qquad (-1)^{3+1}\left(\frac{1}{4^3}\right) = \frac{1}{64} \qquad (-1)^{4+1}\left(\frac{1}{4^4}\right) = -\frac{1}{256}$$

  ➤ Notice that the sum of the first TWO terms is greater than 0 but less than 1/4, and that **every term after the second is so SMALL as to be NEGLIGIBLE**.

- Thus, the sum of first 10 terms of the sequence must be greater than 0 but less than $\dfrac{1}{4}$. The correct answer is therefore (D).

- Here are two practice problems for you:

For every integer n such that $n > 0$, the nth term of sequence T is $(-1)^{n+1} + 1$.

Quantity A	**Quantity B**
The sum of the first 51 terms of T	51

Answer: A. It would be extremely time-consuming to calculate AND add the first 51 terms of sequence T, so let's instead WRITE OUT the first 4 terms of the sequence to see whether we can find a pattern.

If n can only equal integers greater than zero, the first 4 terms of the sequence are:

$n = 1$: $n = 2$: $n = 3$: $n = 4$:

$(-1)^{1+1} + 1 = 2$ $(-1)^{2+1} + 1 = 0$ $(-1)^{3+1} + 1 = 2$ $(-1)^{4+1} + 1 = 0$

As you can see, the terms in the sequence alternate between 2 and 0. Of the first 50 terms, 25 must therefore equal 2 and 25 must equal 0. The 51st term must also equal 2, since the terms in the sequence equal 2 when n is ODD and 0 when n is EVEN.

Thus, the sum of the first 51 terms of T must be 52, since the sum of 26×2 and 25×0 equals 52. The correct answer is therefore (A).

If $A_n = 5^{6n} + 6^{12n}$, what is the units digit of A_6?

(A) 1   (B) 2   (C) 3   (D) 4   (E) 6

Answer: A. According to the problem, A_6 should equal $5^{36} + 6^{72}$. Since both terms are exceedingly difficult to compute, let's instead look for patterns within the respective powers of 5 and 6:

Powers of 5	Powers of 6
5, 25, 125, 625, ...	6, 36, 216, 1,236, ...

Notice that every power of 5 ends in a 5, and that every power of 6 ends in a 6. Therefore, 5^{36} must end in a 5, and 6^{72} must end in a 6. As such, $5^{36} + 6^{72}$ must end in a 1, since $5 + 6 = 11$.

(9) Embedded Functions – Some of the most daunting Function questions feature one Function EMBEDDED inside another.

- Here's an example:

> **For all values x, the functions f and g are defined as**
> $$f(x) = 6x - 1 \text{ and } g(x) = 2x + 5.$$

Quantity A	**Quantity B**
The value of $f(g(-2))$	5

- Embedded functions are essentially Functions WITHIN Functions. To solve them, first solve the INSIDE function.

  ➤ In the problem above, the inside function is $g(-2)$, since $g(-2)$ is literally "inside" $f(g(-2))$. To solve it, we simply need to plug -2 into $g(x) = 2x + 5$:

  $$2x+5 \;\rightarrow\; 2(-2)+5 \;\rightarrow\; -4+5=1$$

- Once you've solved the inside function, INSERT the solution into the OUTSIDE function to complete the problem. Here, because $g(-2) = 1$, we can therefore rewrite $f(g(-2))$ as follows:

  $$f(g(-2)) \;\rightarrow\; f(1) \qquad \text{Substitute 1 for } g(-2)$$

- Thus, to complete the problem, we simply need to determine the value of $f(1)$ by plugging 1 into $f(x) = 6x - 1$. The correct answer is therefore (C), since:

  $$6x-1 \;\rightarrow\; 6(1)-1 \;\rightarrow\; 6-1=5$$

  ➤ If this problem had instead asked us to determine the value of $f(f(2))$, the "inside" function would be $f(2)$.

- To solve the inside function, we would thus need to plug 2 into $f(x) = 6x - 1$:

  $$6x-1 \;\rightarrow\; 6(2)-1 \;\rightarrow\; 12-1=11$$

- Since $f(2) = 11$, we could then rewrite $f(f(2))$ as $f(11)$. The "outside" function, therefore, would equal 65, since plugging 11 into $f(x) = 6x - 1$ gives us:

  $$6x-1 \;\rightarrow\; 6(11)-1 \;\rightarrow\; 66-1=65$$

➤ To ensure that you've got the hang of embedded functions, let's work through a practice example together.

- Consider the following:

  For all x, the function f is defined as $f(x) = x^2 - 4x$, and the function g is defined as $g(x) = 6 - x^2$.

  <u>Quantity A</u>   **<u>Quantity B</u>**

  The value of $f(g(-2))$ **The value of $g(f(-2))$**

- At first glance, you may be tempted to assume that the two quantities are equal. This would be a mistake.

  ➤ Getting the value of $g(-2)$ and plugging it into function f, however, is NOT the same thing as getting the value of $f(-2)$ and plugging it into function g.

- To prove it, let's do the work. $\boxed{\text{In Quantity A}}$, the inside function is $g(-2)$. If we plug -2 into function g, we get a value of 2:

$$6 - x^2 \;\rightarrow\; 6 - (-2)^2 \;\rightarrow\; 6 - 4 = 2$$

- The outside function, therefore, has a value of -4, since plugging 2 into function f gives us a value of -4:

$$x^2 - 4x \;\rightarrow\; 2^2 - 4(2) \;\rightarrow\; 4 - 8 = -4$$

  ➤ $\boxed{\text{In Quantity B}}$, the inside function is $f(-2)$. If we plug -2 into function f, we get a value of 12, since:

$$x^2 - 4x \;\rightarrow\; (-2)^2 - 4(-2) \;\rightarrow\; 4 - (-8) = 12$$

- The outside function, therefore, has a value of -138, since plugging 12 into function g gives us the following:

$$6 - x^2 \;\rightarrow\; 6 - (12)^2 \;\rightarrow\; 6 - 144 = -138$$

- The correct answer, therefore, is actually (A), since -4 is greater than -138.

Chapter 6: Functions & Sequences

Practice Questions

(10) Problem Sets – The following questions have been arranged into three groups: fundamental, intermediate, and rare or advanced.

- Whether you're aiming for a perfect score or a score closer to average, mastery of the concepts in the FUNDAMENTAL questions is absolutely essential.

  ➢ As you might expect, the INTERMEDIATE questions are more difficult but are essential for test-takers who need an above-average score or higher.

- Finally, the RARE or ADVANCED questions test concepts that are very sophisticated or seldom encountered on the GRE. Mastery of such questions is required only if you need a math score above the 90th percentile.

- As always, if you find yourself confused, bogged down with busy work, or stuck, don't be afraid to fall back on your "Plan B" strategies!

Fundamental

1. If function f is defined as $f(x) = 4(1 - x)$, what is the value of $f(-3)$?

   (A) –8   (B) –3   (C) 3   (D) 8   (E) 16

The operation $*$ is defined as follows, for all a and b: $a * b = \dfrac{1}{a^2} + b^2$

	Quantity A	Quantity B
2.	$\dfrac{1}{2*0}$	$(-2)*(-2)$

3. If the sum of the first p positive integers is given by the formula $\dfrac{p(p+1)}{2}$, then the sum of the first 17 positive integers is

   (A) 81   (B) 82   (C) 153   (D) 305   (E) 306

Sherpa
Prep

For all positive numbers x, the function of f is defined by $f(x) = \dfrac{1}{\dfrac{1}{x} + \dfrac{1}{5}}$

Quantity A	Quantity B
$f(10)$	$f(25)$

4.

5. If $a * b$ is defined as $\sqrt{a+b}$, then what is the value of $128 * (160 * 96)$?

For each positive integer n, $a_n = \dfrac{1}{n} - \dfrac{1}{2n}$.

Quantity A	Quantity B
$a_1 + a_2 + a_3$	$\dfrac{11}{12}$

6.

7. The function g is defined for all numbers g as $g(x) = x^2 + 8x$. If n is a number such that $g(2n) = 20$, which two of the following could be the number n?

Indicate two such numbers.

A -5 B -2 C $\frac{1}{2}$ D 1 E $\frac{3}{2}$

$\lfloor x \rfloor$ represents the greatest integer less than or equal to x, and $\lceil x \rceil$ represents the least integer greater than or equal to x.

Quantity A	Quantity B
$\dfrac{\lfloor 2.6 \rfloor + \lceil 2.6 \rceil}{2}$	2.6

8.

$$p(x) = 25\sqrt{x} - 15$$

9. The profit for the sales of a particular hammer can be determined by the function above, where p represents the profit, in dollars, and x the number of hammers sold. How many hammers must be sold to generate $110 in profit?

(A) 4 (B) 9 (C) 12 (D) 16 (E) 25

Let $\boxed{n}$ = 5, if n is an odd integer. Let $\boxed{n}$ = 10, if n is an even integer.

p and q are integers, $7p$ is odd, and $p + q$ is odd.

Quantity A	Quantity B

10. $\boxed{p}$ $\boxed{q}$

$$C = \frac{5}{9}(F - 32)$$

11. The temperature in degrees Fahrenheit, F, can be converted to temperature in degrees Celsius, C, by the formula given above. What is the temperature at which the temperature in degrees Celsius is equal to the temperature in degrees Fahrenheit?

For all real numbers n, let $n^* = 2 - n$.

Quantity A	Quantity B

12. $((-2)^*)^*$ 4^*

13. The operation Δ is defined by the equation $x \, \Delta \, y = \frac{x - y}{x + y}$, for all numbers x and y such that $x \neq -y$. If $g \neq -k$ and $g \, \Delta \, k = 0$, then what does k equal?

(A) $-g$ (B) $-\frac{1}{g}$ (C) 0 (D) $\frac{1}{g}$ (E) g

Function h is defined as $h(x) = 4x - 13$, and $3h(z) = 21$.

Quantity A	Quantity B

14.   The value of $h(3z)$ 63

For any non-negative integer n, let $n^{\circ} = n - 2$

Quantity A	Quantity B

15. $\qquad (x+y)^{\circ} \qquad\qquad\qquad\qquad x + y^{\circ}$

16. In the sequence of numbers s_1, s_2, s_3, s_4, s_5, each number after the first is twice the preceding number. If $s_5 - s_1 = 25$, what is the value of s_1?

    (A) $\frac{4}{3}$ (B) $\frac{5}{3}$ (C) 2   (D) $\frac{5}{2}$ (E) 4

17. Sequence T_1, T_2, T_3,…,T_n is such that $T_{n+1} = T_n + 5$. If $T_{11} = 22$ and $T_n = -3$, what is the value of n?

    (A) 3   (B) 4   (C) 5   (D) 6   (E) 7

18. The relationship between the area A of a circle and its circumference C is given by the formula $A = kC^2$, where k is a constant. What is the value of k?

    (A) $\frac{1}{4\pi}$ (B) $\frac{1}{2\pi}$ (C) $\frac{1}{4}$ (D) 2π (E) $4\pi^2$

$\boxed{\text{Rare or Advanced}}$

The sequence $Z_1, Z_2, Z_3, \ldots, Z_a$, is such that $Z_a = (Z_{a-1})(Z_{a+1})$ for all $a > 2$.
$Z_3 = 2$ and $Z_5 = 6$.

Quantity A	Quantity B
19. Z_6	12

Function f is defined as $f(x) = x^2 - 4$.

Quantity A	Quantity B
20. $f(f(2))$	$f(f(-3))$

21. The positive quantities a, b, and c vary over time, and $\frac{3a}{4}$ always equal $18bc$. If b is halved and c is tripled, then a is

(A) decreased by 50%

(B) decreased by $33\frac{1}{3}\%$

(C) unchanged

(D) increased by $33\frac{1}{3}\%$

(E) increased by 50%

For all numbers k, $k^* = 14 - k$

Quantity A	Quantity B
22. $(k^*)^*$	k

23. For which of the following functions f is $f(f(m - n)) = f(lm) - f(ln)$?

(A) $f(x) = x + 1$ (B) $f(x) = x$ (C) $f(x) = (1 - x)^2$ (D) $f(x) = |x^3|$ (E) $f(x) = x^2$

$$x_1, x_2, x_3, \ldots, x_n, \ldots$$

24. In the sequence above, each term after the first term is equal to the preceding term plus the constant k. If $x_1 + x_3 + x_5 = 27$, what is the value of $x_2 + x_4$?

(A) 12   (B) 15   (C) 18   (D) 21   (E) 24

25. The first term in sequence S is 7. Each even-numbered term is 2 less than the previous term and each odd-numbered term, after the first, is -1 times the previous term. What is the value of the 63rd term of the sequence?

The functions g and h are defined as $g(y) = 2 + 3y$ and $h(z) = 7 - 3z$, and y and z are each non-negative integers less than 9.

Quantity A	Quantity B
26. The minimum value of $g(y) + h(z)$	-15

27. In the sequence $S_0, S_1, S_2, \ldots S_b$, each term from S_1 to S_a is 4 greater than the previous term, and each term from S_{a+1} to S_b is 3 less than the previous term, where a and b are positive integers and $a < b$. If $S_0 = S_b = 0$, and if $S_a = 12$, what is the value of b?

(A) 5   (B) 6   (C) 7   (D) 10   (E) 12

Sequence s is defined as $s_n = \dfrac{1}{n} - \dfrac{1}{n+2}$ for each integer $n > 1$.

Quantity A	Quantity B
28. The sum of the first 10 terms of this sequence	$\dfrac{3}{4}$

(11) Solutions – Video solutions for each of the previous questions can be found on our website at **www.sherpaprep.com/videos**.

- BOOKMARK this address for future visits!

  ➢ To view the videos, you'll need the LOGIN and PASSWORD that you created upon registering your copy of <u>Number Properties & Algebra</u>.

- If you have yet to register your book yet, please go to **www.sherpaprep.com/activate** and enter your email address, last name, and shipping address.

- Be sure to provide the SAME last name and shipping address that you used to purchase your copy of <u>Master Key to the GRE</u> or to enroll in your GRE course with Sherpa Prep!

  ➢ When checking your answers, we encourage you to watch the solution for any problem that you answered INCORRECTLY

- The same goes for any problem that took you MORE than TWO MINUTES to solve.

- After digesting the explanation, REVISIT your mistake a couple of days later to ensure that the problem no longer poses issues to you.

  ➢ If you struggle to solve the problem a SECOND time, add it to your "LOG of ERRORS" and redo it every few weeks.

- Solving tricky questions MORE THAN ONCE is the best way to learn from your mistakes and to avoid similar difficulties on your actual exam.

Fundamental	Intermediate	Rare or Advanced
1. E	10. B	19. B
2. B	11. –40	20. B
3. C	12. C	21. E
4. B	13. E	22. C
5. 12	14. B	23. B
6. C	15. C	24. C
7. A, D	16. B	25. –5
8. B	17. D	26. C
9. E	18. A	27. C
		28. B

Sherpa Prep

Master Key
to the GRE

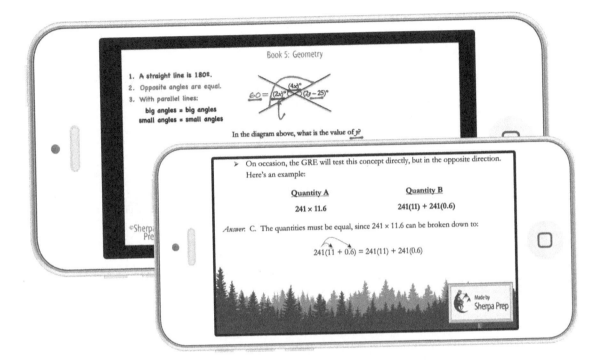